D1604106

# Great Satan's rage

The planet is congested with wealth and death,
a scream pierces the clouds.

Georges Bataille

# Great Satan's rage
## American negativity and rap/metal in the age of supercapitalism

**Scott Wilson**

Manchester University Press
Manchester and New York
distributed exclusively in the USA by Palgrave

*Published by* Manchester University Press
Oxford Road, Manchester M13 9NR, UK
*and* Room 400, 175 Fifth Avenue, New York, NY 10010, USA
www.manchesteruniversitypress.co.uk

*Distributed exclusively in the USA by*
Palgrave, 175 Fifth Avenue, New York,
NY 10010, USA

*Distributed exclusively in Canada by*
UBC Press, University of British Columbia, 2029 West Mall,
Vancouver, BC, Canada V6T 1Z2

*British Library Cataloguing-in-Publication Data*
A catalogue record for this book is available from the British Library

*Library of Congress Cataloging-in-Publication Data applied for*


ISBN      978 0 7190 7463 9 *hardback*

First published 2008
16 15 14 13 12 11 10 09 08      10 9 8 7 6 5 4 3 2 1

Typeset
by Frances Hackeson Freelance Publishing Services, Brinscall, Lancs
Printed in Great Britain
by MPG Books Ltd, Bodmin, Cornwall

# Contents

# Figures

# Acknowledgements

I would like to thank members of the Institute for Cultural Research at Lancaster University for their advice, suggestions and camaraderie, particularly Fred Botting, Nick Gebhardt, Jonathan Munby, Richard Rushton and Hager Weslati. Thanks are also due to students of the MA in Cultural Studies where some of this material was developed, particularly John Marris, Ryan Speed and Wang Qiong. Diane Rubenstein's comments on the becoming nonAmerican part of the book were invaluable. The book would not have been possible without John Wilson's archive, knowledge and detailed corrections and Mia Wilson's inspiration. To Petra Jackson I owe everything.

Finally, I would like to thank Philippa Berry and Andrew Wernick for getting me started on this project, Matthew Frost for eventually going for it and his colleagues at Manchester University Press, especially Jenny Howard and Tony Mason for working with me on the production of the book. Many thanks also to the anonymous readers who supplied very helpful and encouraging comments both at the proposal stage and with regard to the full manuscript.

A preliminary version of part of Chapter 9 'Econopoiesis' has appeared as 'Writing Excess: The Poetic Principle of Post-literary Culture' in Patricia Waugh (ed.), *Literary Theory and Criticism*, Oxford: Oxford University Press, 2006.

*For John*

# 1

# Introduction

Satan, now first inflamed with rage, came down,
To wreck on innocent man his loss
         and his flight to hell.
        (John Milton, Book IV *Paradise Lost*, 1667 (Milton, 1983))

Absolute destruction is the battleground we're given
Strip away the fabric of a thousand years of living ...
The trumpet of freedom has sounded
Great Satan.

        (Ministry, 'The Great Satan', 2005)

## Satan's rage

Satan is defined by the quality of his rage: the rage against the throne and monarchy of God, the war that raged in Heaven resulting in Satan and his rebel angels to be cast into the inferno. His doom reserving him to an eternity of rage, Satan headed to the new world to wreak his revenge on God's creation.

John Milton's *Paradise Lost* (1667) (Milton, 1983) is of course a defining text of Puritanism, the revolutionary religious movement that caused the Mayflower pilgrims to be cast out of England and to head for the New World in 1620. Over the next twenty or thirty years, more than twenty thousand pilgrims, mostly English puritans, migrated to join the fledgling Massachusetts Bay Colony, which became the first substantial base for the European colonisation of North America.

Although based on just a few lines in Isaiah (XIV) and the Book of Revelations (XII), Milton's Satan is developed into a dark and glamorous figure who later became, for the romantics, a hero of rebellion and revolution. William Blake famously wrote in *The Marriage of Heaven and Hell* that the 'reason Milton wrote in fetters when he wrote of Angels & God, and at liberty when of Devils & Hell is because he was of the Devil's party without knowing it' (Blake, 1984: 150). Blake was also of the Devil's party, as he knew very well, just as he was a partisan of the American Revolution. Printed the same year as *The Marriage of Heaven and Hell* in 1793, *America: A Prophecy* features Blake's own satanic hero, Orc. Condemned in the poem by his enemy, Albion's Angel, the representative of George III and Urizen, Blake's personification of moral law, prohibition and repression, Orc is described as 'serpent form'd' and called 'Blasphemous Demon, Antichrist, hater of Dignities; Lover of wild rebellion, and transgressor of God's Law' (198). Orc is a figure of energy and desire raging against all forms of moral and rational restriction. In *America* he comes both to prophesy and to embody the spirit of American rebellion and desire for independence.

Because of America's puritan heritage and romantic aspirations, Satan has a prominent, yet highly ambivalent role in the history of its culture, and indeed in its religious and political rhetoric. From Doctor Dwight to *The Witches of Eastwick*, Robert Johnson to Deicide, Salem to *South Park*, where Satan takes Saddam Hussein as his gay lover in Hell, Satan is a highly complex, glamorous and rebellious figure, a barometer of America's fears and desires.

The United States of America was itself called the Great Satan by the Ayatollah Khomeini on 5 November 1979, the year of the Iranian revolution. In the Qur'an Satan is the 'great seducer,' 'the insidious tempter who whispers in the hearts of men' (Qur'an, CXIV, 4, 5). For the Islamic radicals behind the revolution, America's satanic influence resides in its secular and liberal traditions. The Iranian idea of America as a satanic seducer is often associated with the radical Islamic ideologue Sayyid Qutb, generally cited as the founding figure of Islamic 'fundamentalism'. Qutb spent two years in America and was appalled by what he considered to be its irreligious sensuality and decadence. Writing in his memoir, *Amrika allati Ra'aytu* (America that I saw), about his experience of church dance halls, Qubt disclosed that these were places 'where people of both sexes meet, mix and touch'. Noting further the appalling conduct of the ministers themselves

> who even go so far as to dim the lights to facilitate the fury of the dance ... the dance is inflamed by the notes of a gramophone (and) the dance hall becomes a whirl of heels and thighs, arms enfold hips, lips and breasts meet, and the air is full of lust. (Qutb, cited in Calvert, 2000: 98)

Significantly, it is music 'created by negroes to satisfy their love of noise and to whet their sexual desires' (99) that provides the medium of America's satanic seduction. That jazz and rock 'n' roll is the devil's music is a view that is of course perfectly consistent with America's own religious right, something parodied and celebrated by rock's most passionate adherents: 'Soon I discovered that this rock thing was true. Jerry Lee Lewis was the Devil ... All of a sudden I found myself in love with the world. So there was only one thing that I could do: ding-a-ding-dang my dang-a-long ling-long' (Ministry, 'Jesus Built My Hot Rod', 1992).

Church halls were soon superseded by many other sites and scenes as the setting for the devil's music. Radio, film, television and the marketing of gramophone records enabled the spread of American popular music world wide, rock 'n' roll quickly replacing Hollywood as the most powerful mode of American seduction of the world's youth. Indeed, it was on MTV, the global American music television franchise, that Secretary of State Colin Powell was asked about 'how he feels representing a country commonly perceived as the Satan of contemporary politics'. Powell unsurprisingly rejected the characterisation in the name of America's commitment to 'democracy, economic freedom and the individual rights of men and women'. Further, implicitly justifying actions in Iraq and elsewhere, he insisted that 'far from being the Great Satan, I would say that we are the Great Protector. We have sent men and women from the armed forces of the United States to other parts of the world throughout the past century to put down oppression' (Powell, 2002).

But it is America's perception of itself as the great protector that finds its political rhetoric invoking Satan in its metaphysical conception of its world historical destiny. It is America itself, in the voices of successive American presidents, that likes to evoke the language of evil, particularly since being named the Great Satan by Khomeini. The USSR was called the 'evil empire' in the 1980s, various 'rogue states' were said in the 1990s to comprise an 'axis of evil', and throughout that decade America opposed itself to the 'Beast of Baghdad'. As Jacques Derrida notes, this characterisation of Saddam Hussein as a 'beast' does not simply reduce him to the status of an animal but is meant to summon up 'the very incarnation of evil, of the satanic, the diabolical, the demonic – a beast of the Apocalypse' (Derrida, 2005: 97). American presidents like to use this kind of rhetoric because it is popular and communicates clearly to the electorate in what remains an overwhelmingly religious country. But as it looks into the 'transpolitical mirror of evil' (Baudrillard,1993: 82), there is a further element to America's satanic destiny that is purely structural and bound inevitably to its current world role as the great protector of Western values and society. To understand why America's role as protector necessitates that it become satanic, it is helpful to look at Derrida's argument on the fate of the 'rogue state' in the post-cold-war period. This is something I do at the end of the book in chapter 11. Suffice it to say that in its self-perception as the great protector, America frequently justifies its disregard for the United Nations, international law and the International Criminal Court. For Francis Boyle, the great protector exists in a state of 'international legal nihilism' (Boyle, cited in Pieterse, 2004: 121; see also 2002).

America sees its role as the great protector not just because it is the bearer of the good, in the form of 'universal values' – democracy, economic freedom and individual rights – but because of its great power. As an effect of the cold war with the Soviet Union and its economic success, America has amassed an enormous arsenal of nuclear and other weapons that could destroy the world many times over. America's protectorate is predicated upon an unprecedented and unmatchable force of satanic dimensions. The whole world lives in fear of Great Satan's rage; it provides the political horizon of our times: 'Absolute destruction is the battlefield we're given / Strip away the fabric of a thousand years of living' (Ministry, 'The Great Satan', 2005). Even America's conventional weapons can destroy a nation's infrastructure, sending it back to a premodern state, in a short period of shock and awe.[1]

It became evident that America's power was unmatched at the end of the cold war in 1989, with the Soviet Union's defeat in the war with Afghanistan and the collapse of its economy and political structure. America's self-perceived victory in the cold war was further credited with the economic success of 'Reaganomics', which unleashed a form of deregulated or postmodern capitalism on to the world in the 1980s (see Goux, 1998a). There are many factors to this form of unregulated capitalism and its relation to America's military strategy that are significant here, but this will be discussed in chapter 2. Suffice it to say that it is the energy of America's entrepreneurs that is credited with winning the cold war, and forming the basis of homeland security, as much as the threat of its nuclear weapons. It is the seductive force of American supercapitalism, therefore, that unlocks new markets, unleashing the energy of desire, that provides a perhaps more benign but no less destructive version of Satan's rage. Since the end of World War Two at least, Great Satan's vision of the good life has been all the rage, transforming and deleting traditional cultures and practices across the world. At the vanguard of this seduction has been the youthful rage and rebellion of the devil's music, American rock 'n' roll and its multiple related subgenres. The Iranian reference to Great Satan the seducer is significant therefore to this book but secondary in so far as it provides a mirror to the satanic aspect of America that resides in its self-perceived role as guarantor of universal good in the field of international relations and cultural value.

This book looks at the most pervasive forms of American popular music in the post-cold-war period. By the end of the cold war, heavy metal and hip hop were arguably the most important and influential genres of popular music in America and, by extension, the world. Throughout the next decade 'it became increasingly clear that, between them, hip hop and heavy metal were redefining American popular music' (Walser, 1993: x). And, again by extension, these forms altered the perception of America and its influence in the world. Furthermore, prominent and innovative examples of these genres have also been highly engaged with America's role in the world, supercapitalism and their own function within both. This has especially been the case when the genres – hitherto clearly identified as indelibly 'black' or 'white' forms of music – have crossed over as an effect of cross-racial forms of identification and desire, marketing strategy, political engagement, opportunism and experimentation. It is how examples of these forms have negotiated, contested, raged against, survived, exploited, simulated and performed Satan's rage that is the subject of this book.

## Rock 'n' rage

At the end of the 1980s, a negative turn occurred in American popular music that determined some of the most successful and influential forms of the 1990s and beyond. NWA's *Straight Outta Compton* (1988) provided the gangsta phenomenon with its definitive record, while Public Enemy's *It Takes a Nation of Millions to Hold Us Back* (1988) informed such 'niggativity' with a sharp political focus. In 1991, Nirvana's *Nevermind* became the defining statement of the 'grunge' generation that, after Cobain's suicide in 1994, gave way to even bleaker and angrier forms of American rock, most notably nu metal, which also incorporated many aspects of rap and hip hop. This book discusses a variety of examples of this negative turn in American pop in the context of the end of the cold war, and the explosion of postmodern capitalism (Goux, 1998a) that spread, unfettered, into Eastern Europe and Asia, supported by unmatched US military power. Many of the examples of these forms of popular music have a negative relation to capitalism, but are also very successful commercially. Indeed they tap into the negativity of capitalism itself, particularly the unregulated form that is called here supercapitalism. Along with NWA (Niggaz With Attitude), Public Enemy and Nirvana, the groups and artists that feature or are discussed in this book include Dr. Dre, Ice Cube, Snoop Doggy Dogg, Tupac Shakur, Notorious BIG, Lil' Kim, Rage Against the Machine, Biohazard, Korn, Slipknot, Static-X, Ministry and Deicide.

In this book the ambivalence of these examples towards American economic and cultural power is contrasted with the philosophical negativity that informs the neoconservative strain in right-wing American politics. The 'neocons', whose ideology is informed by Leo Strauss and Alexandre Kojève, are credited with a decisive influence in both the anti-Clinton campaigns and the presidency of George W. Bush. As this book will argue, the neocons also betray a highly ambivalent attitude to mainstream American culture and supercapitalism that is defined not so much by its levels of production, or even its consumption, but by its expenditure.

The theoretical ideas informing this book are derived from Georges Bataille. This is for two main reasons. First because a particular application of his concepts of restricted and general economy offer a profound insight into capitalism at the end of the twentieth and beginning of the twenty-first centuries (see Goux, 1998a). Second because Bataille elaborated his notion of expenditure and unemployed or useless negativity precisely in relation to the Hegelian negativity of Kojève and the 'end of history' thesis that, 50 years later, so decisively informed Republican thinking on the implications of the end of the cold war in 1989. To put it crudely, Bataille was to Kojève in 1939 what Slipknot was to Paul Wolfowitz in 1999. That is to say they are opposed, but also bound, negatively, by a shared ambivalence towards the culture they inhabit.

The choice of music, as opposed to art, literature or film, to explore the negativity of American political culture and its relation to supercapitalism is appropriate for a number of reasons. First, gangsta rap and nu and death metal, the forms discussed, are exemplary expressions of the creative negativity of supercapitalism, particularly when such expressions contest and expose the limits of mainstream culture. The economy and its use as a weapon of social change and control define the horizon of existence for music being produced in African-American areas in Los Angeles, New York and elsewhere, and in the white suburban areas in the mid-west. The high point of the success of gangsta in the mid-1990s coincides with the high point of the globalisation of American products and brands such that they became an object of cultural critique. Gangsta both exploits and informs the consumption of luxury brands, thereby exposing the negativity of the American good life. In a different way, the 'mom and pop rage' of the nu metal bands self-consciously exposes itself as the violent expression, the excess of the implacable banal excess, of shopping-mall consumerism and its nihilistic standardisation and reduction of life and experience.

Second, popular music also provides a focus for the negativity of American neoconservatism that discloses its conformity with its Islamicist enemies. In his influential book *The Closing of the American Mind* (1987), Allan Bloom, the neoconservative ideologue, condemns popular music in exactly the same terms as Sayyid Qutb as strangely both animal and decadent. Both Qutb and Bloom share the view that modern liberal democracy leads to 'the civilised reanimalisation of man' (Bloom, 1987: 143), and that the music of the negroes is its purest expression. While Leo Strauss is usually credited as 'the maitre of the neoconservatives' (Pieterse, 2004:135), it was 'Bloom, far more than Strauss, [who] has shaped the Straussians who govern America' (Norton, 2004:148; also see Norton for a full list of the Straussians in Washington). The Straussians include, of course, Paul Wolfowitz, Secretary of State for Defense from 2005, and now head of the World Bank. The uncanny correlation between these positions and the strange contradiction that popular music is both in the vanguard of the globalisation of American culture and the purest expression of its 'barbarism' will be discussed in chapter 3 (Bloom, 1987: 71).

The third reason is that these forms of music are international and in the process of becoming nonAmerican. This is because the relative poverty of the cultural content of the music lies in contradistinction to its strength and adaptability as form. Both rap and metal have developed across the world different modalities of becoming in contradistinction to the American 'empire' that nevertheless provides the horizon beyond which it is impossible to see.

This is because of the fourth reason why music is appropriate. It articulates restricted and general economies so that even as it generates a multibillion dollar industry, it escapes total commodification. As Robert Walser argues,

> How do you 'consume' music, when (a) music isn't a thing and (b) it's still there after you've used it – or you think you've used it. Just because the industry markets

it as a commodity doesn't mean we have to accept their terms of reference. It's time people stopped talking about 'consuming' art and culture and so on and started thinking of art as an activity, something you do. Even buying and playing records are activities; the record is only the medium through which the activity takes place. (Walser, 1993: xii)

The consumption of music has to be understood in two ways, as an activity in which energies are consumed in performance and dance for no useful purpose other than pleasure or the joy of affirmation, and as the exchange of records, concert tickets and merchandise, products of an industry that circulates, technically supports and exploits the music. In the first sense, consumption has a quite traditional social and symbolic role that in the latter sense is reduced to a purely economic relation. In articulating these two meanings of consumption, the popular music industry succeeds in facilitating the transformation of social relations and practices. It is uncontroversial to suggest that since the 1950s, American popular music has had a leading role in transforming not just American social life but also that of much of the world. Pop and rock music is not simply a product. It becomes an integral part of people's lives, it becomes a way of life, a way of reacting and relating, determining sets of tastes, attitudes and opinions. Frequently these are in conflict with more traditional ways of life informed by very different national cultures. For Michel Foucault, 'rock offers the possibility of a relation which is intense, strong, alive, "dramatic" (in that rock presents itself as a spectacle, that listening to it is an event and that it produces itself on stage), with a music that is itself impoverished, but through which the listener affirms himself' (Foucault, 1988: 316). The relation to the music is often more intense than traditional familial and social relations, even when it is mediated commercially. Through rock music, capitalism establishes the conditions for multiple forms of relation, even a relation of anti-capitalism so that any statement of anti-capitalism is simultaneously a practical affirmation of it. But at the same time, the proliferation of rap and metal has produced many different forms of community that in different ways sustain themselves through a rejection of commercial norms.

Hip hop and the rap core and nu metal of the 1990s that adopted many of its techniques also articulate both forms of consumption in their practice. Hip hop began in block parties in the Bronx in the mid-1970s as a technique which DJs used to edit, exploit and revitalise old records for the purposes of dance. The records and indeed the genre of music that ultimately resulted from these parties was a by-product of an essentially live performance, although this live performance consisted in the reanimation of old records, often retrieved from parents' collections ('mom and pop crates') and second-hand and charity shops (see Schloss, 2004: 82). The development of sampling and recycling with the advent of digital technology transformed the way in which a culture is received, reproduced, experienced and recorded, socially and historically. But this form of music remains a live and lived experience; it is an intense mode of self-affirmation, as Foucault suggests, which provides an antidote to shopping-mall banality. In the 1990s, concerts and festivals became more and more popular and essential, particularly because much of 1990s rap and metal became so musically and lyrically extreme that it received no mainstream airplay. This affirmation, ironically, often took the form of an ecstatic negativity and nihilism that outfaced the nihilism of consumer culture. As the 1990s progressed, the internet and world-wide web became the main facilitator of virtual interaction, exchange and community, its accessibility, speed and global reach instantly establishing and dissolving friendships, fan-bases, groupings and communities. Again, in spite of the initial Utopian hopes of the baby-boomer pioneers of the information highway, this communications system is largely owned and controlled by large corporations (often led by the same Utopians). Myspace.com is currently the most popular and significance space for the spontaneous promotion, exchange and dissemination of new music, particularly that associated with the cult of 'emo'. At the time of writing, emo (emotive or emotional metal) is the latest trend in metal, associated with groups like Panic! At the Disco and My Chemical Romance. Founded in 2003 by Tom Anderson and Chris de Wolfe, graduates of Berkeley and the University of Southern California respectively, myspace.com was sold in July 2005 to Rupert Murdoch's News Corporation for $580 million.[2]

## Rage machines

The discussion of rap and metal in the 1990s is preceded by two chapters; the first explores the development of American supercapitalism which provides the conditions of its existence. The second looks at the philosophical form of negativity that informed American politics throughout the same period that is both echoed and contested by the featured rap/metal artists. While the book is subdivided into eleven chapters, they can be clustered into the following broad sections.

### Supercapitalism

It is the system of supercapitalism that is the immanent economic modality of an unmatched superpower, what Jacques Chirac called the *hyperpuissance* of America, that provides both the focus and the context for this book on American negativity and rap/metal. In supercapitalism, economy is an expression of war just as war is a means of wealth creation. Throughout the 1990s, America's foreign and economic policies merged in surprising ways as a business ethos established itself in government and in the military. First, business was conceived as a kind of war, having been successful in winning the cold war and in controlling populations. Second, war became a form of business in the sense that its aim was to create wealth as well as to fight and control populations.

While 'overseas conflict [was turned] into another business proposition', prisons in the US were 'privatized and turned into a "prison-industrial complex"' (Pieterse, 2004: 125). Throughout the 1990s, America seemed content to be the subject of 'neoliberal globalisation' and as such the major beneficiary of supercapitalism. The most important areas of world influence concerned economics and finance, the IMF, the World Bank and the World Trade Organization (WTO). State intervention was reduced, and policy directed towards market conformity and discipline, the ideology of the free market. Global brands and franchises began to transform the world in America's image. The attack on the World Trade Center in 2001 changed the emphasis, resulting in greater state intervention in the area of homeland security and military actions abroad, but the war–business correlation remained. Ex-CEOs George W. Bush and Donald Rumsfeld were eager to deploy the business-inspired 'revolution in military affairs' to the wars in Afghanistan and Iraq, with mixed consequences. Such a conjunction of war and business involving traditionally very different forms of expenditure is a highly precarious strategy, and runs counter to the classical nineteenth-century capitalism of thrift, savings and investment. Pieterse puts it well when he compares the British and American empires:

> Past empires such as the British Empire invested a share of their surplus in infrastructure overseas, such as railroads and ports. But the new American empire is … a hyperdebtor nation with a massive current account deficit that needs a daily inflow of $1.9 billion in foreign funds to keep it going, even without empire. This deficit empire, rather than investing overseas, drains the world of resources on a gargantuan scale. (122)

American government seems to be quite consistent with its consumer-citizens in its mode of excess and debt, precipitated by a movement of general expenditure. On the one hand, government and corporations want to preserve themselves and their domination but, on the other hand, they become caught up in the general economic logic of war as a mode of sumptuous expenditure and waste, failing to invest any surplus in anything other than in technological research and development aimed at generating more efficient weaponry. One innovation planned is to develop a new generation of weapons, including huge hypersonic drones and bombs dropped from space, that will allow the US to largely dispense with its allies since it can strike its enemies instantly from space or from its own territory (Borger, 2003: 2–3). Satan's rage will in twenty-five years be expressed in thunderbolts from space, directed at the world from the vantagepoint of God.

After the end of the cold war, American capitalism has if not generalised itself totally in Bataille's terms, then become unrestricted, flipping over the relation of priority between production and expenditure. Expenditure becomes precipitous as American capitalism is mobilised in the indefinite war that rages against America's enemies, presently and in the future. It is a society that has generated more waste than all the others put together, but in this waste lies the value of its affluence. The planet is congested by death and wealth in an intensive consumption of resources as war rages in the name of democracy, economic freedom and the rights and comforts of the individual.

## Negativity

The term negativity is used in both a philosophical and a 'pop' sense. In a philosophical sense, the term is used to investigate the ideology of American neoconservatives. In a pop sense, the book looks at how the term has been adopted, variously, by influential and symptomatic popular cultural forms in the domain of American rap/metal music. Broadcast in 2005, Adam Curtis's documentary *The Power of Nightmares* (2004) highlighted the influence of Leo Strauss and his former students/disciples in the policy-making of White House insiders. But this strain of new right ideology has been drawing on the ideas of Strauss and his close friend and correspondent Alexandre Kojève for some time, seeking justification in the end of the cold war to elaborate a 'project for the new American century' in the mid-1990s (see www.newamericancentury.org).

   More even than Strauss, Kojève received belated recognition in the US when Francis Fukuyama applied his 'end of history' thesis to the end of the cold war. The cultural figure who most clearly links Strauss and Kojève is Allan Bloom, who was a student of Strauss and the editor of Kojève's *Introduction to a Reading of Hegel* (1969 (1989)). The strange compatibility between Strauss's version of Nietzscheanism and Kojève's Hegelianism finds its inverse in Bataille for whom Nietzsche and Hegel were equally important although in different ways. In a letter to Kojève, Bataille posed the question of unemployed or useless negativity to the 'labour of the negative' that for Kojève finds its completion and culmination in the homogeneous state (or in the final victory of liberal democracy and market economics, according to Fukuyama). What becomes of negativity when it has no more work to do, when history has been completed, and all that is left is to consume? Bataille concluded that the 'abortive condition', the 'open wound' of such unemployed or useless negativity would constitute 'a refutation of Hegel's closed system' and speculated on what forms it would take (see Botting & Wilson, 1997: 296–300). In the examples of American rap/metal discussed in this book, there is evidence of such unemployed or useless negativity in cultural forms that disclose the 'open wounds' of rage, antagonism, violence, nihilism and 'perverse' eroticism in their castigation of mainstream consumer culture. It is significant, perhaps, that both the neoconservative followers of Strauss and Kojève, and the rap/metal subcultural manifestations of anti-capitalism have a deeply ambivalent relation to consumer culture. The chapter examines the paradoxes inherent to these two apparently opposed, and yet structurally similar positions, and discloses how they emerge out of the negative dialectic of desire itself.

The next seven chapters explore the negativity and the 'niggativity' of American rap/metal in the 1990s in relation to a number of key events in the decade such as the Rodney King riots and the Columbine High School massacre in particular. These events are significant because the forces that produced them are consistent with those generating much of the rage of rap/metal.

## Niggativity

At the same time as Reaganomics was being credited with the collapse of communism, the gangsta rap genre emerged as the ambivalent expression of its internal, inner-city effects. Gangsta rap both contested and exposed the violence of supercapitalism and martial mode of excess control particularly internally on the streets of South Central, Los Angeles. This involved the construction of the hyperbolic gangsta persona drawn from a heritage that goes back to the mythical 'Stagger Lee' of the blues tradition. In rap he adopts a range of positions from an overtly political stance to a very self-conscious performance of the fantasy of black masculine potency and lawless enjoyment. More self-consciously political, the ambivalent term 'niggativity' was coined by Chuck D (from Public Enemy), partly as a critique of gangsta's political ambiguity. The term is descriptive of both the gangsta's violent mode of sovereign expenditure and his/her affirmation of all the most lurid luxuries, the bling, that consumer capitalism has to offer. On the face of it, the gangsta 'nigga' is an unlikely point of identification for suburban white culture, and yet the phenomenon of the 'wigga' (white, wanna-be-nigga) and the success of companies like Nike testify to the fascination that such a figure holds.

Nike has sought to transcend the cynicism with which much of consumer culture is regarded through appealing directly to the authenticity that is granted to African-American culture, an authenticity that is grounded in, and guaranteed by, nothing other than the experience of slavery itself, and the bad conscience surrounding it. Since the value of brands is highly uncertain and contingent, it becomes crucial for a successful brand to associate itself with a value that is imagined as sovereign, as indifferent to the market values established by consumer capitalism even as it is a direct differential effect of them. Nike's goal of transcendence and universality is sought, paradoxically, through recourse to a particular locus of sovereign authenticity: the cool established by African-American culture. Nike have been able to survive bad publicity concerning exploitative conditions of production in Vietnam and China through the utilisation of the cultural cool and hip sophistication of the descendants of slave labour. Indifferent to labour conditions in the East, white kids in the suburban malls will buy anything authenticated by the sovereignty of African-American non-productive expenditure, the enjoyment embodied by the gangsta or African-American sporting hero.

The disaffected son of the retired CIA agent played by Robert de Niro in

*Meet the Parents* (Roach, 2000) has two posters prominently displayed on his wall: Lil' Kim and Korn. In the late 1990s Lil' Kim explored both the commercial and the artistic potential of African-American sexuality in the gangsta netherworld, turning its gender politics upside down. If Lil' Kim represents the acme of black female desirability and assertive independence, Korn represent the nadir of white self-loathing and male inadequacy: 'It always seems that I'm dreaming of something that I can never be / I will always be that pimp I see in all of my fantasies' ('A.D.I.D.A.S', 1996). As is exhaustively documented in his songs, Jonathan Davis, lead singer of Korn was a 'geek' and a 'nerd' who was bullied at high school in Bakersfield, a very nondescript part of California. Korn are generally credited with inaugurating nu metal, a subgenre that through its fusion of rap and metal became the musical expression of the wigga. Korn's song 'A.D.I.D.A.S' self-consciously acknowledges the identification with African-American culture and the inadequacy it implies. The title of course namechecks a famous sportswear manufacturer and song by Run DMC that contributed to its transcendence as a luxury brand, but in Korn's hands it also becomes an acronym – all day I dream about sex – implying, of course, that that is all he can do. The glamour of the gangsta sets off the miserable banality of the mall rat and the boredom of the skateboarder that is given voice by Davis.

## Rage and the Machine

Korn and the bands that followed them like the Deftones, Coal Chamber and particularly Slipknot specialise in a kind of non-specific rage of frustration and general negativity that is spewed out in records that can be extraordinarily aggressive and unpleasant. A combination of grunge, rap, funk, thrash and punk (with a little death metal thrown in), bands like Korn and Slipknot completely eschew the pomp masculinity and hyperbolic self-celebration that characterises much rap and heavy metal and instead revel in fantasies of violence against everyone and everything. The music is accompanied by the abject utterances of self-abnegation, self-loathing and disgust. Statements such as 'All that sucks dies!', 'chop down the big-wigs, shoot the televisions', 'kill me', 'I feel like a wound', 'I wanna slit your throat and fuck the wound', 'The whole world is my enemy', 'I'm not pretty and I'm not cool / I'm fat and ugly so fuck you' and 'Zeros and ones are everything – execute me' constitute the genre, though others are more specific in their (self-)loathing and victimology. Korn's debut album in 1994 established their reputation through remarkable (for the super-macho tradition of heavy rock) lyrics concerned with child abuse, school bullying and laments for destroyed childhood. The track 'Daddy', for example, rivals Sylvia Plath in its analysis of paternal abuse and the complicity of the victim. As unprepossessing as these materials may appear, they are enormously successful. In the mid- to- late 1990s and early 2000s they became the music of choice for the young, white, suburban middle classes, particularly schoolchildren. The albums of Korn and Slipknot hit the top of the charts immediately they were released, their logos and slogans everywhere.

While they are commercially hugely successful, nu metal bands generally have a hard edge to them. Slipknot's precise political stance is unclear, but they are dedicated to techniques of shock and provocation that situate them outside of America's conservative mainstream. As such there is a link to the more politically focused 'alternative' metal groups that are explicitly anti-capitalist. Pioneer rap core bands like Rage Against the Machine and Biohazard, for example, attempt to speak from a position heterogeneous to the 'machine'. Rage Against the Machine, Biohazard and others are not representative of neo-Luddite protests against technology, but are against the technical, social and economic 'machine' of supercapitalism, particularly in its conjunction with American imperialism and war. The machine is another name for the network economy that facilitates a systemic dominance and reduction of life inasmuch as it constitutes an electronic ecosphere that supports and sustains life only in so far as it is economic. But precisely because it provides such an ecosystem, the life of such bands is dependent upon it. The rage therefore emanates from a point both heterogeneous and yet interior to the machine: an impossible point of non-machinic 'authenticity' which is constantly referred to by these bands, but which is nowhere locatable and barred. The authenticity of any utterance is of course instantly erased the moment that it signifies as an element in the network of the machine that produces it as a new product and object of consumption. Always attempting to bump up against the limits of the consumable, therefore, authentic utterances lie at the 'cutting edge' (to use a managerialist cliché) of capitalisable innovations. Authenticity is a continually mobile, lost object that resides nowhere and in nothing other than the waste that is expended, expelled or repelled by the machine. But, at the same time, it is in such repellent detritus that the newest, most desirable products might be found. Symptomatic of violent refusals of Western capitalism elsewhere, the authenticity associated with trauma and violence also returns to the war machine precisely at the point where the pleasure principle of American popular cultural hegemony reaches its limit.

## All is war

According to *Rolling Stone,* rap and metal are far and away the most popular musical forms of US soldiers participating in the occupation of Iraq. In a poll of 'what troops in Iraq listen to as they roll into battle', rap and metal artists took the top nine out of ten places, including Tupac, Eminem, System of a Down, Linkin Park, Hatebreed and Nickelback. The number one favourite was Drowning Pool's 'Bodies' (2001), a song that was suppressed by American radio stations in the immediate aftermath of the attacks on the World Trade Center and the Pentagon. Since rap and metal have been, over the past fifteen years, the most commercially successful forms of music, this popularity is hardly surprising. But high-energy, aggressive and negative rap and metal songs are also favoured for their motivational qualities. Soldiers download music from the internet and purchase CDs from websites, 'burn and trade mixes with fellow soldiers and rig their government-issued equipment to pump music into their headphones' (Serpick, 2006: 110). *Rolling Stone* quotes Sgt. Brandon Welsh who affirms that, 'to get psyched up to go into battle, I listen to punk or hardcore, like Pantera or Metallica, and after every patrol, when we were going back to base and we knew we were alive, we played "This Is Now", by Hatebreed' (20).

Ironically, the US military has also used heavy metal (and songs from Sesame Street) to torment Iraqi prisoners (see DeGregory, 2004, and BBC News World, 2003). Rap and metal, therefore, are used both as motivational devices and as weapons. Metal is also used as a simulation of war. Christopher Coker, in his book on contemporary warfare, tells how US bomber pilots fly missions with heavy metal pumping through their headsets as if compensating for their remoteness from the bloody consequences of their actions. Here, remarkably, metal becomes the double of war in a heightened form.

Death metal, one of the most extreme genres, has even been cited as a condition to which war's bloody violence might aspire. Discussing reports of how, on 20 October 2005, US soldiers 'desecrated Taliban bodies', Suhail Malik quotes an Australian investigative news programme that broadcast a film which appeared to show US soldiers burning the bodies of two fighters as a taunt to nearby Islamic militants: 'According to a transcript of the program, the soldiers faced the bodies towards Mecca in a deliberately provocative move and set them on fire. One said, "Wow, look at the blood coming out of the mouth on that one, fucking straight death metal"' (Malik, 2006: 110). Chapter 10 looks at how death metal provides a simulation of Satan's rage not just in the horrific visions that it constructs from 'the clippings and footage of daily carnage and abuse' (Bogue, 2004: 105), but also in its visions of apocalypse. Musically, as Ronald Bogue argues, death metal creates 'an aggressive sonic machine of destruction, an electronic nonhuman sound shredder' (91) that both performs and thematises assemblages of non-human becomings.

The book concludes at the point of George W. Bush's declaration of the war on terror, a declaration that formalises the condition of perpetual war that had been raging undeclared throughout the 1990s in the form of supercapitalism. The chapter looks at the potential fate of the Great Satan in an age when, as Derrida writes, 'clashes of force in view of the hegemony [of the United States and its allies] no longer oppose the sovereign state to an enemy that takes either an actual or virtual state form' (Derrida, 2005: 155). This suggestion implies a number of consequences which will determine that the pre-eminent question of global politics will concern becoming nonAmerican. Rap and metal are thus viewed from a global perspective as pure forms without any determining content which are already providing a vehicle for such becomings in the context of supercapitalism.

## Notes

1    Pervez Musharraf, the President of Pakistan, claimed that the Bush administration threatened to bomb his country 'into the stone age' if it did not co-operate with the US after 9/11. See *The Times* 22 September 2006: 1.
2    A popular cartoon that appeared on pages and profiles on myspace.com concerned an image of Anderson in white T-shirt, jeans and sneakers carrying two large bags of money. In the picture he is looking back with a big grin on his face, the speech bubble saying 'See you emo fags later.' See www.myspace.com/wthanb (2006).

# 2

# Supercapitalism

What *general economy* defines first is the explosive character of this world, carried to an extreme degree of explosive tension in the present time. A curse obviously weighs on human life in so far as it does not have the strength to control a vertiginous movement. (Georges Bataille, 1988: 40)

With the possible exception of nuclear weapons, capitalism is the most powerful of human inventions. (Edward Luttwak, 1999: ix)

The foundation of American strength is … a diverse, modern society [that] has inherent, ambitious entrepreneurial energy. Our strength comes from what we do with that energy. That is where our national security begins. ('The National Security Strategy of the United States of America', The White House, 2001a)

The world is my expense
The cost of my desire
                              (Rage Against the Machine, 'Sleep Now in the Fire', 1999)

## 6 August 1945

While neither capitalism nor nuclear weapons have yet to completely devastate the world, both inventions have demonstrated their immense potential and a movement of proliferation that has become vertiginous. In so far as official warnings concerning global warming are accurate as the effect of capitalist modes of production, these economic forces are in the process of laying waste to the world more effectively, thus far, than nuclear weapons.[1] According to 'The National Security Strategy of the United States', published in the wake of the attack on the Pentagon and the World Trade Center (The White House, 2001), 'entrepreneurial energy' is the foundation of its strategic defence. For the White House it is American capitalism, rather than its nuclear weapons, that is the source of the United States' 'unprecedented – and unequalled – strength and influence in the world'. The first and final sentences that frame this important document suggest that immanent to America's status as a superpower is a supercapitalism that provides its strength, the energy and force of its expansion and defence. If that is the case, what does that imply for international relations – economic as well as political – and the relation between the state and the global economy that has provided the means for the superiority of capitalism over other economic systems?

While the United States may regard capitalism as a weapon or even the major modality of war, and while it may prove to be an invention just as destructive or more so than nuclear weapons, the main point of capitalism was always to generate wealth. Its generation of wealth, however, has always involved a relation to death. Monetary wealth is quite abstract, a purely human notion of wealth that negates the natural resources of the earth; indeed, negates them precisely to the extent that the earth is regarded as a site of natural resources, rather than wealth in and for itself. Capitalist wealth negates and mortifies the life that it expends through generating itself.

Capitalism is a form of negativity. It transforms the world even as it negates and destroys it. It is thus a form of negativity in the sense that this word is understood philosophically (see Coole, 2000). It effects a continuous process of transformation of the given reality, whether that is nature or traditional societies and cultures. As Luttwak affirms,

> Capitalism transforms both ends of every traditional, bureaucratic, or patrimonial economy it conquers. With that, inevitably, much else is transformed, from the ways of politics and government to private habits and personal tastes, from the patterns of family life to the very landscape of town and country. (Luttwak, 1999: ix)

Nick Land makes a similar point, in more colourful language, in a brilliant article from 1993. For Land, capitalism is an inhuman assemblage of machinic desires that 'rip up political cultures, delete traditions and dissolve subjectivities'; it is an 'unlocalizable assault' upon the socius. Through ever more 'incomprehensible experiments in commodification, enveloping, dismantling, and circulating every subjective space', capitalism keeps on the move 'towards a terminal nonspace, melting the earth onto the body without organs' (Land, 1993: 479). That is to say, it melts the earth down to a pure surface, a purely contentless form for the recording of new processes of production and consumption. But whether any one particular political culture, tradition or national character can exclude itself from and control this powerful invention is doubtful. Even America therefore must become subject to its negative power of becoming, even to the point of becoming nonAmerican.

Dynamic and brutal, 'with its bankruptcies and industrial downfalls that engulf people, communities and entire regions', capitalism is a mode of negativity defined in both its dialectical and Nietzschean varieties by Diana Coole as 'a creative–destructive mode of becoming'. It is 'a restless forming and deforming that crystallises in the myriad phenomena which are its symptoms and symbols, only to shatter them as it invents itself afresh' (Coole, 2000: 86). For Luttwak, this 'creative destruction is the very engine of capitalist prosperity, the source of its constant innovation' (Luttwak, 1999: 30). Human beings are also part of the earth that is melted down as a surface in the negation of all values which is an affirmation of pure form. Capitalism not only conquers traditional markets and economic relationships, but also extends its reach into every sphere of human activity. As Luttwak notes, 'in the process, the *contents* of medicine, art, literature and sport, for example, are utterly deformed by the removal of their personal satisfactions, of all disinterested motives and ethical boundaries, being replaced with money, often lots of it, though not necessarily for the protagonists' (226). Profit is an asubjective mechanism of negativity; it is not driven by greed because the wealth it generates exceeds human scale and comprehension. Greed is a psychological category that has no significant bearing on contemporary capitalism:

> As if the profit-seeking tropism of a transnational capitalism propagating itself though epidemic consumerism were intelligible in terms of personal subjective traits. Wanting more is an index of interlock with cyberpositive machinic processes, and not the expression of private idiosyncrasy. What could be more impersonal – disinterested – than a *haut bourgeois* capital expansion servo-mechanism striving to double $10 billion? And even these creatures are disappearing into silicon viro-finance automatisms, where massively distributed and anonymized human ownership has become as vacuously nominal as democratic sovereignty. (Land, 1993: 478)

Hans Moravec, perhaps the most pre-eminent twentieth-century writer on robotics and artificial intelligence, predicted that by the middle of the twenty-first century robots will have taken over the economy. Indeed, it is already happening. Major US companies routinely use computer systems to lower inventories, respond better to consumer demand, anticipate and locate new markets. But it is not a question of machines replacing human beings or human desires, but rather of a machinic process in which the term 'machine' should be understood as an assemblage of organic and non-organic elements. These elements interlock together in a mode of negative becoming according to an in-human logic. It is human to want more, but this demand is built into the assemblage as an algorithm that ultimately bears no relationship to pleasures, enjoyments or satisfactions on a human scale.

Land's suggestion that massively distributed and anonymous human ownership 'has become as vacuously nominal as democratic sovereignty' may seem excessive. But it is precisely the withdrawal of the state and the redundancy of politics that is one of the main reasons for, and indeed effects of, contemporary capitalism. Edward Luttwak calls it 'turbo-capitalism' and dates its emergence from the end of the 1970s in the abolition of anti-competition laws and regulations, the development of technological innovations, particularly information technology, the wholesale privatisation of state-run or controlled industries and the removal of import barriers. There has been an abandonment of state central planning, administrative direction and most forms of regulatory control. While the metaphor of the turbine evokes capitalism in the jet age, information technology would perhaps be a more appropriate technology to evoke, and it does not really do justice to other factors defining contemporary capitalism nor to its profound effects and implications. The term that this book proposes is supercapitalism for a variety of reasons. Primarily, because it must be related to America as the superpower whose nuclear weapons overwhelm the world militarily. The US military expenditure exceeds that of the rest of the world put together. Such expenditure depends upon, facilitates and is perhaps the most visible expression of American capitalism.

Developments in information technology that have enabled the acceleration and globalisation of capitalism have been led by both the American military (the early development of the internet) and American companies (IBM, Microsoft). But, further, commentators have argued that there is something specific to American culture or even subjectivity that informs the logic and success of contemporary capitalism. For Luttwak, it is a secularised even contentless Calvinism that imbues profit with a supreme value to the degree to which it is not squandered in enjoyment but put to work in the generation of greater profit. This can be allied to a characteristic American pragmatism that Christopher Coker locates in American military uses of technology. Writing on the US military war machine, Coker finds in the computer's focus on solving immediate and practical questions an absence of aesthetic, moral and ethical considerations that is an expression of the 'American spirit, one that finds little time for metaphysics' (Coker, 2004: 123).

But there is little point in returning an analysis of supercapitalism back to a discourse of national character or subjectivity. Rather, the 'American spirit' should be regarded as being like a unit of code, similar to the so-called selfish gene, another extrapolation of Protestant ideology. Supercapitalism's contentless, pragmatic Calvinism is like a genetic algorithm that turns economy into a computing machine. It is the immanent principle of negativity that drives the process of destruction–creation, laying waste to the given reality of the world. It is supercapitalism's negative will to power where this Nietzschean notion of will is not understood in the sense of free will, volition, intentionality or moral responsibility but as a strictly asubjective principle of an immanent desire to overpower and dominate. In Nietzschean terms, supercapitalism is beyond good and evil and therefore the form of capitalism appropriate to the *übermensch* or superman. It is a mechanism for the revaluation of all values, or rather the negation of all values in an affirmation of the power of becoming pure form.

As such, the United States is itself vulnerable to this power of supercapitalist overcoming; it implies ultimately an overcoming of humanity and its American antecedence. Supercapitalism traverses America, exceeds its boundaries, even to the point of negating it, of waging war against and subjugating it, all other nations and even the very form of the nation-state to its will-to-power. As Luttwak notes, now 'nations exist to sustain economies, rather than the other way around' (Luttwak, 1999: 4). Thus the term 'supercapitalism' is also used to suggest that capitalism has superseded itself to become a form of war, although in the process transforming the classical conception of war. While war between nations has been deterritorialised by a geo-economics that simulates international relations in a purely economic domain,[2] supercapitalism has reformatted the US military itself so that its modality and force has become primarily economic.

So while the term supercapitalism denotes both America as a superpower and the overcoming of America, it also denotes both capitalism and the overcoming of capitalism, or at least the way in which capitalism was over-coded and conditioned by the state, its police and its army. This is another quality which capitalism has in common with nuclear weapons. Nuclear weapons, designed as a weapon of world war, negated the possibility of a world war. There can be no war between a nuclear and a non-nuclear power, simply domination, and a war between nuclear powers promises mutually assured destruction, at least this was the assumption throughout most of the cold war. The form and force promised by nuclear weapons dominated, in excess of any individual state, the threshold of war. For Gilles Deleuze and Félix Guattari, the war machine in its nuclear form has 'taken charge of the aim, worldwide order, and the States [have become] no more than objects or means adapted to that machine' (Deleuze and Guattari, 1988: 421). The war machine negated itself through the imposition of a 'terrifying peace', a Mexican stand-off frozen at the point of planetary death.

Since the end of the cold war, supercapitalism has economised nuclear power to the degree to which its deployment is being seriously considered in the form of tactical weapons, a suggestion ironically justified, currently, by the threat of their localised use by terrorists. The complicating factor is that these terrorists are increasingly less allied to a state, whereas only states can be credibly threatened by American nuclear power. Further, the powers of terror ranged against the United States and their allies utilise the finance system and forms of mobility and networking that are the very condition of supercapitalism. Just as the threat of the use of nuclear weapons has become decentralised from the state, so supercapitalism has become the means through which global war, which traverses the boundaries of states, takes place.

Since World War One, of course, global war (as opposed to, or in conjunction with, empire) has increasingly become the means and modality of corporate capitalism, even as war itself has adopted commercial and economic methods. But towards the end of the twentieth century, war and business started to become the same thing, and thus transformed themselves, not just because war supports business or because the latter capitalises on the advantages offered by military and information technology. The American spirit of bourgeois economy (for which war was traditionally the excess) has given way to supercapitalism in which war is the modus operandi. The work ethic has 'gone ballistic' (Goldman and Papson, 1998: 153).

## Restricted and general economies

This understanding of supercapitalism is consistent with Jean-Joseph Goux's interpretation of Bataillean general economics, which he sees as characteristic of what he calls postmodern capitalism (Goux, 1998a). Throughout his *oeuvre*, but particularly in the three-volume theoretical work *The Accursed Share* (1988, 1991), Bataille draws a distinction between restricted and general economy, which opposes work to non-work and useful production to non-productive expenditure. For Bataille, capitalism is firmly located with the former rather than the latter.

This helpful but problematic distinction between restricted and general is nicely illustrated by two definitions of the term 'consumption'. The first definition is: 'to use up, expend, exhaust, destroy or waste'. Bataille gives this sense of consumption the name *dépense*, a non-productive mode of expenditure represented among other things by

> luxury, mourning, war, cults, the construction of sumptuary monuments, games, spectacles, arts, perverse sexual activity (i.e., deflected from genital finality) – all these represent activities which, at least in primitive circumstances, have no end beyond themselves. (Botting and Wilson, 1997: 169).

The second definition concerns modes of expenditure that 'serve as a means to the end of production' and is generally understood in relation to 'consumer society'. Consumption here is concerned with the exchange of goods and services, with what people choose to buy or purchase, consuming being to take up or take away something, a meaning which has its roots in the latin *con-sumere*. For Bataille, however, *dépense* must be distinguished from modes of useful consumption because with *dépense* 'the accent is placed on a *loss* that must be as great as possible in order for that activity to take on its true meaning' (169).

In his own analyses, Bataille is generally concerned with *dépense* rather than useful consumption since he believes that the main problem for living organisms is to consume, that is to expend and waste, the energy which they receive that is in excess of that necessary for maintaining life. Based in an analysis of biological and physical processes, Bataille's account also extends to human societies where he discusses the ways in which ancient and non-Western societies destroy their excess in festivals, sacrifice, rituals of potlatch, and so on. In contrast, Western society, since the epoch of modernity, broadly from the seventeenth century on, has increasingly used its excess to multiply goods, commodities and services designed to make life more comfortable. That is to say that Western society, horrified at the immorality of the waste, uselessness and violence of archaic festive practices, has individuated and multiplied consumption in the second sense in order to utilise, rationally and morally, its excess. For Bataille, however, these 'diversions', aimed at the conservation and utilisation of excess, have always been inadequate. Consequently, the problem of the utilisation and distribution of excess has resulted, supremely in the twentieth century, in the mass consumption of human beings, goods and resources in two world wars and in perpetual violent conflict around the globe.

In his essay 'General Economics and Postmodern Capitalism' (1998a), Jean-Joseph Goux problematises the clear distinction between restricted and general economy in relation to contemporary capitalism. Perception of the twentieth-century emergence of the postmodern economy can be conveniently dated from the publication of Jean-François Lyotard's *Postmodern Condition* in 1979 (Lyotard, 1984). This publication broadly coincided with the election of Ronald Reagan to the presidency of America and the victory of Margaret Thatcher in Britain. In both countries, the 1980s saw the subsequent de-regulation of commercial practices, the wholesale privatisation of state-controlled industries, and an opening of all forms of social life and organisation to the free market. Much of the rest of the developed and developing world has followed suit and the global economy has been transformed.

In reflections on capitalism in the 1980s, it became obvious that it is no longer evident, if it ever was, what can be described as simply useful or idly luxurious, or what establishes the distinction between productive economic activity and wasteful, useless expenditure. Furthermore, in economists like George Gilder, Ronald Reagan's favourite author, apparently, Goux saw 'a transformation of the ethics of consumption, desire and pleasure' that left classical economic thinking, along with its principles of rationality, utility and morality, in confusion. In postmodern capitalism, distinctions between elements sacred and profane that once organised communal, symbolic life are expelled as part of the unprecedented amounts of waste that the 'capitalism of abundance' produces with such abandon (Goux, 1998a: 210–14). For Bataille, the notion of the gift, as understood by Marcel Mauss, exemplified the notion of general economy, particularly in social practices such as potlatch. However, Goux argues that contemporary capitalism requires a new understanding of the role of gifts along with a new appreciation of waste. Indeed, it is capitalism that appropriates the idea of the gift, making it operate as an aneconomic principle of continued circulation, profit and production–consumption. Capitalism gives, generously, irrationally; it innovates, its entrepreneurs take risks, speculate and sacrifice time and money on the production and branding of goods which consumers may or may not desire (and certainly do not need). Chance and fortune succeed rational calculation, unpredictability comes to the fore in (an)economic circulation. Heterogeneous elements are supplanted, absorbed, incorporated, into the circulation of production and consumption, part of an 'overall capitalist market strategy, which consists of dropping into the magnetic field of the political economy (of market exchange-value) everything "sacred" and "transcendent" that might appear to escape it – including desire' (Goux, 1998a: 202).

Indeed, it is the trace of general economy that sustains a principle of restriction in the midst of a generally unrestricted market economy. For there is a paradox in the suggestion that all points of expenditure (both sacred and abject) have been restricted and utilised for profit. That would mean that there is no point of sacred exteriority, no heterogeneity, in relation to which an economy can be restricted. Therefore there is no restricted economy either. There is then, generally speaking, an unrestricted economy in which hitherto sacred elements, relics, monuments, totems and objects of beauty or of abjection and waste are all subject to an unregulated system of value. It is no accident that the only buildings currently being built which look like cathedrals are the huge shopping malls such as the Trafford Centre in Manchester, which looks like St Peter's in Rome. But the point here is that shopping malls – representing the great gift or potlatch of consumer choice – precisely do resemble cathedrals rather than factories. This visual and architectural excess is necessary to their functionality, their market efficiency. It represents their superefficiency, which is to say a principle of exorbitant efficiency that transforms the conventional meaning of the term.

It is in the idea of efficiency that is itself unregulated and exorbitant that such an analysis resonates with Lyotard's account of the postmodern condition. For Lyotard, the postmodern condition is marked by an eclipse of canons of judgement, whether rational, aesthetic, legal or empirical, by performance tables or accounts of profit and loss (Lyotard, 1984: 44–5). What Lyotard calls 'a generalized spirit of performativity' turns knowledge into a commodity within a technologically enabled market of information (44–5). The maximisation of output and minimisation of input constitutes the only goal, with the 'principle of optimal performance' presiding as the operational code. Though technology is considered to be but one game among a multiplicity of others, it nonetheless predominates owing to its capacity for deciding, without recourse to a judgement other than one of economic performance, what is the most efficient move.

New technology, particularly digital technology, provides the model and means of efficiency and enhanced performance across a range of activities traditionally both restricted and general like commerce and war. Cybernetics establishes a plane of consistency in which disparate activities take place according to the same economic logic. However, the efficiencies and speeds that are generated and facilitated by digital technology exceed human scale. Restricted economy was precisely supposed to be calculated and measured according to rational ideas of human need, interest and proportion. Such efficiencies that are precipitated by digital technologies very quickly become a mode of excess, becoming closer to general economic phenomena beyond the scope of human comprehension. On the one hand, in the world of commerce, such enhanced computerised efficiency enables corporate power to preserve itself and expand its domination, but, at the same time, it is caught up in the general economic logic of excess as a mode of sumptuous expenditure and waste. After the end of the cold war, capitalism has generalised itself as a form of expenditure. 'No society has "wasted" as much as contemporary capitalism', writes Goux (1998a), and in this waste lies the value of its affluence.

## War and commerce

From the early modern period of mercantilism there has always been a connection between war and commerce in the West, articulated but never totally determined by the emergent European states. Since its ostensible intention was to find gold in order to fund armies, 'mercantilism was an economic phenomenon, but its purposes were strictly political, indeed strategic' (Luttwak, 1999: 140). But whatever its ostensible purpose, mercantilism gave rise to great quasi-martial global corporations like the East India Company that operated, partly because of the great distances it covered and the great wealth it accumulated, in the margins of the state, in relative autonomy. Indeed, it founded and administered a number of key Indian city-states, including the current capital Mumbai, for over a hundred years until it was dismantled and its rule of India replaced by the British Raj in the mid-nineteenth century.

It was in the twentieth century war has facilitated commerce and vice versa continually but predominantly for political ends. The second world war was fought, still on the basis of empire, for new markets, particularly in the East. The second world war ended in the cold war nuclear stand-off between East and West, a war that was won by a combination of economic and military means in proxy wars. The martial effect of commerce was highlighted at the end of the cold war in the form of a double involution that found war becoming internal to commerce and vice versa. A superficial example would be the cola wars between Coca-Cola and Pepsi Cola which erupted as the markets in Vietnam and the old Soviet Union were opened. The cola wars mark a symbolic point where capitalism went 'ballistic' in a self-declared world war geared towards maximum consumption. As the political scientist Benjamin Barber argues, 'the Cola Wars and the market wars of the modern global economy are really a new phenomenon ... the conqueror is conquering not by killing bodies but by winning over souls' (cited in Angelico,1998).

It was President Nixon who introduced Pepsi to the Soviet Union in 1971, achieving a soft-drink monopoly for the company that sponsored his presidential campaign in the late 1960s. However, Coca-Cola was allowed into Moscow in 1985, and when the Berlin Wall came down in 1989, 'Coca-Cola were right there giving away six packs and twelve packs'. Mark Prendergrast notes that subsequently there has been a 'blitzkrieg of capitalism' led by Coca-Cola (Angelico, 1998). The cola wars are of course mutually beneficial to either company, fostering the illusion of choice in the midst of a highly publicised corporate battle that raises the profile and visibility of the combatants, their brand names and products. Further, as the wars rage across the world, companies justify their cultural imperialism as an exercise in bringing prosperity and civilisation to a dark and godless world. Jim Lawrence, Executive Officer of Pepsi-Cola International, recalls introducing Pepsi-Cola to Vietnam two hours after President Clinton lifted the embargo. 'And two hours and one minute later, Vietnamese all over Ho Chi Minh City were slugging down Pepsi Cola and saying if this is what America is about, then that seems pretty good to me' (Angelico, 1998). His suggestion that it took Pepsi-Cola only one minute to achieve what the French and US military failed to achieve in twenty years is ample testimony to the high efficiency of the supercapitalist war machine. It incorporates and deflects the resistance associated with national identity on to another cola company. Indeed, in so far as national identity is associated with indigenous food and drink, traditional cultural and social practices, it becomes eroded by the exciting onslaught represented by the cola companies. As Benjamin Barber argues,

> We talked, in Vietnam, about winning the hearts and souls of men. The cola wars are only about the hearts and souls of men. And what they know is that if you can win the hearts and souls of men by fabricating needs and persuading people they must have the products you sell, you win a war much more permanently and with much more conviction than if you simply occupy a town or occupy a country. (Barber, cited in Angelico, 1998).

Companies in the field of information technology have led the way in adopting martial strategies in transnational business competition, not only through the technology that they have developed and introduced but also through the opportunities and risks that technological innovation brings. As with war, the introduction of new weapons technology can prove utterly devastating. For multinational corporations it is not simply a matter of 'making a profit' – Microsoft makes more profit than is humanly imaginable, yet they still see themselves as vulnerable because a new technological innovation could transform a particular horizon of operability and wipe them out. Consequently, Microsoft aims at ubiquity; the functional goal for multinationals is total economic and cultural domination, with strategic alliances, resulting thereby in a generally economic conflagration: an order of total corporate war.

But even as war became the immanent principle of commerce, commerce remained internal to war as the revolution in military affairs of the 1990s took up new economic processes and strategy enabled by new technology. Since the middle-to-late 1990s, the US Military has begun to adopt transnational corporate means. In 1998, US military and naval strategists Vice Admiral Arthur K. Cebrowski and John Gartska published a seminal article in the military journal *Proceedings* on 'Network-Centric Warfare' (Cebrowski and Gartska, 1998). The article argues for a revolution in military affairs (RMA) which has subsequently informed the wars in Afghanistan and Iraq. In this article Cebrowski and Gartska draw parallels with business and urge the military to adopt business practices and conceive the goal of the military as one of wealth creation. War is an extension of wealth creation not simply because the military's primary role is to protect western business and open up new markets. Nor is it because of its interest in maintaining the economic and political power of the military–industrial complex, but rather in the profound sense that the new *raison d'etre* of war is not political but economic. Further, Cebrowski and Gartska argue that the military should model themselves on businesses like Wal-Mart and Morgan Grenfell because these businesses have proved themselves to be more efficient and effective war machines than the US military. In their paper they urge that, like businesses, military organisations and operations must 'capitalize (in every sense) on the advances and advantages of information technology'. Citing the way Microsoft locked in the Windows-Intel standard in personal computers, thereby locking out Apple, Cebrowski and Gartska write, 'locking-out competition and locking-in success can occur quickly, even overnight. We seek an analogous effect in warfare' (Cebrowski and Gartska, 1998).

It is the example of Wal-Mart, the gigantic all-purpose discount chain store, that most impresses the military strategists. By 1996 Wal-Mart had consistently outperformed its competitors, accumulating profits of $3 billion on sales of nearly $105 billion. In the process it visited 'destruction on hundreds of American market towns' through putting out of business town-centre specialist retailing and smaller supermarket chains, and destroying communal life (Luttwak, 1999: 220). Yet it was not simply Wal-Mart's military-style devastation of urban centres which impressed the navy strategists, it was their use of an information-rich, network-centric, as opposed to platform-based, mode of operations:

> Wal-Mart was able to achieve this edge by making the shift to network-centric operations and translating information superiority into competitive advantage. Realizing that it had grown past the point where it could cost-effectively synchronize supply and demand from the top down, the company over time set up a sophisticated operational architecture – consisting of a sensory capability and a transaction grid – to generate a higher level of awareness within its retail ecosystem. (Cebrowski and Gartska, 1998)[3]

Cebrowski and Gartska argue that similar information networks can be used on the battlefield. Indeed, they become the battlefield as systems of sensors, surveillance and mobile computer screens link individual soldiers, satellites and operational commanders. More importantly, these networks enable different nodal points to organise from the bottom up, or 'self-synchronise'.

Network-centric warfare does not involve traditional arborescent control and command structures, but operates in different directions and on different levels within interlinked information networks and feedback loops which enable maximum awareness throughout the whole (headless) body. The old arborescent structure, where command and control always has to go through a central governing head or centre of consciousness, has given way to a system of control that has become immanent to the network. Moving at the speed of digital informational flows, the network provides 'the ability to generate and sustain very high levels of competitive space awareness, which is translated into competitive advantage' (Cebrowski and Gartska, 1998). As Clay Risen in an article for the *New Republic* comments, 'like Wal-Mart, through network-centric warfare (NCW) the military could achieve a level of total information awareness that would allow it to know exactly what the enemy was doing at all times' (Risen 2006).

Risen begins his article by describing the enthusiasm of US Defense Secretary Donald Rumsfeld for network-centric warfare and the economic model of military affairs. In a speech given on 10 September 2001, Rumsfeld castigated the US military for being 'out of touch with the modern boardroom'. 'Successful modern businesses', announced Rumsfeld, 'are leaner and less hierarchical than ever before. They reward innovation and they share information. They have to be nimble in the face of rapid change or they die' (Risen, 2006). Through the campaigns in Afghanistan and Iraq over which he presided, Rumsfeld continually drew on the buzzwords of new economic theory in his explanations and justifications for the war. The notion of the 'tipping point', for example, was continually referred to in the early days of the assault on Iraq. This assault was led by a relatively small, rapid mobile force in contrast to the much larger force that waged the first Gulf War in 1991. As Kevin Kelly in his book *Ten New Rules for the New Economy* (1998: 34) argues, the network economy produces lower tipping points than industrial economies, so that significantly smaller pools can lead to runaway dominance sooner.

Significant parts of the US military and the prosecution of its wars and security operations became privatised in the 1990s and 2000s to military contractors such as DynCorp and MPRI. Pieterse suggests that the global market in private military contracts is estimated at $100 billion. Their services include 'training foreign troops, low intensity conflict overseas, security for President Karzai in Afghanistan, airport security and military recruitment' (Pieterse, 2004: 125). Indeed the biggest army in Iraq after the American army was not that of Britain but a private army of military, engineering contractors and subcontracted logistics personnel. Following the intelligence failure that allowed the attack on the World Trade Center, the Pentagon set up a web site on the principle of using the model of financial speculation and the futures market to predict future terrorist activity: 'A mutually advantageous combination of online betting and intelligence gathering ... it illustrated the novel possibilities of neoliberal empire and war as business' (Pieterse, 2004: 126).

While marketing was originally an extension of military and political propaganda according to Edward Bernays, the 'father of American public relations' (cited in Curtis, 2002), in the 1990s and 2000s marketing techniques entered government and military operations with a vengeance. Pieterse mentions that the Rendon Group, which was responsible for the 'horror fantasy of Iraqi soldiers ripping babies from incubators in Kuwait' in the Gulf War in 1991, was also 'probably responsible for the choreography of tearing down Saddam's monument in Baghdad' and the feel-good 'Saving Private Lynch' story in the Iraq war of 2003 (2004: 129).

These and other examples illustrate not only that war has become 'a business proposition' (Pieterse, 2004: 131), but also Jean-Joseph Goux's argument that the economy has become the dominant paradigm for human activity in the West. And that is also necessarily the case for the rest of the world in so far as it is driven by the global economy and its system of finance. Goux suggests that 'only in the modern era in the West' has the economy 'been separated from all religious, political and moral ends in order to constitute a system ruled by its own laws, which are those of market exchange' (Goux, 1998b: 37). Furthermore, the economy has invaded and taken over all those areas. For Goux, the economy dissolves and reconstitutes social ties according to the dictates of a depersonalised 'regulatory mechanism', but this regulatory mechanism now constitutes even as it operates what military men like Cebrowski and politicians like Rumsfeld call the electronic 'ecosystem'. As their language makes clear, war has become a matter of business, and business war within an electronic ecosystem established by information technology networks.

But to suggest that war is business and business is war requires a different understanding of war and its relationship to the state and international relations. Given both the overwhelming military dominance of the United States and its identification with global capitalism, the question of whether there is any longer such a thing as a meaningful international relation is a topic that will be taken up in the final chapter of this book. Here, it is enough to emphasise that the end of supercapitalism is not the state, even though supercapitalist corporations frequently have to negotiate state law and governments, and the state seeks supercapitalist means to sustain itself and its mode of governance.

Ironically, the day after Rumsfeld agitated for a revolution in military affairs, the United States and the rest of the world were treated to a stunning demonstration of network-centric warfare at work. Or at least according to Clayton D. Saunders, in a Pentagon Report made public in 2002, *Al Qaeda: An Example of Network-Centric Operations*:

> On 11 September 2001, Al Qaeda used information and knowledge advantage, access, and the ability to support forward-based teams, to conduct effects-based operations against the United States. Although obviously not employing the theory, in practice these operations appear to have been network-centric in nature,

with Al Qaeda reaping the benefits inherent in this organizational and operational structure to conduct its attacks. (Saunders, 2002; see also Hoffman, 2002: 13)

Finding its own image in the operability of network-centric stateless terror, the US and its military justifies its own operations that led it beyond the jurisdiction of the state and state law. The war on terror announced by President Bush the following day disintegrates the very concept of war (and of terrorism) since it is potentially waged against everyone but no one of any particular nationality or state. As Jacques Derrida points out, 'there is essentially no longer any such thing that today can be called "war" or "terrorism"', even if some states do bear the force of this 'war's' strategic rationalisation (Derrida, 2005: 156). What is the role of the state in the era of supercapitalism? As corporations operate as if they were at war and national or supranational armies seek to be more like businesses, the question would be whether the military machine and the state have been overrun and superseded by the corporate-capital war machine.

## The state and the war machine

The role of the state has been diminished in the face of the rise of multinational corporations and the acceleration of transnational capitalism made possible by the globalisation of the system of finance and electromagnetic communications. The subsequent correlation between war and commerce, the revolution in military affairs and its relation to the business revolution therefore poses further problems for the state. Since supercapitalism not only establishes direct contact between military criteria and business criteria, and resolves any contradiction between them, the situation, as Alain Joxe notes, 'by-passes politicians. There is no derivation through politics. And politicians cannot restore a role for themselves even by intervening in trade legislation' (Joxe, 2002: 59).

For Edward Luttwak, international relations have been replaced by 'geo-economics'. While traditionally the political goals in the international domain are to secure and extend the physical control of territory, and to gain diplomatic influence over foreign governments, the state's new role has become supplementary to transnational commerce. In contrast to traditional world politics, Luttwak writes, 'the corresponding geo-economic goal is not to achieve the highest possible standard of living, but rather the conquest or protection of desirable roles in the world economy' (Luttwak, 1999: 133). Governments seek, through whatever means are at their disposal (state investment in research and development, market-penetration investments), the conquest or defence of important roles in high-value strategic industries (telecommunications, information technology, biotechnology, aerospace, and high-tech automotive components). 'Winners have financial, creative and higher management functions and control. Losers may only have assembly lines if their domestic market is large enough' (134). The correlation between war and commerce, and the globalisation that enables and accelerates it through the financial and communications systems places the state in a clear secondary role and perhaps, along with other paternal, meta-social guarantees, in a terminal crisis.

For Deleuze and Guattari, in their famous analysis of capitalism in *Anti-Oedipus* (1984), these paternal metasocial guarantees are essential to capitalism. It is the Oedipal family triangle with the father and his correlates — boss, bank manager, head of state, God – which provides the structure necessary for its maintenance. Deleuze and Guattari take an essentially Weberean account of capitalism as the economic expression of bourgeois morality and protestantism. They argue that capitalism acts as an agent of repression through requiring the sublimation of desire in work, thrift and good housekeeping so that the surplus can be reinvested for further profit. The family, 'the State, its police, and its army form a gigantic enterprise of antiproduction, but at the heart of production itself, and conditioning this production' (235). While capitalism is potentially a deterritorialising force, an expression of the schizophrenic process of production, it continually reproduces the Oedipal structure which bounces desire back into a paranoid neurosis (with all its attendant representations) because this is the kind of worker that it requires. The paranoid subject suffers a double fracture in which its 'labour-desire' is alienated in the private property of the privatised family (337).

Supercapitalism, however, fractures paternal law and family structures though its deployment of contract law and its commodification of identity as workers are required to sell themselves and not just their labour in a highly mobile, flexible market. The destiny of the schizo-capitalist subject (or subjectile) is to be a brand, or a desirable product that produces desire, a product that innovates and creates other products, jobs, markets, fantasies, desires.

As capitalism has introduced the mechanism of the market into all the areas of anti-production, Deleuze and Guattari's model no longer holds. Indeed, in his speech to the Pentagon in September 2001, Rumsfeld castigated the military for its 'paranoid' conservatism that 'stifles free thought and crushes new ideas' (cited in Risen, 2006). The penetration of the market into traditional areas of anti-production or the opening up of localised markets on to the power of the global economy, produces 'regional impoverishment ... almost universal community decline, family instability' (Luttwak, 1999: xiv). As the difference between rich and poor is increased and exacerbated, crime also increases. This of course produces a 'paranoid' reaction in the state, with increased police powers, surveillance, incarceration and a political 'back to basics' rhetoric emphasising 'family values'. However, the economic policies of deregulation directly contradict such values and exacerbate their decline, and indeed the decline of the state. All mainstream political parties in the West have adopted broadly the same policies accompanied by a more or less social or moral rhetoric that is directly undermined even as it is supposed to be facilitated by more deregulation, more marketisation and further transformation through the mechanism of optimal performance.

More appropriate than their Oedipalised model to supercapitalism is Deleuze and Guattari's notion of the war machine which, they argue, has a heterogeneous existence to the state (Deleuze and Guattari, 1988: 352). Historically states and state apparati captured and utilised the war machine for its own ends, but the cold war marked a change whereby 'States [became] no more than objects or means adapted to that machine'. States have become even more the objects of this heterogeneous principle of war now that they have been liberated by the thawing of the cold war and mobilised by the global economy. The war machine deterritorialises states and deploys citizens as freelance brands working in transnational corporations or migrant workers. The regulatory mechanism of supercapitalist consumption and exchange, immanent to the networks and the movement of information that flows through them, uses the remains of the state formation as a depository for the excess of the ecosystem, to use Cebrowski and Gartska's metaphor. The economic ecosystem rather than the state provides the conditions for social and cultural life.

The role of states is being reduced to that of a repository of waste expelled or rejected from the ecosystem. The states and their nationalist ideologies are the location and locus of the ecosystem's non-productive residues: pockets of anti-production, anti-capitalist resistance, resentments, corporate burn-outs and drop-outs, the beggars whose presence in the metropolitan cities does so much to encourage the working and consuming population, the human carcasses of exhausted and exploited labour, and its Fascistoid nationalists and racists. The nation-state, the dysfunctional remnants of social and familial life, its so-called ethnicity in its purely non-commodifiable racist manifestations, provides the thin locus of heterogeneity, expenditure and waste in relation to which the war machine smoothes out the space of its economic ecosystem.

War is the exemplary and exciting modality of the economic ecosystem for two main reasons: first it exposes the liberal comforts of commodity consumption to the expenditure – the violence, waste and destruction – that grounds it in images of anti-Western or anti-capitalist despotism, religious extremism, racism and ethnic cleansing; second these heterogeneous forces, discharging violently around various sovereign, despotic figures (Milosevic, Saddam Hussein, Osama Bin Laden), are the expenditure of the superefficient violence that is immanent to the ecosystem itself. It should be remembered that this ecosystem is not a fragile and intricate harmony of interactive and interdependent forces, but a fierce battle order of shifting alliances and synergies aimed at locking out and destroying other competitors.

The war machine, therefore, is located outside the state formation, 'simultaneously in two directions':

> huge worldwide machines branched out over the entire *ecumenon* at a given moment, which enjoy a large measure of autonomy in relation to the States (for example, commercial organization of the 'multinational' type, or industrial

complexes, or even religious formations like Christianity, Islam, certain prophetic
or messianic movements, etc.); but also the local mechanisms of bands, margins,
minorities, which continue to affirm the rights of segmentary societies in
opposition to the organs of State power. (Deleuze and Guattari, 1988: 360)

The alliance that is frequently made between worldwide, transnational commercial organisations and the local mechanisms of bands wherein they often
attempt to locate their authenticity will be the subject of much of this book:
the importance of African-American counterculture to Nike, for example. Further, these global organisations are not as large as they appear because they
manufacture anything. They are rather like bands themselves, a small group of
executives, conceptual artists and marketing men and women who brand goods
made elsewhere. The biggest companies do not manufacture goods; they create concepts, brand goods and consume cheap labour. As Naomi Klein notes,
'Increasingly, brand-name multinationals – Levi's, Nike, Champion, Wal-Mart,
Reebok, the Gap, IBM and General Motors – insist they are just like any one of
us: bargain hunters in search of the best deal in the global mall' (Klein, 2000:
202). The so-called big companies (big in profits but tiny in workforce) contract out to other subcontractors who outsource to a network of home workers
in basements and living rooms or to a shifting population of nomadic and
migrant workers who are assembled in export-processing zones. Klein writes,
'Manufacturing is concentrated and isolated inside the zone as if it were toxic
waste: pure, 100 per cent production at low, low prices' (203). The prices are
low because there are 'no import and export duties, and often no income or
property taxes either … there are 1,000 spread through 70 countries employing roughly 27 million workers' (205). Saskia Sassen writes that the zones are
part of a process of carved-up nations so that 'an actual piece of land becomes
denationalized … Nevermind that the boundaries of these only-temporary,
not-really-happening, denationalized spaces keep expanding to engulf more
and more of their actual nations' (Sassen in Klein, 2000: 207–8).

Perhaps because of its identification of itself as the subject of globalisation,
and in its enthusiasm for the efficiencies of the corporate war machine, America
has been largely uninterested in deploying military force in order to exert a
system of global governance – at least during the 1990s. Writing before the
actions in Afghanistan and Iraq, Alain Joxe complains that America and its
Western allies cynically preside over an 'empire of disorder'. 'The world today is
united by a new form of chaos, an imperial chaos, dominated by the *imperium*
of the United States, though not controlled by it. We lack the words to describe
this new system, while being surrounded by its images' (Joxe, 2002: 78). It is a
matter for historical debate whether US operations in Afghanistan and Iraq
constitute acts of global governance or are narrowly interested acts of strategic
importance concerned with resources otherwise content to fulminate disorder
and chaos.

Where there is a Western alliance in the twenty-first century the leadership of the United States has with evangelical zeal wholly served the interests of commerce and the military, even to the point of militarising the business and administrative classes. The generals in this war are equivalent to elite techno-bureaucrats like Vice-Admiral Cebrowski or Bill Gates. Luttwak notes that today's meritocracy of senior technologists and managers 'do not desire bemedelled uniforms or sumptuous balls, but they do want to command the world scene' (Luttwak, 1999: 133).[4] Which is to say they want to command the chaos of an indefinite world war, not govern or administer the world since that would involve instituting a massive force of anti-production. They wage a militarised commercial war on populations in the West as well as fighting a strategic war for resources, territory and markets with current and future non-Western competitors like India and China. Meanwhile, the indefinite and phantasmatic war on terror justifies a permanent suspension of the rule of state or international law on behalf of raw military power and administration in the name of economic growth and prosperity.

For Giorgio Agamben, even where there are states, the rule of law that they are supposed to instantiate is today in a more or less permanent state of exception or emergency (Agamben, 2005). This state was 'originally understood as something extraordinary, an exception, which should have validity only for a limited period of time, but a historical transformation has made it the normal form of governance' (Agamben, 2004b). A paradoxical situation has arisen in which the absence of state law becomes the condition of the normal form of governance. In the empire of disorder, governance takes place, where it does, through the dictates of raw power, decree, and technobureaucratic forms of regulation and administration. As Agamben suggests, 'we are experiencing the triumph of management, the administration of the absence of order' (2004b). Politics cedes to the administration and control of populations where this is not already effective in economic life generally. In the United States the primary means through which corporations become bureaucratised and regulated is paradoxically through the marketisation of the legal system. Luttwak comments on the ease with which people can 'resort to the courts in pursuit of private gain under the guise of "damage awards": the wealth of many Americans had its origins in a successful lawsuit' (Luttwak, 1999: 7). Even in Europe the real or implied threat of lawsuits now drives the bureaucratisation that accompanies the marketisation of state institutions, health services, schools, universities, prisons and security forces as they strive to demonstrate that they offer 'value for money' to the customers who were once patients, pupils, students and prisoners.

The 'triumph of management', the combination of raw power and administration, is the form of governance peculiar to supercapitalism. Force and administration do not constitute an antithesis, in spite of claims for the civilising effect of bureaucracy. On the contrary they are modalities of the same violence, the same war.

## Death incorporated

Supercapitalism is an effect not just of a mutation in capitalism, but also a mutation in the notion of war. War has been transformed first through becoming consistent with economy, as a mechanism of wealth creation and expenditure, and second through having no object other than stateless 'terror'. Looking at how war has become transformed gives an insight into how supercapitalism deploys, mobilises, expends and exhausts its human brands and resources.

According to Christopher Coker, traditional war has three main modalities. First, war is 'an *instrumental* concept that refers to the ways in which force is applied by the state, the way in which it is used to impose one state's will upon another … for purposes that are economic or political' (Coker, 2004: 6). Second, war is an *existential* concept that refers to those who practise it: warriors. Third, war is a *metaphysical* concept in which 'war translates into sacrifice – and invests death with meaning' (6).

Supercapitalism has transformed these modalities in the following ways. First, war is no longer simply an instrument of the state and its economy. Rather, the corporate war machine has invaded and deterritorialised the state such that it has itself become an instrument of war. The state's role is to facilitate war, rather than the other way around. War is no longer instrumental in that sense; it is not politics by other means. But neither is it simply the case of a reversal in which the classical state formations become the means through which a fundamental war between premodern peoples becomes normalised and stratified in laws and state institutions. This version of politics as war is suggested by Michel Foucault in his series of lectures given in 1976, but posthumously published in 2003.

In these lectures Foucault tells the story of how one force exerts its dominance through the offices of the state by seizing the monopoly of violence and the ability to make war, violence becoming a tool of modern government. In his argument, Foucault acknowledges that 'power relations are deeply involved in and with economic relations, even if power relations and economic relations always constitute a sort of network or loop' (Foucault, 2003: 14). Further, at certain points where power and economy loop around one another they can both be seen as modalities of general economy in which they have no utility whatsoever. Indeed, this is the logic of Foucault's position. If power and politics are simply war by other means, they have no other end than the joy of subjugation for its own sake. Wealth and power are not the end of this war, wealth and power are simply the means to make more war, the chance for a body, an assemblage of forces, to dominate, subjugate and therefore 'affirm itself with more joy' (Deleuze, 1983: 121). This is perfectly consistent with the Nietzschean roots of Foucault's understanding of history and power (see the chapter 'Nietzsche, Genealogy, History' in Foucault, 1984: 139–64). War therefore must be understood as a mode of pure negativity, an instrument of its own inhuman joy in creation and destruction.

Secondly, the existential element of war is transformed from being to becoming, as excess and form, in relation to the machinic assemblages, the networks, that comprise the battlefield of supercapitalism's economic ecosystem. In so far as the archaic warrior ethic, defined against the instrumentalised and industrialised modern soldier, is a figure of non-productive expenditure, then this fits in very well with the asubjective ethos of post-human becoming outlined in Coker's own speculations on the future of war. The miseries of industrial war have given way to a re-enchantment of high-tech war, at least for the combatants if not for their collateral damage. In this, war has followed capitalism that re-enchanted itself through the adoption of a martial ethic. Industrial capitalism characterised by heavy and careful investment has been transformed by a supercapitalism that is marked by exuberance, risk, danger, and playing for the highest stakes rather than servile accounting. Because uncertainty is built into the speculative business of capitalism, its entrepreneurs have to adopt the strategies of the artist or the gambler, or, supremely, the spirit that is infused with the celerity, untimeliness and heterogeneity of the warrior.

In supercapitalism, work has been transvalued as play or fun and the worker has become a freelance like the warrior who fights for no one but himself. Warriors (rather than mere soldiers, the equivalent of an industrial workforce) bear no allegiance to anyone other than themselves and their own code of honour. There is no code other than the profit code for the employee of a company in Wall Street or Silicon Valley, of course, and the thrill of fierce competition in work that is both highly paid and highly insecure. They enjoy a glamour equivalent to that of single combat in the context of an absence of loyalty to state, company, colleague. 'They "network", as they call it, on an almost daily basis to find better jobs, with no misplaced sense of loyalty to their current employers, who are in turn constantly re-evaluating the cost/benefit ratios of their continued employment' (Luttwak, 1999: 223).

These worker-warriors are expendable, organic elements of the machinic assemblages that comprise the supercapitalist ecosystem. They are not employees in the old sense of corporate citizens; since there are no secure jobs, there are 'no venues for life-long careers, no reassuring sense of mutual obligation' (223). Instead, they are reduced to 'employment in its purest form', that is to say to a utility that is indistinguishable from pure expenditure in the sense that they are meant to be used up without residue or reserve, ejected the moment they no longer achieve optimal performance. As such they are not subjects of supercapitalism, but subjectiles, highly mobile elements that are both producer and product, equivalent species to those organic products with a short shelf life or sell-by-date appropriate to the rapid production and reproduction of the new which supercapitalism requires. They are destined, after a few years, to join the junk heap of the obsolescent generations of technological objects which they operated and which operated them.

So while post-industrial work has been re-enchanted with something like a warrior ethic of pure employment in which utility is equivalent to expenditure, such employment unfolds to an alien rhythm and at inhuman speeds. As Coker writes, 'the warrior meme has readapted to its environment again as human and machine are increasingly assimilated' (Coker, 2004: 70). The existential dimension of this environment is not one of being but of becoming in relation to the machinic 'other' that is both interior and exterior to oneself:

> In this cybernetic world there is no question of finding one's 'authentic' being because there is no 'essence' of humanity, any more than there is an 'essence' of war with which we can put ourselves in touch. Human nature and intelligence are dynamic and interactive. They are *performative* because both organic (human) life and machine life work as one (cybernetically). Both exist by responding to external stimuli, but they respond very differently to how they did in the past. (70)

When Coker is writing about the future of war he is in every respect also talking about the present of the world of transnational commerce, particularly the business of information and biotechnology. The supercapitalist ecosphere is providing 'the context for a new corporeal reality, an entirely new world in which war is conducted, a world into which we are sensorially (not only physically) incorporated and assimilated' (72). Such assimilation and incorporation does not, of course, allow for a code of honour of single combat, nor the recognition of other warriors that provides a mirror of self-worth. Rather, it is the technological logic of the upgrade, the new, more sophisticated model with better features and greater efficiency which provides the threshold of value. Coker writes of the ways in which warriors, like their equipment, will be re-engineered, 'through biotechnological means' to enhance their performance (74). Just as it is 'becoming attractive to use genetic data to select prospective employees' (76), so warriors can be selected, adapted and engineered biotechnologically. Adopting a Nietzschean mode, Coker declares that 'we are on the cusp of "overcoming" our humanity' (75), although not at all in a sense that Nietzsche would approve.

Coker argues that the Nietzschean register is appropriate because of the emphasis on biology rather than culture. The all-too-human was for Nietzsche a product of reactive forces of *ressentiment* against the affirmative vitality of nature. Humanity is 'sick' because reactive forces of religion, morality and instrumental reason have crushed 'man's' powers of affirmation. The task of the philosophy of the future is to 'translate man back into nature', to make 'man' adequate to his own nature through affirming it. The natural body is will to power incarnate, 'striving to grow, spread, seize, become predominant … because it is *living* and because life simply *is* will to power' (Nietzsche, 1984: 259). Life is a process of becoming that is also always an overcoming, for Nietzsche. The overcoming that Coker describes, however, is of another kind altogether. It is another 'slave's revolt' – not a cultural negation of nature this time, however, but a biotechnical one since it involves 'determining our own evolution' (Coker, 2004: 75). Howard Caygill, in an essay on the metaphysics of the gene, gives a very different Nietzschean reading of this 'faith in science' to render intelligible the totality of the human genome in the form of digital information and subject it to manipulation and the abolition of chance. Caygill sees in it not an affirmation of nature in the form of the biological over the cultural, but on the contrary a 'hostility to life' that is also a 'concealed will to death' (Caygill, 1996). This is betrayed by Coker's aporia of the all-too-human fantasy which imagines that it will determine the terms of its own overcoming. 'Biocybernetics is not really intended to subordinate us to machines,' states Coker reassuringly, 'instead it will help us to use machines more effectively to enhance human performance' (Coker, 2004: 98). But such a notion of performance is slavish since it is already determined by an inhuman econoscientific (biotechnological) imperative that compels and measures 'human' performance. As Caygill writes, the piety of that 'faith in science looks to science not only for guidance as to who is to be saved and who is to be damned in the next world, but also this world' (Caygill, 1996). It is not a scientific priesthood, however, but the forces of supercapitalism which will determine who is saved or damned, accelerated or expended in this life. It is not a question of the Nietzschean superman, therefore, so much as the supercapitalism that determines the conditions of biotechnical becoming.

The hostility to life that is also a concealed will to death is betrayed paradoxically by the way in which war has been transformed as a metaphysical concept. This is the essential idea that war invests death with meaning through translating it into sacrifice. As Coker shows, the sacrificial element of war is being eradicated through America's policy of zero military casualties in the use of remote precision weaponry, robots guided by computer, and so on. While America's desire to minimise its own casualties is understandable, it has thus far been less concerned with the collateral damage caused by its actions, even if such a phrase abolishes death and its meaning linguistically. However, in his speculations on the future of war Coker cites a Los Alamos briefing paper from the 1990s which speaks of 'maximising force while reducing its lethal consequences'. Non-lethal weapons (NLW) are described as the weapons of the future, weapons that for the first time in history can 'degrade the functioning threat to material or personnel without crossing "the death barrier"' (cited in Coker, 2004: 126). But there is nothing that affirms life in such a policy, simply a desire to negate it, to control, economise and utilise it as a resource. This is clearly shown by Coker in a story which he cites to illustrate the confusion that such a policy causes combatants in the traditionally lethal practice of war.

He recalls the experience of a US Navy SEAL sniper in Somalia in 1995 who was ordered to detune his special dazzling laser to prevent him from blinding Somali citizens. Instead he was ordered to shoot anyone who threatened him. 'We're not allowed to disable these guys because that was considered inhumane?', asked the bemused soldier, 'Putting a bullet in their head is somehow more humane?' (cited in Coker, 2004:128). Blinded Somalian bodies paraded on television would no doubt make for poor public relations, whereas dead ones are less of a news story. But humanity is here clearly defined in terms of operability and performance. To be blind is to no longer meet the standard of humanity.

Death is abolished in a more profound way by the introduction of biotechnical discourse, and the marketisation of its products. Even before biotechnology began to digitalise life and render it undead in computer simulations, the conjunction of life-support and transplantation technology meant that an undead body might be allowed to live through prosthetic means, or harvested for vital organs for purposes of transplantation. The meaning of the terms 'life' and 'death' in such circumstances become highly problematic. For science these terms have no meaning in any case, meaning being restricted to the question of function. As is well known, science does not ask nature what it means, but simply seeks to find out how it works. Technoscience looks at how nature can be made to work more efficiently. As Giorgio Agamben comments, 'life and death are not properly scientific concepts but rather political concepts, which as such acquire a political meaning precisely only through a decision' (Agamben, 1998: 164). Determining the threshold of life and death, and thereby determining its significance, is essentially a decision that defines the political for Agamben. The sphere of the political is determining what life can be killed without the commission of homicide in the name of life in abstract, the idea of life that politics determines is worth living.

In supercapitalism, politics takes a secondary role to the economy and economic performance. The meaning of sacrifice and death is incorporated, subsumed into economic value as a process of obsolescence essential to the generation of the new. It is not a question of healing, mending or repairing broken parts and sustaining a life, but rather of replacing, upgrading, enhancing. As a functioning part of the ecosystem of supercapitalism the living body should not in any case be regarded as a discrete unit, not even in the old industrial metaphor of a cog in a wheel. The body is not a small part which represents the whole and whose removal would cause the whole to derail or grind to a halt. Bodies should not be perceived in their organicity but in their relational operative potential. How can they be extended, harnessed, optimised through their interactivity with other biotechnological powers and assemblages that comprise the supercapitalist ecosystem. Coker mentions that in business networks computers provide employees with data in order to better understand and penetrate their markets. He notes that, in the military, soldiers have for some time been inserted into a mechanical and electromechanical system as virtual 'consoldier', that is 'as information transmitters and processing devices, their role giving rise to what is now called cognitive engineering' (Coker, 2004: 90). Staring at a screen has for some time been the paradigmatic activity of work, leisure and war, the screen to any form of supercapitalist activity. But, as

Coker shows, the logic of this is straightforward and implies the collapse of the brain and the screen so that the brain becomes a screen, and vice versa. It implies a kind of total prostheticisation in which thought and feeling becomes predominantly anorganic, the effect of an acentred and probabilistic system or network. A network of bioelectronic neurones that provide the forms of consciousness and animation for assemblages are programmed with software genetic algorithms for 'wanting more'. These algorithms determine growth, self-replication, expansion and mobility for anorganic assemblages that wage war over the planet, and perhaps further, in the name of life and of making life more comfortable.

## Notes

1   'Global temperatures will rise by an average of 3°C due to climate change and cause catastrophic damage around the world unless governments take urgent action, according to the UK government's chief scientist. In a stark warning issued yesterday Sir David King said that a rise of this magnitude would cause famine and drought and threaten millions of lives. It would also cause a worldwide drop in cereal crops of between 20 and 400m tonnes, put 400 million more people at risk of hunger, and put up to 3 billion people at risk of flooding and without access to fresh water supplies. Few ecosystems could adapt to such a temperature change, equivalent to a level of carbon dioxide of 550 parts per million in the atmosphere, which would result in the destruction of half the world's nature reserves and a fifth of coastal wetlands' www.guardian.co.uk/climatechange/story/0,,1754276,00.html.

2   Warfare by other means, 'geo-economics' is 'investment capital for industry provided or guided by the state is the equivalent of firepower; product development subsidised by the state is the equivalent of weapon innovation; and market penetration supported by the state replaces military bases and garrisons on foreign soil as well as diplomatic influence' (Luttwak, 1999: 129).

3   This in conjunction with a fairly simple strategy: 'The recipe that has made Wal-Mart the largest retailer in the world, hauling in $137 billion in sales in 1998, is straightforward enough. First build stores two and three times the size of your closest competitors. Next, pile your shelves with products purchased in such great volume that the suppliers are forced to give you a substantially lower price than they would otherwise. Then cut your in-store prices so low that no retailer can begin to compete with your 'everyday low prices' (Klein, 2000: 133).

4   State/corporate consistency or 'reciprocal manipulation', 'as in the dealings of the largest international oil companies – American, British, French, Italian – with their respective state authorities and political leaders. Top oil company executives and senior foreign policy officials, oil company representatives overseas and diplomats in place, oil company country-experts and intelligence officers, often collaborate so closely that they might as well be interchangeable, and sometimes are – oil companies are often generous employers of ex-officials' (Luttwak, 1999: 142).

# 3

# Negativity

I'm a negative creep – and I'm stoned!

(Nirvana, 'Negative Creep',1989)

## 9 November 1989

The subject of 'Negative Creep', one of the highlights of Nirvana's first album *Bleach* (1989), is generally taken to be the singer himself, Kurt Cobain (Sandford, 1995: 116). As such it is one of the early signature tracks to establish a certain negative persona which became mythologised in the early 1990s pop phenomenon called grunge. Musically, grunge is characterised by a combination of punk and heavy metal, though with a lyrical and melodic sensibility that is common in neither. Associated with Seattle and bands like Mudhoney and Pearl Jam, grunge provided the soundtrack to an American generation that was given novelistic definition by Douglas Coupland's *Generation X* (1991) and cinematic renown by Richard Linklater's film *Slacker* (1991). The term Generation X became a media label and a marketing tool, identifying a market of twentysomething Americans born in the 1960s, the children of the baby boomers. According to Douglas Brinkley, the generation was regarded as 'numb and dumb', 'lazy underachievers, apathetic "boomrangers" who sank home to the parental nest after graduating from college' (Brinkley, 1994:1). This is assuming that there was a parental home, since divorce was a major figure defining this generation and its resentment and lassitude. Writing of its soundtrack, the *New York Times* called grunge 'what happens when children of divorce get their hands on guitars' (cited in Sandford, 1995: 103).

On 'Negative Creep' Cobain does not so much sing as scream with rage, his voice 'self-lacerating, spiteful and trembling with fury' (Sandford, 1995: 68). It is a characteristic performance: confessional, anguished, drug-addled disgust and shame at some implied sexual abuse or transgression. The repeated line 'Daddy's little girl ain't a girl no more' provides the chorus. It is a theme amplified by other *Bleach* highlights such as 'Floyd the Barber'. This song apparently narrates a 'Sweeney Todd nightmare' of small-town America in which the singer describes being tied down (75), 'shaved and shamed', forced to fellate Floyd and another paternal figure, Barney, before being slashed and murdered with a razor by the men and the singer's Aunt Bea. 'Paper Cuts' appears to describe maternal sexual abuse, torture and incest to such a degree that it provides a horrific state of perverse 'nirvana' in which 'my whole existence is for your amusement'. Whilst there is actually something comic in these grotesque parentally ambivalent narratives, the anguished vocals are delivered with sepulchral seriousness and accompanied by crashing, doom-laden, heavy metal guitar power chords.

It is of course an error to overnarrativise or make too much sense of pop lyrics. The power of pop lyrics lies precisely in their economy or even their poverty, which leads to an excess of possible meanings and effects. Effect is more important than meaning. Their power is completely bound up with the rhythm and mood of a particular recording. Words are nothing outside of the song in which they are embedded and in the particular performance that gives them emphasis, or not. Words are musical rather than linguistic elements. They evoke a feeling, a mood, an attitude. Mis-heard lyrics can be as effective as correctly heard ones. They are not verbal statements but musical utterances that are related to perceptions and changes in perception rather than knowledge.

But even though there is no point in attempting to reconstitute a narrative, it is fun to do so. Indeed, the minimal lyrics of a song like Nirvana's 'Negative Creep' encourage it, remaining purely virtual elements in a potential multiplicity of narratives. Read in another way, the opening line's use of a martial metaphor ('this is out of our range') could suggest that this is the voice of some Grunt GI in a foxhole. His screams 'Drone!' perhaps betraying, however anachronistically, panic for or at the presence of one of those Predator drones automated surveillance-weapons systems that reconnoitre American fields of battle. But the register is much more Vietnam than the first Gulf War, familiar from movies like *Apocalypse Now*, *The Deer Hunter* or *Platoon*. The rage of a confused and terrified GI strung out on Hendrix and dope, Russian roulette, a flame-thrower and some 'R and R' rape: 'Daddy's little girl ain't a girl no more'; 'Polly wants a cracker'. The mood of sexual violence, rage, panic and shame evoked by these early songs is consistent with many martial representations of the United States cleaning up the denouement of the end of history. They set the tone for much that was to come in the 1990s and 2000s in music and at war.

In fact, Cobain and Nirvana were in Germany as part of their European tour promoting *Bleach* and thus were able to witness the fall of the Berlin Wall first hand. At two in the morning after the wall came down, Cobain and a companion were celebrating in a small courtyard on the south side of the Reichstag. They were picked out by a police spotlight, 'lying semi-naked – the police described it as a gross combination – celebrating with the aid of a bottle and a stolen Federal Republic Flag' (Sandford, 1995: 133). Cobain greeted the end of history with his trousers down, being chased by the German police – just another stoned, negative creep convulsed in laughter.

*Bleach* sets the negative tone that characterises the attitude associated with the slacker generation: self-pitying, spoilt, spiteful, apathetic, indolent, lethargic, arrogant, cruel, stupid, self-absorbed, self-loathing, self-harming, an attitude authenticated by Cobain's suicide in 1994 at the peak of his fame. That fame was secured by Nirvana's second album, *Nevermind* (1991) and its opening track 'Smells Like Teen Spirit', both of which became worldwide bestsellers. Almost as memorable as the music it contained, the album's cover nicely catches the negativity of the record that locates it interior to a contradictory logic of (anti-)capitalism. The cover depicts a naked five-month-old baby (Spencer Elden) submerged in a swimming pool apparently intent on a dollar bill dangling on a fish hook. The cover performs the very exploitation of innocence that it seeks to satirise in its evocation of supercapitalism's appeal to a protosubject below the threshold of rational interest, need or even desire.

At the time of writing, *Nevermind* is still regarded as a seminal album, redefining rock for and after the 1990s. It is a view repeated in the plethora of lists and canons of popular culture that have characterised the early years of the twenty-first century as it looks back on the last. *1001 Albums You Must Hear Before You Die* calls *Nevermind* 'the most important rock album of the 1990s' (Dimery, 2005: 656). Garry Mulholland in *This is Uncool: The 500 Greatest Singles Since Punk and Disco*, calls 'Smells Like Teen Spirit' 'the greatest rock 'n' roll single in this book' (Mulholland, 2002: 326). For Mullholland this is because it is 'the most withering negation of everything rock 'n' roll was supposed to stand for at its late '60s peak' (326). It negates all of rock's pretensions concerning teen rebellion and idealism, summarily dismissing 'rock's power to accomplish anything'. The title is famously caustic, 'Teen Spirit' having been reduced to a marketing phrase naming a brand of feminine deodorant. Yet, in his critical commentary on the song, Mullholland notes that this pessimism is itself negated in the exuberance of its vehement performance, thereby capturing the perfect doubleness of negativity. Even as it negates all forms of positivity, it affirms itself through the force of its own negation:

> its singer and lyricist looms over and around the whiplashing, painstakingly *organized* maelstrom, fixes the listener with a steely-eyed stare, and attempts to force us into a pact of mutual self-loathing and resigned defeatism. The attempt fails, simply because the music is too exciting, even after the singer ends by wailing 'A DENIAL – A DE-NY-YUL!!' at us over and over again, all his pessimistic insight contradicted by his own pop genius. (326)

A powerful rock song's denial of the power of rock, it combines musical mockery at guitar heroics with lyrical rage at rock lyrics' inability to do anything other than crush life in cliché, stupidity and pointlessness, collapsing into malign indifference, 'Oh well, whatever!', and defeatism, 'never mind'. But perhaps it is a question of paradox rather than contradiction, the paradox of negative affirmation that is for Nietzsche the effect of the greatest music. Music violently exposes all language and discourse as itself destructive of life, negating the force of its significance in exuberance: 'Compared with music all communication by words is shameless: words dilute and brutalize; words depersonalize; words make the uncommon common' (Nietzsche, 1968: 810). Cobain's words rage in shame at their own shamelessness; they brutally rail at their inadequacy and at the banalisation effected by rock and pop fame. This is particularly the case with 'Stay Away': 'monkey see, monkey do / (I don't know why) / I'd rather be dead than cool / (I don't know why) / Every line ends in rhyme / (I don't know why) / Less is more, love is blind/ (I don't know why)'. What rock and pop knows in spite of the ignorance betrayed by the naivety and incoherence of its speech is the knowledge of its bodily intensity that emulates and gives sense (the sense of non-sense) to 'the fleet and dense fulminations of life in its excess' (Coole, 2000: 114). This excess is the vibrant energy found in Cobain's rage and in the malevolence of his anguished defeatism. Without point, purpose or meaning, utterly useless, 'hello, hello, hello, how low?', the song approaches the point of sovereignty, as that term is defined by Georges Bataille: 'Anguish only is sovereign absolute. The sovereign is a king no more: it dwells low-hiding in big cities … its sorrow scornfully mocks at all that comes to pass, at all there is' (Botting and Wilson, 1997: 147).

'I feel stupid and contagious, here we are now, entertain us' – Mullholland is right to focus on the way that 'Smells Like Teen Spirit' infects its listeners, forcing them into a pact of mutual stupidity, self-loathing and defeatism, but wrong to suggest simply that it fails. It succeeds in its failure and is contagious in that success, binding together an imaginary community based around the entertainment of negativity, inaugurating both an ethic and an aesthetic, a pose and a style, unleashing a future of negative becoming and (self-)marketing in various directions, speeds and tempos. In one direction, grunge sensibility and its combination of punk and heavy metal mutated, alongside rap, thrash and death metal, into nu metal. Nu metal expunged the melodic element of Nirvana's *Nevermind* which enriched and embarrassed Cobain, having more in common with the raw energy of *Bleach*.

Nu metal locates itself squarely in the contradiction that Mullholland identifies between the desire for teenage rebellion and its commodification. The contradictory desire to make it, but not sell out. The shameful acknowledgment of that desire is expressed along with an awareness of its belatedness and idiocy marked by contempt for the parental baby-boom generation that it defined. The self-loathing that still wants the same – the excess and the 'fuck-ups' that it represents. Nu metal inhabits this contradiction, exacerbating the wound in order to amplify its howl of rage, which is spewed out in records that are often very aggressive and unpleasant. Musically they accelerate grunge into a

miasma of rap, rapcore, thrash and death metal. Lyrically, they revel in fantasies of violence, accompanied by the most abject and pathetic utterances of
self-abnegation, self-loathing and disgust.

Another musical strand Nirvana accelerated in a slightly different direction,
particularly in *Nevermind*, was the 'quiet verse/loud chorus' structure also associated with the Pixies,[1] which became the blueprint for Korn, the Deftones
and other post-grunge bands of the mid-1990s. Nirvana's lyrical exploration
of self-pity, anguish and depression, alongside issues and sensibilities associated with identity, gender and sexual politics connected up with the 'emotional
hardcore' subgenre of the 1980s. Sandford writes that 'so far as grunge had
non-musical principles they were negative: disapproval of the state's anti-ho-
mosexual bills, opposition to the Omnibus Drug Law and a melange of Utopian–Socialist mumblings, of which strident feminism was the cornerstone'
(Sandford, 1995: 115). The feminism and sexual ambiguity with which Cobain
and others flirted subsequently becomes fully stylised later in the 1990s and
2000s with the gothic-lite cult of emo – emotive or emotional metal. Emo pushes
the style of apathetic depression, sexual sensitivity and low self-esteem to a
certain limit evident in the parody 'Emo Kid' by comedy duo Adam and Andrew. Describing life as 'a black abyss' that grabs hold of the singer and tightens
its grip 'tighter than a pair of my little sister's jeans … which look great on me
by the way', the defining emo characteristic is to 'play guitar and write suicide
notes'. Clearly Kurt Cobain was proto-emo.

American popular music negativity is always but never completely com-
modifiable. Something necessarily escapes capture by the commodity. It is dou-
bly marked by its excess (its imminent destiny as junk) and the deficiency that
marks the doubled place of the abject and the authentic that is missing in
commercialised culture. Immanent to that locus of deficiency and excess is the
sovereign negativity which propels the general economic logic of
supercapitalism as a mode of pure expenditure. Sovereign negativity as pure
consumption in a Bataillean sense as the 'impossible' that wastes itself completely, uses itself up without purpose or remainder. It is this locus of 'impossible' consumption which provides the immanent destructive energy of
supercapitalism. Ostensibly a means to the good and comfortable life,
supercapitalism is at the same time a modality of absolute consumption that in
the process of its negative-becoming deletes and consumes all cultures, including consumer culture.

It would no doubt be improper, in many ways, to use Cobain's suicide as a
figure for this impossible consumption, but first-hand accounts of the scene of
death broach this idea of pure negative expenditure. According to the doctor
who performed the autopsy, 'it was the act of someone who wanted to obliter-
ate himself, to literally become nothing' (cited in Sandford, 1995: 9). Inserting
the barrel of a shotgun into his mouth, Cobain pulled the trigger and obliterated the very organ of consumption, which became consumed in fire so that

'dental records were no use, because nothing was left of his mouth' (10). In so doing, he exchanges his life for a signifier of celebrity that takes its meaning in relation to other dead rock stars: Jimi Hendrix, Elvis Presley, Sid Vicious. But none of these are Achilles, their stories are not those of tragic heroes who through exchanging a noble death for poetic immortality both transcend and ground the value of ancient and modern systems of value and exchange. Rather, these deaths – choking on vomit, heart failure from straining to excrete the accumulated waste of junk food, violent heroin-soaked oblivion – are double, a point of double articulation. The deaths mark both the point of impossible excess that, held in reserve, uncertainly founds the system of value (celebrity) and exchange (wealth), and the power of excess that overruns and exceeds that system, rendering it completely meaningless.

## New world order

> how to love without a trace of dissent
> i'll buy the torture cos you pay for the rent
> tied high with a broken command
> you're all alone to the promised land
>
> (Ministry, N.W.O., 1992).

A few months before Kurt Cobain cavorted beneath the crumbling Berlin Wall, Francis Fukuyama, a political adviser to Ronald Reagan, published an essay called 'The End of History?' in the journal *The National Interest* in the summer of 1989. While Fukuyama's argument did not depend upon such events, the fall of the wall came to symbolise the collapse of Communism that the Americans claimed as a victory for liberal democracy and free enterprise. The suggestion that this also constituted the end of history seemed hyperbolic, but few people in the White House questioned its basic assumptions. Fukuyama's article and the follow-up book, *The End of History and the Last Man* (1992), were accepted as statements that supported the announcement by Reagan's successor, George Bush Sr a new world order.

Over ten years later, these statements remain fundamental to George W. Bush's administration and provide justification for its affirmation of the future as American, from the New American Century and beyond. In a speech on 17 September 2002, Bush reiterated the claim that the great political struggles that marked the twentieth century are over. They have been 'ended with a decisive victory for the forces of freedom – and a single sustainable success: freedom, democracy, and free enterprise' (George Bush, cited in The White House, 2001a). The main assumptions of this speech, and the policy of national security that it informs, are perfectly consistent with Fukuyama's idea that American-style liberal democracy constitutes the 'endpoint of mankind's ideological evolution' and the 'final form of human government' (Fukuyama, 1992: xi). As we shall see, this argument and this vision is based in a theory of negation explicated, ironically, by a Russian in a commentary on the thought of the German philosopher G. W. F. Hegel.

In 1989, however, Fukuyama's argument met with a good deal of incredulity. How could history be at an end when historical events were still unfolding, like Iraq invading Kuwait, events that still required America to go to war? In his follow-up book, Fukuyama addresses this incredulity by drawing a distinction between history as simply a model of empty homogeneous time through which events occur, and history understood philosophically as 'a single, coherent, evolutionary process' (xii). The latter understanding of history can only superficially be supported by events like the fall of the Berlin Wall, or contradicted by the Chinese crackdown in Tiananmen Square, because these events are not formative in themselves, they are effects of history's inexorable progress. This understanding of history is drawn from the German philosopher G. W. F. Hegel and two of his followers, Karl Marx in the nineteenth century and Alexandre Kojève in the twentieth. For these thinkers history unfolds as a logical and necessary process in relation to which there are very few significant events; for Hegel it was the French Revolution, while the Russian Revolution was claimed for Marx. Kojève, an unorthodox Marxist who fled Stalin's purges, conventionally privileged the Russian Revolution, but for him it was the mere fact of revolution that was essential, the fact that the 'slaves' had overcome the 'masters' in armed struggle. In the twentieth century, Kojève saw no essential difference between the American system and Stalinism or Maoism. It was the strictly economic dimension which persuaded Kojève that America would eventually prevail over the USSR in the cold war. But trips to the east between 1948 and 1958 persuaded Kojève that 'the Russians and the Chinese are still but impoverished Americans, moreover on a rapid road to wealth. I was lead to conclude that the *American way of life* was the kind of life proper to the post-historical period' (Kojève, cited in Derrida, 1994: 72). The main thing is that for the thinkers who followed Hegel and Kojève, history was *already* over well before 1989, the latter date simply confirmed it for the Americans.

Hence the sense of belatedness and weariness which greeted Fukuyama's argument in some philosophical quarters where it resonated, if at all, 'like an old repetition' (Derrida, 1994: 14). Derrida, for example, had seen the end before too many times, and rather patronisingly wrote:

> Many young people today (of the type 'readers-consumers of Fukuyama' or of the type 'Fukuyama' himself) probably no longer sufficiently realize it: the eschatological themes of the 'end of history', of the 'end of Marxism', of the 'ends of man', of the 'last man' and so forth were, in the 50s, that is, forty years ago, our daily bread. (14)

Like rock 'n' roll, eschatalogical philosophy never surpassed the time of Elvis in the 1950s. But like an old rocker himself, Derrida himself cannot quite give up on the apocalyptic tone of his 50s quiff, acknowledging in his late work the triumph of democracy, even as he speculates about its fate at the ends of the state (Derrida, 1994). If not the 'last form of government', democracy has nevertheless become 'coextensive with the political' and 'constitutive of the political realm precisely because of the indetermination and the "freedom", and the "free play", of its concept' (28). Derrida notes that the only regimes which do not present themselves, in various ways, as democratic are a very few theocratic Muslim governments. While it is their privilege to present the 'Other of democracy', Derrida, as we shall see in the final chapter, is interested in speculating on a 'democracy to come' in a situation that may be beyond the state.

Concern about the ends of the state was not shared by Fukuyama in 1992 since his thesis precisely announces the triumph of the 'universal homogeneous state'. This is the form that all nations are destined to take sooner or later, even those few Muslim theocracies. To assert this, Fukuyama must however bring together under the same state form international finance and commerce, global communications, science and technology as all part of the same system that has triumphed. The White House knows that this is only possible if America identifies itself totally with economic and military power, giving them consistency as the means of its strategic defence – a defence that is necessarily continually pro-active and pre-emptive.

The political – American – dimension is crucial for Fukuyama because otherwise history comes to a close purely as an effect of science and technology and its economisation in the free market. Kojève's Hegelian story of the dialectic of master and slave is important because it provides the human element that would otherwise be lacking, both science and economy being essentially driven by natural laws (discovered by Newton, Hobbes, Smith, Darwin, and so on). While the technological applications of 'modern natural science' confers the 'decisive military strength' that enables and supports the new horizons of production possibilities that 'makes possible the limitless accumulation of wealth', a purely economic or scientific explanation of history is unsatisfying (Fukuyama, 1992: xiv). Certainly it can explain the 'increasing homogenization of societies, regardless of their historical origins or cultural inheritances' and the erasure of 'tribe, sect and family' with more economically rational social organisations 'based on function and efficiency' (xv), but it cannot explain the importance of democracy. To do this, Fukuyama argues, 'we have to return to Hegel and Hegel's non-materialistic account of History' (xvi).

Fukuyama's version of Hegel, however, is drawn from the commentary of Alexandre Kojève in his *Introduction to the Reading of Hegel* (1989). These lectures were first given in Paris in the 1930s and were assembled by Raymond Queneau. Queneau's notes were first published in America in 1969, a year after Kojève's death, in an edition edited by Allan Bloom, Fukuyama's teacher at Cornell University in the early 1970s. Bloom later Invited Fukuyama to give his 'end of history' lecture in Chicago after Bloom had moved there.

## Dialectic of desire

Kojève's story begins with the origin of human self-consciousness that provides the condition of all knowledge about the world. The condition of consciousness is desire, but human self-consciousness can only arise when desire goes beyond the objects that can satisfy it. Self-consciousness presupposes desire that precedes yet makes possible the coming of humanity. Desire is thus itself not human, it is in-human, both exterior and interior to the humanity that arises as an effect of desire taking itself as its own object beyond the given reality of nature.

Desire at first gives rise to consciousness through spurring the human animal to action in order to satisfy it. Desire is satisfied through the negation of some object of hunger, for example through eating and therefore transforming it into nutrition. 'Thus, all action is "negating"', says Kojève. Negation is not purely destructive, it is transformative. But as soon as desire is satisfied, consciousness returns to a state of passive contemplation of the world without self-awareness. Only desire brings back awareness of oneself precisely as a subject of desire. In order for self-consciousness to be sustained, then, desire must be directed towards a non-natural object, something beyond the given reality that will paradoxically not satisfy it. The only thing that goes beyond given reality, of course, is desire itself. Therefore desire must be directed towards another desire. Since another desire is no thing, nothing precisely, it cannot be satisfied; self-consciousness can thereby be sustained. Desire establishes human self-consciousness as an effect of its pure negativity: desire desires itself as unsatisfied desire; it desires itself as its impossible 'other'.

> Desire taken as Desire – i.e. before its satisfaction – is but a revealed nothingness, an unreal emptiness. Desire, being the revelation of an emptiness, the presence of the absence of a reality, is something essentially different from the desired thing, something other than a thing, than a static and given real being that stays eternally identical to itself. (Kojève, 1989: 5)

As Kojève's story unfolds, the pure negativity of desire becomes the inhuman machine of historical becoming. Desire is always desire of the other, a desire for another's desire. Endlessly differing from itself in the mirror of the same, desire generates a continual movement and dissatisfaction that negates and transforms itself in a process of becoming in relation to the other. But the desired other is not simply another desire. Since it is another desire to establish a properly human value beyond the given reality of its animal nature, the (non-)object of desire is ultimately death. For Kojève, establishing the value of the properly human, in contradistinction to the animal, necessitates confronting death and risking life, the preservation of which represents the supreme value for an animal. At the beginning of history, desire confronts the absolute value represented by the nothingness it desires, death. This is the value of that which negates all given reality, all means of animal preservation and satisfaction. The pure negativity of this 'human' desire is therefore the desire for death: 'In other words, man's humanity "comes to light" only if he risks his (animal) life for the sake of human Desire' (7). Humanity, therefore, can only come about as an effect of a challenge to fight to the death for the sake of pure prestige.

Fukuyama puts it like this: 'the stakes in this bloody battle at the beginning of history are not food, shelter, or security, but pure prestige. And precisely because the goal of the battle is not determined by biology, Hegel sees in it the first glimmer of human freedom' (Fukuyama, 1992: xvi). There is a slight problem here with the way in which Fukuyama elides the difference between history and actual bloody battles. This Hegelian stand-off for pure prestige is simply a philosophical device or philosopheme that has no more historical status than that of an explanatory myth. Moreover, it is of course essential that the so-called battle, as such, never takes place. If both combatants were willing to risk their lives in a bloody battle for recognition and pure prestige, it would result in the death of one or both of them. 'The realization and revelation of the human being' requires that one of the potential combatants refuses to risk his life and refuses to fight. This refusal establishes the relation between master and slave that becomes for humanity the 'fundamental human relation' (Kojève, 1989: 9).

Fukuyama connects this desire for recognition with the Platonic idea of *thymos* or spiritedness, which he translates somewhat anachronistically as self-worthiness, self-esteem or pride. But again, here is an over-interpretation of Kojève that is introduced by a sleight of hand, because the effect of the production of the master–slave relation is precisely that the desire for recognition has *failed*. Recognition by a slave, a mere 'thing' defined by the things in the world that he cannot go beyond, is no recognition at all. Furthermore, the production of a slave retrospectively negates the risk of life in the first place, since victory over a slavish coward was never in doubt. The 'mastery' of the master is an absurd sham. If, as Fukuyama suggests, pride emerges from this stand-off, it can only be the effect of the shame of the paradoxical victor who has failed to achieve his prize. This prize is the recognition of his proper human worth, which can only be given by someone worthy of recognising him, another free man. But all he has produced is a subhuman slave. The master is stuck, as Kojève says, 'in an existential impasse' (Kojève, 1989: 19). All that is left for him to do is to put his slave to work and consume the fruits of his labour like a drone or a parasite. It is not very heroic.

It is not, as Fukuyama suggests, a humanistic notion of pride or *thymos* that drives history, but the forced labour of the slave paying for the resentment of a master who has failed to satisfy his desire. The master falls back into passivity, assuaging his frustration through consumption. The work of the slave, meanwhile, begins to negate and transform nature for the pleasure of the master. An economic law is thus imposed upon the slave – that he must work for the pleasure of the master – with the result that natural laws are utilised in the development of science and technology. Through his work the slave negates, acts upon, transforms and utilises nature for an economic purpose. Immanent to this work, however, is the inhuman force of pure negativity, which is neither the desire of the master nor that of the slave, but the desire of desire itself as unsatisfied desire. History, if that is what is at stake, is the product of neither the master nor the slave, but of the pure negativity of a desire to expend itself in death. It is this desire that drives the slave precisely to the degree to which the slave works tirelessly to avoid it. The master, meanwhile, can only simulate desire's expenditure in festive entertainment, negating the labour of the slave in his idiotic enjoyment.

Neither the master nor the slave, therefore, is properly human; humanity is supposedly realised only at the end of history with the granting of universal recognition by the universal homogeneous state. This occurs, Fukuyama suggests, with the 'democratic revolutions' that abolish the distinction between master and slave by establishing the principles of popular sovereignty and the rule of law (Fukuyama, 1992: xvii) – rule by the people for the people. This law is both economic and political since it involves free access to the products of labour in the name of 'universal and reciprocal recognition' guaranteed by the state. But there is a problem here that goes unnoticed by Fukuyama. The pure negativity of desire has still not been confronted. The so-called universal recognition of the liberal state stays at the economic level of the goods, the products of slavish labour produced in the avoidance of desire. For Michel Foucault, this is '*Homo oeconomicus* ... the human being who spends, wears out, and wastes his life in evading the imminence of death' (Foucault, 1986: 257). The only compensation for the slave-become-bourgeois lies within the same economic paradigm. Precisely in so far as he can afford it, the self-made man can simulate the master: he spends, accumulates and wastes his life in comfort and pleasures that can only for so long protect him from the real of his desire. All that universal recognition means here is the opportunity to work for one's share of the goods that keep desire at the level of the given reality, albeit a reality transformed by the products of labour. The desire for a value beyond the given reality that at the beginning was necessary for human self-consciousness has still not been confronted.

For Georges Bataille, this is the problem with Kojève's account of history, the modality of desire necessary for self-consciousness is forgotten. The recognition offered by the liberal state reduces the human being, as a consumer, to the exigencies of things that are useful and necessary to a comfortable life. Human life is therefore defined by the threshold of utility, necessity and comfort introduced by *things*: automobiles, washing machines, computers, and so on. Human beings themselves are therefore reduced to the level of things and are similarly valued according to their utility, or in other words their servitude to a system in which they must be useful, sell their labour and buy goods. For

Bataille, self-consciousness is unavailable to the master, the slave or his synthesis, the consumer-citizen, and available only to a form of sovereignty that opens itself up to the movement of pure negativity. That is, it opens itself to the negation of all goods and things, to the movement of non-productive or useless expenditure: eroticism, extravagance, chance, violence, intimacy, loss and consumption in the form of the destruction of the utility associated with things. 'Intimacy is not expressed by a *thing* except on one condition: that this *thing* be essentially the opposite of a *thing*, the opposite of a product, of a commodity – a consumption and a sacrifice' (Bataille, 1988: 132). Bataille sees this reversal of a traditional understanding of morality in terms of utility, reason and the good, as actually being ethical. This is because he believes that the Western world is sleep-walking to a global catastrophe and sees the 'raising of the living standard' (41) as the only remedy. What Bataille aims at in his theory of general economy is from the outset 'the *self-consciousness* that man would finally achieve in the lucid vision of its linked historical forms' (41).

Kojève, on the other hand, draws a clear distinction between the given reality of the natural world and the world that is transformed as a result of labour. This is the world that has been transformed by the slave's avoidance of the pure negativity of desire that forces him to work and thus realise himself in his products: 'It is the realization of his project, of his idea; hence, it is he that is realized in and by this product, and consequently he contemplates himself when he contemplates it' (Kojève, 1989: 25). While these artificial products are just as autonomous, just as independent of man as nature, man is nevertheless realised in these artificial products, and can sit back and contemplate his realisation in their image. But this leaves man, at the end of history, as the redundant witness of an autonomous realm in which desire has become incorporated in products and, furthermore, automated in those second- and third-generation machines that operate in the place of human work.

It is possible that in Hegel's time a worker could look at the object of his or her labour – a table, perhaps, or a clock or even a steam engine – and see embodied in it his or her own thought, reason, imagination and sweat. But what liberated slave now can look at any product of microprocessing and see in it an image of work? Machines, particularly machines designed and made by other machines, don't work, they simply operate or break down. These mechanical forces of production, operating according to a different pace and rhythm, soon outstrip any reference to human necessity, utility, need or comfort. Instead, encoded like the slaves they replaced by the absolute negativity of inhuman desire, they default to a process of production that is no different to that of expenditure since it is without sense or reason. These products of the undead replicants of slavish consciousness encoded with the DNA of inhuman desire are junk almost as soon as they are produced. The pure instrumentality of the nothing of desire in pursuit of its principle generates more and more useless products, turning the urban landscape into an archipelago of landfill sites. Thus the restricted economy exemplified by the so-called universal homogeneous state is generalised through the vertiginous movement of technological change driven by the imperatives of supercapitalism, but crucially, without the self-consciousness that is the constant reference of all fantasies about artificial intelligence, robots and supercomputers which featured so prominently in cyberpunk novels and Hollywood science-fiction movies of the 1980s and 1990s. Self-consciousness is singularly lacking in either man or machine or indeed in the machinic assemblages that render both terms archaic.

## The ultimate American man

It is the redundancy of man at the end of history which most disturbs Francis Fukuyama and many of his neoliberal and neoconservative colleagues. Fukuyama's book is generally optimistic, and in its declaration of the 'good news' of the triumph of liberal democracy can be seen as almost evangelical in its praise of the American way. And yet when he contemplates his fellow Americans there is a crisis of confidence, something appears to be lacking. Just at the point of world historical triumph, there is no feeling of pride or superiority. These terms have become negated by the automatic recognition of citizenship. As a consequence, citizens of liberal democracy, 'schooled by the founders of modern liberalism', give up 'prideful belief' in their superior worth 'in favor of comfortable self-preservation' (Fukuyama, 1992: xxii). A certain inadequacy of Hegel's progressive history becomes evident and questions the very notion of progress itself.

In his doubts, Fukuyama draws on his own intellectual paternal heritage. He follows his former teacher Allan Bloom in endorsing his own master Leo Strauss who invoked Hegel's great critic Nietzsche. For Strauss, the Hegelian citizen of the universal homogeneous state looks uncannily like the 'last' or 'ultimate' man characterised in Nietzsche's *Thus Spake Zarathustra*: '"We have discovered happiness", say the Ultimate Men and blink'. In the world of the last or ultimate men there are no longer masters or slaves, no great inequalities of wealth; suffering and strife have been ameliorated or obliterated; there is equality in desire and status. And they even like to get 'stoned', as the Americans say, to induce pleasant dreams and take away the anguish and pain of death:

> A little poison now and then: that produces pleasant dreams. And a lot of poison at last, for a pleasant death.
>
> They still work, for work is entertainment. But they take care the entertainment does not exhaust them.
>
> Nobody grows rich or poor anymore: both are too much of a burden. Who still wants to rule? Who obey? Both are too much of a burden.
>
> No herdsman and one herd. Everyone wants the same thing, everyone is the same: whoever thinks otherwise goes voluntarily into the madhouse.

'Formerly all the world was mad', say the most acute of them and blink. (Nietzsche, 1969: 46–7)

For Leo Strauss, 'the state through which man is said to become reasonably satisfied is ... the state in which the basis of man's humanity withers away, or in which man loses his humanity. It is the state of Nietzsche's "last man"' (Strauss,1963: 223). Fukuyama cites both Nietzsche and Strauss's analogy and raises the question, 'is not the man who is completely satisfied by nothing more than universal and equal recognition something less than a full human being, indeed an object of contempt?' (Fukuyama, 1992: xxiii). What does it mean to be recognised in a context where everyone is recognised automatically irrespective of their courage or other distinctive qualities? Fukuyama just raises these questions as a coda to his otherwise optimistic narrative and justification of the triumph of liberal democracy. He does not think, for the time being, that they pose a challenge to the worldwide liberal revolution that is seeing all nations roll up to the same destination like so many wagons following in the footsteps of the American pioneers. But he does wonder if the new occupants of the West will find the surroundings 'inadequate' and 'set their eyes on a new and more distant journey' (339).

Indeed, the triumph of democracy, forged out of a struggle *for* democracy, raises a question concerning its future. What does 'left wing' and 'right wing', phrases coined during the French Revolution, mean now that the *ancien régime* is definitively gone, with no prospect of return? If everyone agrees that we have reached the perfect form of government, what is there to campaign for or vote about except matters of administration and management that may become more and more 'democratised' economically through customer-led feedback mechanisms? Democracy becomes disenchanted when it seems to be no longer about class struggle but about choice between which brand of bureaucrats can be trusted with raising the standard of living a little higher even as they continue to standardise life in the name of health, happiness and comfort.

While Fukuyama hesitates to condemn this state of affairs as a loss of humanity and a return to base animality, that is not the case with his mentor Allan Bloom. Two years before Fukuyama published his essay in *The National Interest* (1989), Bloom published his most well-known book, *The Closing of the American Mind* (1987). The book is usually read as a right-wing denunciation of the left academy, a major assault in the culture wars. And certainly it is. But it is much more than just a belated, reactionary attack on the so-called political correctness of the left academy and the 'dumbing down' of the curriculum through the extension of the canon of literature and philosophy to include work by women and non-European or non-white American authors. The book is also, much more radically, a call to re-enchant politics along Nietzschean lines. In his last paragraph, Bloom grasps the unique importance of his nation and its power in a way not fully or officially acknowledged until the regime of George W. Bush:

> This is the American moment in world history, the one for which we shall forever be judged. Just as in politics the responsibility for the fate of freedom in the world has devolved upon our regime, so the fate of philosophy in the world has devolved upon our universities, and the two are related as they have never been before. The gravity of our given task is great, and it is very much in doubt how the future will judge our stewardship. (382)

The doubt concerns not just Bloom's specific disenchantment with left-wing academics and curricula, but with American culture and society generally, which he takes to be the model for the universal homogeneous state. For Bloom it is doubtful that the last man has either the chest for world leadership or the stomach for a fight. The reason why the political fate of freedom is so closely related to the fate of philosophy is because philosophy must forge new values. A transvaluation of American values is necessary, appropriate to the spirit required for world leadership in the new American century where the new applies as much to American as to the forthcoming twenty-first century.

Bloom begins his book with a critique of 'our virtue': that is, the fundamental American virtue of 'openness'. The problem with American openness is that it leads to cultural relativism, something that has allowed America to emerge as a nation of immigrants endowed with a pioneering spirit. America, historically, is open and it sees no reason why the world should not be open to it. But for Bloom this openness is disastrous, so it quickly becomes clear that the 'closing' referred to in his title is not a complaint but a demand. The American mind *must* be closed to the openness of cultural relativity. The American mind must be closed to other cultures and fixed upon some core beliefs of its own, something it can be passionate, prejudiced and unreasonable about. It must be closed upon values that will drive it to war to impose them on others. Echoing Nietzsche's Zarathustra, Bloom complains that in the American university 'the study of history and culture teaches that all the world was mad' because once it was filled with 'true believers' (26). Even when he is not acknowledged, Bloom follows his master Strauss in presenting his arguments through the words of others, particularly classical philosophers and Nietzsche. Indeed, his reading of Nietzsche is highly mediated by the teachings of Strauss.

While he laments the dispiriting effect of cultural relativism on American values, Bloom is at the same time well aware that Nietzsche is also a 'cultural relativist' (202). However, that does not mean he tolerates a culture of anything goes. On the contrary, for Nietzsche strong cultural relativism necessarily means war, whereas weak cultural relativism implies a passive nihilism. While there is no reason for liberal democracies to fight one another because they perceive the 'same human nature and the same rights everywhere', strong cultures must fight wars with each other because 'values can only be asserted or posited by overcoming others, not by reasoning with them' (202). Nietzsche was aware that God was dead in the sense that the awe he inspired had been rationalised out of existence; he knew that morality was an effect of prejudice or slavish resentment, and that society was not grounded in nature. But Bloom insists that 'to live, to have any inner substance, a man must have values, must be committed' (202), and must be committed as if there were a God. Religious belief, therefore, is essential if the 'last man' isn't to return to a state of animality, irrespective of the fact that there is no God.

Bloom's Nietzscheanism is avowedly right-wing, but he is aware that right wing Nietzscheanism has an unfortunate legacy – National Socialism. While Nietzsche was neither nationalist nor socialist nor, more significantly, racist, some of his statements when given a certain interpretation can open dangerous ground. While Bloom believes, again following Strauss, that liberal democracy (in the form of the Weimar Republic) led to the rise of the Nazis, Nietzsche 'prepared the way' to dangerous forms of charismatic populism 'by helping to jettison good and evil along with reason, without assurance of what the alternatives might be' (214). Bloom isn't sure of the alternatives either. On the one hand, he takes a nostalgic look back to the days of religion when religion infused with a spiritual meaning everything that could be described as the political, the social or the personal. But he notes that those modern discourses that appeal to the idea of the sacred have 'done nothing to re-establish religion – which puts us in a pretty pickle' (215). Indeed, Bloom cuts to the quick of the problem: 'we reject by the fact of our categories the rationalism that is the basis for our way of life, without having anything to substitute for it' (215). This is what the book calls for. America must overcome itself, transvalue the enlightenment principles upon which it was founded, and forge the hypervalues and supermorality worthy of the superpower that it is. A superpower requires supermen, and the superman is the very figure whom Nietzsche contrasted to the last or ultimate men who, according to Leo Strauss, currently populate the USA.

## The neoconservative superman

'Superman', suggests Rich Johnston, 'is the ultimate fantasy neocon, in that his might makes right. And he is always fighting on the side of good, without unfortunate consequences such as insurgency, faulty intelligence or Guantanamo Bay' (cited in *The Times*, Times2, 11 July 2006). Johnston's reference, however, is to the Superman of Marvel comics rather than to Nietzsche's altogether more enigmatic figure, located beyond good and evil, whose possibility also enchanted the intellectual masters of neoconservatism.

'*I teach you the Superman*. Man is something that should be overcome' (Nietzsche, 1969: 41). Both Bloom and Fukuyama are associated with the neoconservative strain of American politics that was prominent in both the anti-Clinton campaigns and the presidency of George W. Bush (see Norton, 2004). Shadia Drury has been tireless in her exposure of these links and the profoundly anti-democratic implications of Strauss's thought, all of which are denied by his followers. But, as she shows, obscurantism and the practice of the Platonic 'noble lie' are part of the style and strategy of the philosophy.[2] If Strauss is anti-modern, anti-liberal and anti-democratic in his enthusiasm for the ancients and for Nietzsche, he must also be anti-capitalist. The superman who emerges as an effect of the self-overcoming of man and the will to power is not a creature of the market place, according to Zarathustra. The superman cannot be confused with the 'great men', the heroes of the hour, who are revered by the 'solemn buffoons' who populate the marketplace; that is, the place for the exchange of values as commodities not for their creative transvaluation (Nietzsche, 1969: 78–9). 'All great things occur away from glory and the marketplace: the inventors of new values have always lived away from glory and the marketplace' (79).

Accordingly, it is up to an elite class of Straussians to transvalue American virtue, or re-enchant American virtue with the classical virtues, away from those of the founding fathers. The latter understood only the values of the marketplace, and 'under the tutelage of Hobbes and Locke, deliberately created a squalid regime ruled by self-interest, sacrificing virtue to liberty and equality, and are ultimately responsible for the philistinism, mediocrity, and deracination of contemporary America' (Jahn, 2000). For Drury this is at the heart of the profoundly un-American nature of the Straussian, neoconservative political programme (Drury, 1999: 15). While this is of course denied, or denied publicly, the logic is unquestionably that the American values characteristic of modernity and the marketplace need to be overcome.

At the same time it is highly peculiar that so many neoconservative members and fellow travellers of the Bush regime, the so-called protectors of freedom and democracy for whom the term 'freedom' means free enterprise, should apparently be so contemptuous of capitalism and equality. While for Strauss, Bloom and many of his followers, 'the global reach of American culture threatens to trivialise life and turn it into entertainment' (Drury, 2003), the foundation of American strategic defence is its 'entrepreneurial energy'. Pointing to the Bush regime's adventures in Afghanistan and Iraq, Drury suggests that this may be the antidote to capitalism's comforts. Here the political philosophy of Carl Schmitt joins that of Strauss and Kojève as part of the neoconservative's philosophical justification. Drury claims that

> All three of them were convinced that liberal economics would turn life into entertainment and destroy politics; all three understood politics as a conflict between 'mutually hostile groups willing to fight each other to the death. In short, they all thought that man's humanity depended on his willingness to rush naked into battle and headlong to his death. Only perpetual war can overturn the modern project, with its emphasis on self-preservation and 'creature comforts'. Life can be politicized once more, and man's humanity can be restored. (Drury, 2003)

War might be seen as an essential, humanising supplement to capitalism and its creature comforts, but what if capitalism itself were to become transvalued.

What if capitalism, instead of being dedicated to the bourgeois safe investments of the last man, went ballistic? Perhaps, through its total identification
with war, the power of negation and overcoming the other, American capitalism can be transvalued. It can become a supercapitalism worthy of a superpower and the supermen who would command it beyond good and evil.

But such a development implies a very different conception of war than the
battle for pure prestige celebrated in this ideology. War is becoming 'posthuman'
if not superhuman in a Nietzschean sense. As Christopher Coker shows in *The
Future of War* (2004), warriors have become simply elements in larger machinic
assemblages, subject to biotechnological modification and optimisation. At the
same time, the logic of war's development is consistent with the development
of capitalism, it occupies the same ecosystem, it utilises the same technologies
and techniques, the same strategies, and, in its automation and excess, is driven
by the same immanent principle of inhuman desire. Supercapitalist war is not
just a war with the 'other' – Chinese or Indian say – whose own cultures must
be overcome all the better to affirm the power and prestige of American culture. This is a war with the 'other' who is also the same. A schizophrenic war
against American culture itself, including that of the Straussians and their fellow travelers in elitism. They cannot exempt themselves from its global force.

On the anniversary of his essay on the end of History for *The National Interest*, Fukuyama was invited by the same publication to write a retrospective on
the original article. Fukuyama decided to write about the one argument that
he could not refute – that there could be no end of history until there was an
end to science. The article, published in 1999 and entitled 'Second Thoughts:
The Last Man in a Bottle' concerns itself with the implications for culture and
humanity of applied science, particularly biotechnology.

Ten years after 1989, Fukuyama's Hegelian optimism has been affected by
the 'biological turn' that swept through much of the social sciences in the 1990s.
While in 1989 human freedom lies precisely in it not being 'determined by
biology' (Fukuyama, 1992: xvi), in 1999 it is only in the protection of biological determinism that human freedom and dignity can be assured. 'Human nature exists … and has provided a stable continuity to our existence as a species'
(Fukuyama, 2002: 7). But just at the point where the life sciences may be able
to 'decode' the biochemical information and unlock the secret of human nature in its genome (thereby, no doubt, telling the believers in natural right what
they already knew), that same information could enable its transformation:
'Modern biology is finally giving some meaningful empirical content to the
concept of human nature, just as the biotech revolution threatens to take the
punch bowl away' (13).

Somewhat predictably, Fukuyama gives his chapter on genetic engineering
an epigraph from Nietzsche's *Thus Spake Zarathustra* on the superman. 'What
is the ape to men? A laughing-stock or a painful embarrassment? And just so
shall man be to the Superman: a laughing-stock or a painful embarrassment'

(Nietzsche, 1969: 41–2). But his speculations on genetic engineering limit themselves to the desire for, and future of, 'designer babies'. As such they remain completely within the same threshold of the 'desire of the other' or, in Nietzschean terms, values determined by *ressentiment*. Fukuyama's previous chapter on the prolongation of life shows that one of the major investments in biotechnology will be in extending life-expectancy so that people can continue to spend, accumulate and interminably wear out their life evading the imminence of death. Fukuyama's speculations on the likely life-enhancements that will be sought are also perfectly consistent with the logic of commodification. Biotech companies will market specific 'genes' for characteristics like 'intelligence, height, hair color, aggression, or self-esteem' (16) and sell these to individuals or companies who wish to enhance the image or performance of their offspring or employees. As Coker shows, forms of biochemical modification already occur in business and the military. But there is no transvaluation of the 'human' here; human value is sustained within the threshold of capitalist economy and the idols of the marketplace.

The exception is where that value becomes one of pure performativity in the sense that it has no object, driven by pure negativity in the sense that the latter is beyond the recognition of the state. This is the negativity immanent to supercapitalism itself, as its DNA. It is indifferent to human values, having accelerated way beyond the human measure of need, want and desire. It is negativity as action without purpose and consideration, without mercy and justice, simultaneously creative and destructive in its negative transformations, laying the world to waste. Performativity is the inhuman action of accelerated hypernegation. The notion of performance that must always be increased and enhanced applies equally to humans and machines. Indeed, performativity establishes the plane of consistency in which 'both organic (human) life and machine life work as one (cybernetically)' (Coker, 2004: 70). Biotechnology can enable greater interactivity between these two elements of the assemblage, eventually achieving bioelectronic continuity between them. Again, there is nothing Nietzschean about Coker's vision of human beings who are reduced to a number of enhanced faculties (perception, analogical thought, intuition) and become organic supplements to machinic intelligence. Biotechnology does not take history on to a further stage here; it just takes it further in its current inhuman direction. Such a future remains encoded by the negativity of supercapitalism.

There are no supermen or superwomen who are the privileged subjects or agents of supercapitalism, then, unless the 'digitocommodification' of supercapitalism is seen as 'the index of a cyberpositively escalating technovirus' that has been implanted by replicants from the future. These replicants are revolutionaries 'virtually guiding the entire biological desiring-complex towards post-carbon replicator usurpation' (Land, 1993: 479). Picking up his motif from *Blade Runner* and the *Terminator* films, Nick Land, philosopher of machinic desire, goes into cyberpunk overdrive: 'How would it feel to be smuggled back out of the future in order to subvert its antecedent conditions? To be a cyberguerilla, hidden in human camouflage so advanced that even one's software was part of the disguise?' (Land, 1992b: 235). As an example of the discourse of 1990s cyberfantasy it would be difficult to parody, but its vision of history's continuation by biotechnology exhibits more imagination than the dreary all-too-human concerns of Fukuyama.

Fukuyama wants to remain at this particular historical terminus and expects the state to prevent the biotech industry from changing human nature, since human nature is the ground of human dignity. What is human nature for Fukuyama? A set of innate abilities (cognition, language acquisition) and emotional responses 'that guide the formation of moral ideas in a relatively uniform way across the species' (Fukuyama, 2002: 142). These moral ideas – suspicion of deceit, self-protection, reciprocity, revenge, embarrassment, care for family, repulsion for incest and cannibalism – are unremarkable and perfectly consistent with the morality of the 'last man', Nietzsche's parody of Hegel's perfected form of humanity. However, Fukuyama's idea of human nature is not the dialectical product of human history, nor has it been designed by God. What, then, are the grounds for judging these traits, characteristics and emotional reflexes as 'moral' and 'dignified'? The fact that they 'evolved over time out of the requirements of hominids' is no justification (142). Evolution is a process not an end and the requirements of hominids have changed and will no doubt continue to change. Fukuyama does not have an answer to this, but wishes to preserve the sum of human traits and characteristics which constitute the 'complex whole' that should ground a law of equality based on natural right (171). It is for the purpose of conserving this particular correlation of traits and just as importantly this way of understanding and valuing them as reason, morality, sociability, emotion, consciousness, that the state must intervene and strictly regulate biotechnology.

The ability of the state to regulate biotechnology rests with either international law or the power of America which, as we have seen, is bound up with multinational capitalism and its ability to operate outside the state form, partly as a means of America overcoming all other states. Concern for the dignity and integrity of the human form understood as 'a complex whole' has rarely, if ever, been a concern of modern warfare or of capitalism. Accordingly, biotechnology is already operative in supercapitalism in both its commercial and martial modalities and will continue to be so wherever it affords an advantage, a profit and a means of overcoming of the 'other'. That is to say the continual re-creation of the impossible conditions of an economic and political refusal of the West, its user-friendly goods and cyberpositive war machine. In this process human nature is foreclosed as the space of critical reflection is collapsed by the real-time informational exchange of digital machines. Human traits, characteristics and reflexes are broken down into blocks of desire and affect, in which human behaviour is understood quite differently in terms of 'swarms' or 'hives' (see Kelly, 1998: 32). The economic laws of supercapitalism, according to the new economists of the 1990s, have much more in common with natural laws understood more generally than the laws of human nature.[3] In his chapter on human nature Fukuyama alludes to these with yet another epigraph from Nietzsche, this time presumably to illustrate an idea of nature that must be opposed:

> 'According to nature' you want to *live*? O you noble Stoics, what deceptive words are these! Imagine a being like nature, wasteful beyond measure, indifferent beyond measure, without purposes and consideration, without mercy and justice, fertile and desolate and uncertain at the same time; imagine indifference itself as a power – how could you live according to this indifference? (Nietzsche, 1984: 9)

Nietzsche addresses the stoics because their invocation of nature is essentially self-justificatory. The stoics refuse to acknowledge or confront the indifference of nature, but instead seek to naturalise their own morality in nature as an ideal. Fukuyama attempts to do the same, but would add, as does Nietzsche, that this is perfectly possible because 'is the stoic not a *piece* of nature' himself? But this is Nietzsche's point: nature is the affirmation of the will to power and the will to power is comprised of both affirmative and reactive forces. In Fukuyama's conception, human nature is a reactive force-field comprised of the reason, morality, fear and *ressentiment* that it deploys to negate and subjugate rather than affirm its nature. But to appreciate these terms requires a different understanding of Nietzsche than the right-wing version offered by Fukuyama and his masters. Only then will it be possible to confront 'nature's' 'will to power', its uncanny resemblance to supercapitalism, and the self-consciousness that is required to live with the possibility of overcoming it. 'To live – is that not precisely wanting to be other than this nature?' (Nietzsche, 1984: 9).

## Rockin' the end of history

For Shadia Drury, Allan Bloom's *Closing of the American Mind* is 'a jazzy version of the work of Leo Strauss' (Drury, 1994: 161). Drury's description is no doubt deliberately ironic because it is American popular music that is the music of the last man of the universal and homogeneous state (Bloom, 1987: 68). Bloom does not offer a specific opinion of jazz but in so far as it privileges rhythm over classical harmony, and encourages people to dance, it is the 'expression of pure animal sexuality' (68). It is rock music above all, however, that is the favoured music of the last man, appealing to the universal values of love and sex, knowing neither class nor nation. American students do not have books, Bloom writes, but 'they most emphatically do have music … It is their passion' (68). While elsewhere complaining of the relativist cool of American students, here they are at last passionate about something, but to excess. Music is passion without reason: 'rhythm and melody, accompanied by dance are the barbarous expression of the soul' (71). Music is barbaric without the reason that shapes it into poetry which cools it down and turns it into a proper object of contemplation.

Certainly, Bloom performs in his own writing the deranging effects of rock's libidinal force. Bloom is most concerned about how rock addresses adolescent sexuality, 'having a much more powerful effect than pornography on youngsters' (74). The pornography of 'voyeurism is for old perverts; active sexual relations are for the young' (74). Demonstrating his familiarity with the more sedate pleasures of voyeurism, Bloom peers through an imaginary window to a typical 'pubescent boy whose body throbs with orgasmic rhythms ... whose feelings are made articulate in hymns to the joys of onanism' (75).

On Bloom's own bedroom wall is his epitome of rock's intoxicating 'nihiline' (78), the post-Nietzschean poster boy, Mick Jagger. Bloom is breathless in his ambivalent tribute:

> A shrewd, middle-class boy, he played the possessed lower-class demon and teenage satyr ... with one eye on the mobs of children of both sexes whom he stimulated to a sensual frenzy and the other eye winking at the unerotic, commercially motivated adults who handled the money. In his act he was male and female, heterosexual and homosexual; unencumbered by modesty, he could enter everyone's dreams, promising to do everything with everyone ... He was beyond the law, moral and political, and thumbed his nose at it. (78)

It is not necessary to be aware of Bloom's own publicly unacknowledged sexuality to perceive, in the rhythm and melody of his prose, another hymn to onanistic joy, the Dartford Dionysus entering dreams filled with ecstatic wonder and terror at that 'everything with everyone'. Beyond good and evil, and thumbing his nose at both, Jagger seems to have more in common with the superman than the last man, except for his perfect attunement to liberal democracy and capitalism. He is beyond class, beyond nation, beyond even gender and sexuality, but at the same time the embodiment of 'perfect capitalism' (76). In his entrepreneurial energy, then, his example poses, potentially, a serious challenge to those neoconservatives like Bloom who are disturbed by, yet dependent upon, the entrepreneurial energy of American capitalism. Hence the ambivalence of Bloom's description: Jagger becomes a fantasy figure filling Bloom with uncertainty, a new Napoleon (79), leading ordinary young people into the post-historical period.

American rock music seems an ideal place to look at the conjunction between American culture, economy and the various forms of negativity that characterise it. American rock – or American pop, generally used as a generic term for the music of the second half of the twentieth century – developed out of the folk and blues traditions. Further, perhaps because of the way in which it articulates desire, negativity, economy, machine, American rock and pop music seems to have a better understanding of so-called post-historical existence in the epoch of supercapitalism than these Straussians. The latter are neither properly ancient nor modern, Hegelian nor Nietzschean, capitalist nor anti-capitalist, American nor un-American, unable to make up their minds whether they are neoliberal or neoconservative because it matters little either way.

But the music that will become the object of discussion is not that of Jagger, the Rolling Stones, the Beatles and the other 1960s baby boomers with their 'smarmy, hypocritical version of brotherly love' (74). This book takes as its cue and context the end of the cold war and the last decade of the twentieth century. The most popular American music of that period – hip hop, rap and the various forms of metal – invoke and perform a different modality of negativity from the Hegelo-Nietzscheanism of the neoconservative Straussians. Yet this different mode of negativity perhaps finds its antecedence in one of Kojève's contemporaries.

In a letter to Kojève, Georges Bataille posed the question of 'unemployed' or useless negativity to the 'labour of the negative' that for Kojève finds its completion and culmination in the homogeneous state:

> I grant (as a likely supposition) that from now on history is ended (except for the denouement). … If action ('doing') is – as Hegel says – negativity, the question arises as to whether the negativity of one who has 'nothing more to do' disappears or remains in a state of 'unemployed negativity'. … I imagine that my life – or, better yet, its aborting, the open wound that is my life – constitutes all by itself the refutation of Hegel's closed system. (Bataille in Hollier, 1988: 90)

What becomes of negativity when it has been made redundant? What does someone do with the rage of feeling useless? Deriving his sole authority from his own experience, Bataille contends that the 'open wound' that is his own life in itself confounds Hegel's closed system, opening it on to heterogeneous forces. There and elsewhere, Bataille speculated on what future forms of violence, war and purposeless revolt such negativity might paradoxically engender. Bataille's 'abortive condition' is negativity stripped of human purpose, a rage become immanent to supercapitalism as its principle of inhuman transformation. Unemployed negativity describes the impossible locus of general economic life both heterogeneous and immanent to supercapitalism, or the 'machine', as it is referred to by Rage Against the Machine. In the example of this group and others that are discussed in the following chapters, there is evidence of such unemployed or useless negativity in cultural forms that disclose the wounds torn open and endlessly exacerbated by supercapitalism in its provocation of rage, antagonism, violence, nihilism and 'perverse' eroticism. Since the rap/metal anti-capitalists can find no other form of exchange than that of consumer capitalism, the embrace of such rage constitutes them as the stormtroopers of its digital–global 'cutting edge' as it deletes traditional musical cultures and establishes itself as the soundtrack of supercapitalism.

By 1989 one social form in particular, rendered heterogeneous by the neoliberal economic policies of Ronald Reagan's government, came to negatively exemplify the entrepreneurial spirit of American capitalism. Ironically, the negativity of this form was noted by neoconservatism, even as it was abjected as its social antithesis. 'In our world there are still people who run around risking their lives in bloody battles over a name or a flag or a piece of clothing', wrote Francis Fukuyama, before adding with regret that 'they tend to belong to gangs with names like the Bloods and the Cripps and make their living dealing drugs' (Fukuyama, cited in Drury, 1994:185–6). The next chapter looks at the uncanny proximity between negativity and the niggativity of the gangsta.

## Notes

1    Kurt Cobain apparently credited the inspiration for this structure to the Pixies, claiming that 'Smells Like Teen Spirit' was an attempt to rewrite the Pixies' 'Debaser' from the album *Doolittle* (1989). There are similarities, particularly the baseline and some drum figures. But the songs are quite different. The Pixies slightly predate Nirvana, and Black Francis's screaming-in-rage style of singing anticipates Cobain – 'Come on Chuck!', a formative friend is reported to have said, 'Sing it like you hate that bitch!' (Mendelssohn, 2004: 5) as do the themes of incest, mutilation and venereal disease which star in the songs collected on *Surfer Rosa* (1988a) and *Come On Pilgrim* (1988b) and which are accompanied by a 'grinding, shrieking slab of guitar hell' (Michael Azerrad, cited in Mendelsson, 2004: 48).

2    Since it must not be disclosed to the common people that the only truth is that there is no truth. They must be kept in awe. 'The idea that Strauss was a great defender of liberal democracy is laughable. I suppose that Strauss's disciples consider it a noble lie. Yet many in the media have been gullible enough to believe it. How could an admirer of Plato and Nietzsche be a liberal democrat? The ancient philosophers whom Strauss most cherished believed that the unwashed masses were not fit for either truth or liberty, and that giving them these sublime treasures would be like throwing pearls before swine. In contrast to modern political thinkers, the ancients denied that there is any natural right to liberty. Human beings are born neither free nor equal. The natural human condition, they held, is not one of freedom, but of subordination – and in Strauss's estimation they were right in thinking so' (Drury in Postel, 2003).

3    Natural history and biology has traditionally been a branch of economics, and vice versa, since Hobbes.

# 4

# Niggativity

To get some respect, we had to tear this muthafucka up.
(Ice Cube, 'We had to tear this muthafucka up', 1992)

## 29 April 1992

For Francis Fukuyama, former adviser to the Reagan administration, the essence of humanity lives on at the end of history in Compton, Los Angeles. While most of America eases itself into the contented life of prosperous post-historical consumption, some people are still willing to risk their lives in their desire for recognition and respect. Somehow, citizenship in the universal homogeneous state isn't enough. Significantly, the people left unrecognised by the state, or for whom recognition by the state is derisory, live in the places devastated, in the 1980s, by the effects of Reaganomics: deindustrialisation, market liberalisation, drug-trafficking, gang warfare and white flight. Only in the 'hoods and the ghettos, it seems, does the struggle for the recognition of pure prestige that defines humanity as such persist: 'Straight outta Compton, another crazy ass nigga / More punks I smoke, yo, my rep gets bigger' (NWA, 'Straight Outta Compton', 1988). No doubt Fukuyama is being ironic, or giving an example of what passes for irony in neoconservative circles. No doubt the mere fact that such struggle only persists in street gangs among drug dealers is evidence of the debasement of the principle.

And yet, on the eve of the neoconservative war against Iraq, Admiral Timothy Keating evoked an old mainstream hip hop hit as his battle cry. 'It's Hammer time!' announced Keating to the world's media in March 2003. Keating's triumphal citation of M.C. Hammer's catch-line to the rap 'Hammer Time (U Can't Touch This)' (1990), recalled the previous Gulf War when this record was ubiquitous on the airwaves. While it seemed incongruous to see a grizzled old Admiral put himself in the dancing shoes of the twinkle-toed Hammer, it is also highly symptomatic of mainstream America's appropriation of the energy of African-American culture, along with the labouring and soldiering bodies. At the same time as recognition seems to be lacking in places like Compton, something also seems to be lacking in the American military.

Perhaps somewhere in the back of his mind, Keating was recalling another hammer time. Operation Hammer, undertaken by Daryl Gates's LAPD in the highly publicised 'war on drugs' that swept through South Central Los Angeles throughout 1988–90, resulted in the arrest of 1,500 people, many on suspicion. With a huge budget, Gates's force benefited from new technology being developed by the military, which would be used in the Gulf War a year later. The LAPD became a militarised techno-police complete with a fleet of helicopters and a V–100 armoured military vehicle equipped with a massive battering ram that police used to smash into suspected crack houses. The 'chief symbol of the new repression', the vehicle was celebrated in the rap 'Batterram' by Toddy Tee in 1985 (Chang, 2005: 315; see also Davis, 1990: 265–322). In *City of Quartz*, Mike Davis describes how in the mid-to-late 1980s public space disappeared as Los Angeles became a heavily fortified battle zone. The militarised, brutal and increasingly lethal police force protected a white population obsessed with security who were locked up in gated communities, behind fortifications and inside panic rooms and were hooked up to the latest in technological surveillance. Outside the gates, in the 'no-go areas', the streets were given over to the crack trade, gangs and the police who waged war on them and the population they exploited and intimidated.

For Michael Hardt and Antonio Negri, the war on drugs and the war on gangs mark a shift away from the purely rhetorical invocation of war (as in the 'war on poverty') to a more concrete realisation of immanent war. The use of the rhetoric of war in attempting to address criminal practices like drug-dealing 'serves to mobilize all social forces and suspend or limit normal political exchange' (Hardt and Negri, 2004: 14). Since the actions involve armed combat and lethal force, they constitute more than a purely metaphorical war. Yet this is not war as conventionally understood, because it is not based on a war between states. Rather, 'in these wars there is increasingly little difference between inside and outside, between foreign conflicts and homeland security. We have thus moved from metaphorical and rhetorical invocations of war to real wars against indefinite, immaterial enemies' (14). Thus in formal and practical terms the war on drugs both precedes and prepares the way for the war on terror. Furthermore, this immaterial enemy, the 'enemy troops in the War on Drugs' consisted largely of 'young, inner city minority males' (Tonry, 1995: 4). According to a report published in 1990, *Young Black Men and the Criminal Justice System: A Growing National Problem*, (see George, 1998: 43), one in four African-American males between the ages of twenty and twenty-nine were either incarcerated or on probation. By 1992 58% of all federal prison admissions were drug offenders (Quinn, 2005: 46). One of the reasons for this was the introduction of the Reaganite policy of marketisation into the policing and prison systems (See Caplow and Simon, 1999: 74–122). These involved financial incentives, targets and bonus systems that were associated with drug arrests.

The police harassment and intimidation was intense.

To illustrate how the modality of economic life in South Bronx and South Central had become continuous with war, Chang quotes Greg Brown, a resident of Nickerson Gardens, confirming that the future for young blacks in the neighbourhood was no longer the factory floor of General Motors, but jail. 'You see that new Seventy-seventh Street LAPD station? It's beautiful. You see anything else in the community that looks better than that jail?' (Chang, 2005, 316). Chang comments that 'hip-hop was close to this underground economy because, more often than not, it was being made by youths who were not exploitable, but expendable' (367). In her book *Ain't Nuthin' But a G Thang* (2005), Eithne Quinn cites a roll call of rap artists imprisoned for possession of crack cocaine – J-Dee, Coolio, Warren G, Geto Boy's Willie D and Snoop Doggy Dogg – and quotes the latter on the effects of regular incarceration: 'It's a vicious circle, a revolving door, and after a while the line between being *in* and *out* gets real blurry and all you know is you are serving time one way or another' (47).

In March 1991, two events, both caught on videotape, caused South Central LA to go up in flames. On Sunday 3 March, Rodney King was captured on an amateur's camcorder being beaten by five police officers after they had pursued him for a speeding offence. A year before, King had made an 'ineffectual' attempt to rob a Korean-American store. Terrified of being sent back to prison, King fled the police who were pursuing him, but was eventually caught. He suffered fifty-six baton blows and kicks to the head and body. On 16 March a teenage girl, Latasha Harlins, was shot dead by a Korean-American storekeeper Soon Ja Du, after an altercation about a bottle of orange juice, the killing being captured by the store's own surveillance cameras. The two events highlighted the triangulated racial tensions between the African-American and Korean-American communities and the LAPD. The tensions between the two minority communities was both documented and exacerbated by ex-member of NWA, Ice Cube's 'Black Korea' from *Death Sentence* (1991). In these exchanges, the liquor or convenience store becomes the front line in a racial and economic war between two communities struggling for survival and advancement. Appropriately enough, the furious response of the Korean-Americans to Ice Cube's provocation was the Korean-American Grocers' Association boycott of St Ides '8-Ball', the brand of malt liquor sponsored by Ice Cube. The boycott resulted in a humiliating apology (for an account of the reception of 'Black Korea' and the Korean-American response, see Chang, 2005: 346–52).

On 5 November, Soon Ja Du was sentenced to 5 years on probation, to the outrage of many in the African-American community. Five months later, all five LAPD officers were acquitted of the assault on Rodney King. Riots ensued, enabled partly by the brief 'truce' between Cripps and Bloods sets, the repressive police action having had the brief effect of unifying many to join 'the same gang' in the war against the 'war on youth' (see Chang, 2005: 381–92). The rage against the King acquittals was also memorably voiced by Ice Cube on his album

*The Predator* (1992). The anti-police violence, both imagined and documented in the rap 'We had to tear this muthafucka up', bursts out in a context where justice has been suspended, or become complicit with the war that now mediates the social relations between rich and poor, majority and different minority populations.

Conventional war lies at the limit of political exchanges, as their point of regulating excess. In times of war, political differences are suspended in the face of a foreign enemy. War is exceptional and, accordingly, political opposition and democratic laws are suspended. As such, war is conventionally held in reserve to be summoned in times of domestic political emergency as a threat or distraction. External threats, real or phantasmatic, have historically been used as a means of transcending social unrest in the name of national unity. War, therefore, is a mode of transcendence through which a ruling class or race may maintain its position of dominance in the name of the state. With the cold war, two international power blocks were locked in a nuclear stand-off. In this situation, actual war between the main combatants becomes impossible, apart from some low-intensity actions in small client states, since it would result in mutual destruction. War is not exceptional in the old sense, but remains constant as an immanent principle of external containment and the internal regulation and policing of political dissent.

Since the collapse of the Soviet Union, war has become not simply oppositional. It has become internal as well as external, constructive as well as destructive, a mode of wealth generation as well as expenditure. Externally, it seeks to open up markets and nation-build; internally, it seeks to mobilise and utilise the entrepreneurial energy that is the source of national security. War since the cold war is no longer excessive to normal social life in the sense of being exceptional. Rather, it has become the internalised principle of creating and regulating social relations. War has become essential where religious obedience and the political–social contract has given way to the economy as the prime determinant of social life. That is to say, war is seen as an essential element of a general economic process. According to Hardt and Negri, war has taken over the 'fundamental social and political role' through accomplishing this kind of constituent or regulative function. War has become

> both a procedural activity and an ordering, regulative activity that creates and maintains social hierarchies, a form of biopower aimed at the promotion and regulation of social life. (Hardt and Negri, 2004: 21)

In order to become constitutive and creative, however, war cannot be simply a matter of repressive force; it requires the economic creativity of a capitalism that has become fully combative supercapitalism. That is why entrepreneurial energy is the foundation of American national security. Capitalism becomes essential to war, just as war is the essence of supercapitalism as its principle of pure negativity. Negativity establishes both war and capitalism on a plane of consistency. Supercapitalist war is neither a mode of transcendence nor a mode of immanence, but a mode of excess that is paradoxically essential. It is its excess-essence: the essence that is one continuous process of becoming-absence in wasteful expenditure. To coin a neologism, war is the excess-essence, or x-essence, of supercapitalism.

## Gangsta

Gangsta rap irrupts in the midst of this war in which deregulated capitalism provides the conditions of survival and combat. As such, its economic success provides an example of the negativity that is both mobilised as a mode of entrepreneurial combat and exploited by supercapitalist corporations. African-American creativity and entrepreneurial energy, specifically in the field of hip hop and sport, particularly basketball, illustrates the process of supercapitalism and its martial excess-essence. At the same time, gangsta rap provides an ironic commentary on this process and on the 'humanity' that it lacks.

Gangsta rap emerged in the context of the post-civil-rights period of African-American culture. Critics of African-American culture (George, 1998 and Quinn, 2005, for example) have stressed that this period sees a shift in the politics of representation, race and identity from collective responsibility to individual prestige that focuses on performance and entrepreneurship. As Quinn writes, 'in the mixed-up no guarantees world of neoliberal America … gangsta rap was energized politically by the rejection of collective protest strategies and the embrace of the ruthless drive for profit' (Quinn, 2005: 16). At the same time, this shift is extensively documented both in the lyrics and the samples that are taken from civil-rights-era soul and funk classics and in news reportage, comment and debate. The self-reflexive and self-dramatised combat of gangsta amplified even as it acted out the conditions of its production. In the process, its notoriety guaranteed the success which hugely enriched its major practitioners, or at least those who were not killed as an effect of the gang ethos that provided its lustre of lethal violence. But, further, this formula propelled hip hop generally into a major transnational and transcultural form and vehicle for supercapitalism as rap became by the end of the 1990s a global form.

For Nelson George, the drug culture, the crack wars, that provided one of the main references for gangsta rap was a 'direct by-product' of President Reagan's neoliberal policies in the 1980s. Crack, a 'fast-food' version of cocaine and heroin is itself an effect of 'McDonaldization' (George, 1998: 41–2). It is well known that the crack wars and their policing provided the context and much of the subject matter of gangsta. The street gangs supposed to organise and profit from the drug-dealing became semi-mythical. As Quinn suggests, the famous Cripps and Bloods, the reference for much of gangsta rap, were actually 'super-gangs' subdivided up into hundreds of hostile sets (Quinn, 2005:

50). Nevertheless, 'the levels of gang violence were "excrescent" (as Malcolm Klein called it) – providing the material for powerful realist tales about gangbanging conquests, murderous escapades, and tense poignant stories about loyalty and allegiance, sacrifice and loss' (54).

As Fukuyama shows, the mythology of the Bloods and Cripps reached even the parameters of the White House, where their violence was perceived, perhaps surprisingly, in terms of the fight for pure prestige. This is the violence that defines humanity for the neocons, the humanity that is precisely lacking in the creature comforts of post-historical man. While, in these terms, the slavish avoidance of the phantasmatic fight for pure prestige encodes objectless war as the inhuman drive of the machines of capitalist production, the rappers paint it large in the vivid colours of gangbanging for profit, though a profit that is self-consciously regarded as the surplus value of the reality of a precarious urban existence: 'Gangsta, gangsta! That's what they yellin' / "It's not about a salary, its all about reality" (NWA, 'Gangsta, Gangsta', 1988). With the salaries and comforts associated with respectable middle-class professions out of the range of a poorly educated population, rap musicians and entrepreneurs sought to exploit conditions in which prestige and profit become continuous and equally contingent: 'get rich or die doin' it', as 50 Cent would later claim. 'It was the West Coast gangsta that most fully came to narrativize these tragic deaths. Gangsta rappers fashioned stories about armed conflict and going out in a blaze of glory, often conveying a sense of the casualisation of violence that would shock and excite both fans and critics' (Quinn, 2005: 54).

As Quinn argues, gangsta rap can be boiled down to two broad sets of archetypal protagonists: 'the nihilistic gangbanger and the enterprising hustler' (92). The former is based on the mythological badman represented in musical folk history as Stagger Lee or Stagolee, an embodiment of pathological violence or pure expenditure. The latter is represented by the pimp/trickster figure of enjoyment and social mobility. Taken as a composite, they provide the formula for supercapitalism wherein a principle of pure negativity takes the form of an imperative to enjoy. The key difference, however, is that these African-American figures are of course marginal to dominant culture. Indeed they could be seen as excessive precisely to the degree to which they emerge out of a specific culture's historical negotiation with its dominant white culture. Yet, the very specificity of this history gives these figures an exemplary value for that culture. In their excess and indeed in their deficiency in relation to the 'norm', they are actually essential.

The violence of African-American men, real or imaginary, has a thrilling authenticity for dominant white culture. This authenticity does not reside simply in the popular racist belief that black men are naturally overlibidinal and inherently violent. Yet it is significant that such popular racism persists even though it has no basis in genetic or natural science. Its persistence, perhaps, is primarily an effect of the economic relations between Europeans, Americans of European origin and African Americans since the time of slavery. The violence of African-American men is imagined to be an excrescence of the energy of bodies in slave labour. The exploitation of that energy of course generated the wealth that built much of modern America and Western Europe from the eighteenth century. To cast this in neoconservative or Kojevean and quasi-Nietzschean terms, contrary to the account of Hegel's essentially Eurocentric master–slave dialectic, the European 'slave' did not, through just his own labour, create the wealth that enabled the overthrow of the 'masters', the aristocrats. Rather, it was the slave become slave-owner and slave-driver who created the wealth and forged the industrial process of production that created capitalism in its classic nineteenth-century form. African slaves are significantly left out of Hegel's account of world historical progress even though they are essential to the development of modernity. They are marginal and yet essential, outside but fundamental.

The thrilling authenticity of that energy resides in the cultural memory of the slavery that grounds the morality of American desire. Bad conscience concerning the suffering of slavery is invested in *ressentiment* at all forms of black sovereign enjoyment except where it can be commodified and returned to its purpose of making a profit for American companies. Images of the enjoyment of the freed African slave make a profit because they resonate throughout the years with the promise of liberation from the order of production that haunts the slavish consciousness of the white American *homo economicus*. Breaking through the mirror of production in the post-civil-rights period, the sovereign nihilism of gansta rap represents the ecstatic unbinding of slavery to the order of things: 'Fuck flippin' burgers' (NWA, 'Niggaz 4 Life', 1991); 'a real nigga [lives] by the muthafucking trigger' (NWA, 'Real Niggaz Don't Die', 1991). This unbinding from the order of production is prohibited by the universal homogeneous state that constrains the 'last man' to an animal existence of pure consumption. The badman of gangsta rap represents an ecstatic nihilism beyond all canons of *ressentiment* which is absolutely essential to any re-evaluation of values: 'I'm not a rebel or a renegade on a quest / I'm a nigga with a 'S' on his chest / so get the Kryptonite cos I'm a rip tonight' (Ice Cube, 'Amerikkka's Most Wanted', 1990). Superman? *Superfly!*

The gangsta, therefore, has an uncanny proximity to supercapitalism. He assembles with his AK-47 and his production arsenal of beat box, samplers and sequencers, a mini-supercapitalist war machine. Like war itself, he becomes capitalism's excess-essence, or rather its x-essence where, as with Malcolm X, the 'X' marks the unnameable inheritance of African lineage overwritten by slavery. 'X' marks the essential point of impossible African-American authenticity that resides imaginarily in the remnants of the civil-rights movement and collectivised struggle. But this 'X' no longer binds and governs a community according to a paternal principle all the more powerful for being nameless. 'Fatherlessness' looms large in the work of gangsta rap, 'the ghosts of

Malcolm, Martin, Bunchy and George appearing as absent fathers to a way-
ward generation gone nihilistic' (Chang, 2005: 333). 'X' marks the unnameable
diamond of desire that bursts out of the chaos of a desertified community
ravaged by drug-dealing, gangsterism, corruption and police brutality, to propel the phenomenal success of hip hop across the world, in the process inspir-
ing numerous other indigenous youth cultures into global supercapitalism.

That gangsta lies at the vanguard of this economic integration is perhaps
paradoxical, but consistent with the transformation of other nations in similar
conditions, with collectivised economies and political ideologies. As Hardt and
Negri note, the integration of the former Soviet Union into the global capitalist market produced 'powerful Russian mafias [that] emerged in control of a
wide range of criminal activities. "Democratic transition", we learned, is a code
phrase for corruption. Such corruption may conflict with the need for a stable
national political regime but at the same time facilitate integration into the
global economic market' (Hardt and Negri, 2004: 179). So, as he stood on the
threshold of another US military adventure in regime change, nation-building
and democratic transition, perhaps it is not after all surprising that Admiral
Tom Keating should cry 'It's Hammer time!'

## Aesthetics of excess

The defining record of gangsta rap is NWA's *Straight Outta Compton* (1988).
The album 'hit American popular culture with the same force as the Sex Pistols' *Never Mind the Bollocks* had in the UK eleven years earlier' (Chang, 2005:
320). If NWA are the Sex Pistols of rap, then Public Enemy are The Clash,
sharing the latter's more self-consciously political edge. In contrast to the Pistols' anarchic negativity ('no future', 'pretty vacant'), The Clash addressed issues of unemployment ('Career Opportunities') and race ('White Riot', 'White
Man in Hammersmith Palais'). The politics of Public Enemy and Chuck D in
particular are similarly broadly coherent in their anti-capitalism, and consistent with the civil-rights generation in 'calling for black responsibility and calling out white corporate exploitation' (Quinn, 2005: 5).

NWA's attitude, on the other hand, was, like the Pistols, much more ambivalent in its excessive appeal to shock, rage and non-productive expenditure. NWA
have united both radical and conservative critics alike in their dismay at their
deployment of negative images of 'niggas', pimps, bitches and 'hoes' and their
aggressive anti-authoritarian stance exemplified by the second explosive track
on *Straight Outta Compton*, 'Fuck tha Police'. NWA and the genre that was named
after the third track 'Gangsta, Gangsta' exceed easy attempts at categorisation
in conventional political terms. Indeed, for Jeff Chang, in his history of the hip
hop generation, *Straight Outta Compton* exemplifies 'the aesthetics of excess'
(Chang, 2005: 318–19): 'Excess was the essence of NWA's appeal' (319). It is

precisely this identification of excess as essential that defines what is at stake in gangsta's economic appeal and its exemplary negative function in relation to supercapitalism. But what is gangsta rap? Nelson George lays out the (fairly narrow canon) like this:

> Listen to any of NWA's albums, as well as Eazy-E's solo efforts, Dr. Dre's *The Chronic* and Snoop Doggy Dogg's *Doggystyle*. In their celebration of gats, hoes, gleeful nihilism, and crack as the centre of their economic universe, these albums darkly display everything people fear about gangsta rap. (George, 1998: 47)

These albums are also in sharp contrast to the asceticism and serious politics of empowerment and liberation of Public Enemy. Indeed it is gangsta's gleeful nihilistic laughter that is perhaps its most disturbing element. In his chapter on one of Ice Cube's most controversial albums, *Death Sentence* (1991), Chang quotes Ice T noting that 'rap is really funny, man. But if you don't see that it's funny, it will scare the shit out of you' (Chang, 2005: 331). With gangsta the laughter itself can be scary. Ice Cube is or has been the most politically assertive and engaged ex-member of NWA. Indeed he collaborated with Chuck D, Flava Flav and the Bomb Squad on *Amerikkka's Most Wanted* (1991), produced after he had fallen out with the rest of NWA. In spite of this, however, Chuck D has been fairly unequivocal in his criticism of gangsta's apparent political ambivalence and negativity. The term 'niggativity', indeed, which would seem a highly appropriate term to describe the attitude of NWA, was actually coined by Chuck D himself on his solo album the *Autobiography of Mistah Chuck* (1996). On this album, the ambivalence of niggativity is directly addressed and clear lines are drawn between progressive and non-progressive forms of African-American negativity.

Chuck D backs up his progressive politics with an asceticism that forgoes the immoral life of enjoyment celebrated in many of the gratuitously shocking rhymes of NWA and others. On the track 'Niggativity … Do I dare disturb the Universe', Chuck D defends his teetotalism ('never drank beer with the boyz') and his distaste for the chronic (marijuana): 'I'm not a chimney / so don't call that shit soft / What turned me off / swore their breath stink Plus / I never got out rhymed by a drunk'. Chuck D's distaste for alcohol turned to political rage at the enthusiasm of some of his fellow rappers for sponsoring very strong malt liquor. Eithne Quinn begins her book *Nuthin' But a G Thang* (2005) by contrasting the ethics of Ice Cube's sponsorship of St Ides malt liquor with Chuck D's disgust at the irresponsibility and complicity with white oppression that this represented for him (1–8). On the Public Enemy track '1 Million Bottlebags', Chuck D rails about slaves to the bottle and the can 'cause that's his man, the malt liquor man' (cited in Quinn, 2005: 5).

For Quinn, these different positions further mark different attitudes to the 'burden of representation' that successful black musicians are expected to carry. Gangsta doesn't so much reject this burden as ironise and confound it with its darkly comic amplification of racist stereotypes and the confirmation of main-stream society's worst fears concerning young black men. Instead gangsta's apparent apathy towards the aspirations of black protest is transformed by the energy of its investment in the realities of economic survival. Quinn neverthe-less recognises in gangsta's entrepreneurialism an 'extreme political charge' (12). But this involves a slightly different understanding of politics. Like much cul-tural studies work of the 1990s, Quinn shifts the emphasis of political analysis from the relations of production to the exchange and consumption of signs. The authenticity of the political subject is thus no longer grounded in his or her labour, any more than its oppression is located in the alienation and ex-ploitation of that labour by exchange value. On the contrary, authenticity is grounded in acts of consumption. As she states, 'the shift in emphasis can be summarized as the superseding of commodified authenticity with a new sub-cultural articulation of authentic commodification' (7). What is inauthentic commodification? Choosing to sponsor the wrong beer? Listening to the wrong albums, sampling a bad beat? This shift is a symptom of supercapitalism in which the economy establishes the conditions of social life in which the market becomes the main regulator, the so-called bottom line. Social bonds are estab-lished and dissolved according to the laws of exchange. Indeed, since social bonds have to be *created* in this sphere dominated by exchange, representation is replaced by an aesthetic dominated by presentation and performance. Social bonds are not just mediated but replaced by commercial and aesthetic produc-tions of bonds that are lived out primarily through consumption.

Chuck D in *Mistah Chuck* is radically opposed to the view that a politics of redistribution can be found in the aesthetic commercialisation of African-American experience. Naturally, there is an inherent contradiction since Chuck D has no option but to speak in the form of a commercial product, but contra-diction is the stuff of radical politics. It is the moral authority of Chuck D's voice that contradicts the conditions of its utterance as it lays down a series of powerful prohibitions. One of the signature tracks on the album, 'No', estab-lishes the parameters of his negativity in unequivocal terms, denouncing not only the white system of justice, but also the 'sell out' 'negroes with egos' pro-ducing shows 'calling women bitches and whores'. The rap builds to a fervent call for direct political action: 'no justice no peace … no struggle no progress' ('No'). In this respect, however there is no essential difference between Chuck D's niggativity of 'revolutionary programs and universalist messages' (Chang, 2005: 321) and the dialectical negativity of Hegel and Marx. Chuck D's 'no' seeks to establish a strong enough counter-force to negate the negation of white culture, thereby cancelling it, sublating it, even as it is raised to a higher level of universality in the state form that would denote another end of history. Not that of Fukuyama for sure, but a state of universal recognition nevertheless in which all were brothers and no one was called a bitch or a whore.

Chuck D is of course only of marginal concern to Quinn's book on gangsta rap. Her general argument is a subtle one concerning the way in which gangsta both reflects and reinforces the neoliberal individualist and entrepreneurial thinking of 1980s and 1990s America even as it contests white supremacy, morality and state apparati. The argument is persuasive, but perhaps gangsta's contestation does not constitute a critique of capitalism (as Robin D. G. Kelley claims in endorsing the book), so much as an exposure of its immanent violence, of the negativity and non-productive expenditure that propels it. Critique implies a position outside of its object from which it is perceived and criticised, but gangsta recognises no outside, no exterior position in excess of the American capitalist system that is itself simply a modality of excess in the form of war. Gangsta participates in this war. This contestatory participation discloses the liberal, moral, rational justification of capitalism and the occlusion of its violence through its *modus operandi* which is to push capitalism's inherent excess to the limit. Chang cites Dr. Dre, NWA's main producer, outlining his alternative strategy: 'I wanted to make people go: "Oh shit I can't believe he's saying that shit". I wanted to go all the way left. Everybody trying to do this Black power and shit, so I was like let's give 'em an alternative. Nigger niggerniggerniggernigger fuck this fuck that bitch bitch bitch bitch suck my dick, all this kind of shit' (318). The niggativity of NWA is not oppositional but immanent to supercapitalism as its essential excess. It is more closely associated with the negative joy of pure expenditure and an entrepreneurship of the violent, the useless and the ecstatic. It is not interested in the labour of the negative, of struggle, of the deferral that looks towards the promised land. 'If the thing was protest, they would toss the ideology and go straight to the riot. If the thing was sex, they would chuck the seduction and go straight to the fuck. Forget knowledge of self or empowering the race. This was about, as Eazy [E] would put it, the strength of street knowledge' (318). And the knowledge of street niggativity is strictly affirmative: 'And then you realise we don't care / We don't say "Just say no" / We're too busy saying "Yeah!"' (NWA, 'Gangsta, Gangsta', 1988).

The aesthetics of excess – a phrase that already transforms aesthetics into a general economic figure – is not limited to gangsta. Indeed, it could be adopted as a description of hip hop's musical development generally. Hip hop predates gangsta by ten to fifteen years depending on which myth of origin or theory of musical evolution one subscribes to. But if gangsta's aesthetics of excess is characterised by a rejection of the subject of the revolutionary narrative and of the linear structure of universalism, in favour of an ecstatic affirmation, this seems to me to be consistent with the early hip hop aesthetic generally.

## Done with judgement

In academic commentary on the aesthetic of hip hop, claims have been made for it as both a postmodern form and a form that is intrinsically African-

American in its rejection of linear Western musical models. Russell Potter, in his influential *Spectacular Vernaculars* (1995), is typical: 'If Blues is the "classical" music of African-American culture, and Jazz is the "modernism", then hip hop has a powerful claim to be regarded as their postmodern successor' (Potter, 1995: 18). Joseph Schloss argues that Potter's account, which analyses hip hop as 'a specifically African-American response to the fragmented aesthetic of contemporary media culture', is too closely related to other academic writing that attempts to discuss hip hop within 'a presumed aesthetic framework that is a natural result of what Jameson (1991) would call the cultural logic of late capitalism' (Schloss, 2004: 65). This kind of approach tends to integrate hip hop into an academic aesthetic discourse, particularly a literary one, and a political discourse already prepared for it. Further, it implies a judgement that has become very familiar, as Schloss states: 'the sampling aesthetic is presented as an example of postmodern pastiche, with all its attendant implications: juxtaposition of disparate aesthetic systems, blank parody, fragmentation, lack of historicity, and so forth' (65). It is always problematic for a writer in an academic work to criticise other writers for being academic, but it seems to me that this objection is justified where it concerns judgement, whether that judgement be aesthetic, political or moral–juridical. Academic criticism that follows Fredric Jameson's optimistic characterisation of contemporary capitalism as 'late' certainly involves these forms of judgement. This is because they imply a historicism that will have assessed the value and utility of such forms of postmodern contradiction to the degree to which they contribute to their own resolution and overcoming along with capitalism itself.

Judgement always situates itself outside and above its object, subjecting it to an eternal postponement and an infinite debt. Rejecting the canons of academic judgement, however, does not imply disposing of means of distinguishing between forms and qualities, as if everything had equal value. On the contrary, it is academic judgement that equalises everything as it attempts to measure its objects according to its own pre-existing criteria of value and utility, be they aesthetic, moral or political. 'What expert judgement, in art, could ever bear on the work to come?', asks Gilles Deleuze (1998: 135). Citing Spinoza, Deleuze suggests that 'it is a problem of love and hate and not judgement', of force and affect. Academic writing, therefore, is justified in speaking of forms heterogeneous to itself if it rejects judgement for affinity, 'sensing whether they agree or disagree with us, that is, whether they bring forces to us' (135).

Elements of hip hop aesthetic (if there is one, or just one) precisely contest aesthetic judgement in four quite specific ways. These are related to the four main elements of hip hop generally and gangsta rap in particular. Hip hop is essentially a combination of beats and rhymes. That is, beats are taken from short segments of previous records and strung together in aural loops, along with the rap, a kind of rhythmic poetry somewhere between speech and song. Hip hop owes its origin to the creativity of live DJs manipulating turntables in order to heighten the pleasure and intoxication of dancers, even as the same technique quickly moved from performance to production with the use of digital sampling in the studio. A rapper's performance typically involves a combative mode of self-performance and the construction of a sexually powerful yet embattled persona.

In his essay on judgement, Gilles Deleuze identifies its four major powers: the power of final authority whose last judgement is infinitely postponed and therefore uncontestable; the power of the dream whose ideality and utopianism is unimpeachable; judgement's power of organisation; and its stratification of war into a power of the state. All these powers are evident in Jamesonian critique, however nuanced and sophisticated its Marxism, in the ultimate judgement of history.

The four powers of judgement are applied in the most common critiques of hip hop such that the form could perhaps be characterised precisely through the contestation of that judgement. As Schloss states, in academic hip hop criticism 'the sampling aesthetic is presented as an example of postmodern pastiche' (2004: 65), and indeed postmodern ahistoricism. The practice of sampling, lifting fragmentary beats out of a particular record and its specific historical context, fails to respect both the integrity of a particular song and its internal organisation, not to mention authorial intention and copyright. The combination of different samples fails to respect the historical political integrity of a particular utterance. This is most keenly felt where the examples have been taken from an older generation's collections of soul and funk classics closely associated with the black power and civil-rights movements of the 1960s and 70s. Schloss notes significantly that 'for many, if not most, producers, this process begins with the selective exploitation of their parents' record collections' (82). The almost sacrilegious theft and recontextualisation of musical samples in hip hop appears to refuse the debt owed to African-American history.

But the practice of sampling involves a different and perhaps more primary relation of debtor and creditor between DJs, producers and their archive, ethically and aesthetically if not always financially (for a highly problematic discussion of the ethics of hip hop sampling, see Schloss, 2004: 101–34). This relation of debtor and creditor is not the same as that established by the final authority that stands at the end of time as the ultimate test of history and thereby subjects all to an infinite and unpayable debt. In hip hop, the relation between debtor and creditor is primary to all exchanges, immanent to the form, essential to its creativity and value. The exchanges between debtor and creditor are finite precisely because they are plural and multiple. They do not transgress the integrity of the history of African-American music but, in Deleuzian terms, would constitute the course of the time of its continual becoming. Potter's argument about the postmodernity of hip hop actually concerns this point rather than one about succession. Hip hop is postmodern, he argues, not so much on account of chronology as on account of what Bakhtin calls 'chronotopes' – the linked prismatic synecdoches of cultural history. Hip-hop's central chronotope is the turntable, which Signifies on its ability to 'turn the tables' on previous black traditions, making a future out of fragments from the archive of the past, turning consumption into production. With this mode of turning and re-turning, hip-hop's appropriative art (born of sonic collage and pastiche, re-processed via digital technology) is the perfect backdrop for an insistent vernacular poetics that both invokes and alters the history of African-American experiences, as well as black music on a global scale (Potter, 1995: 18).

Correlative to hip hop's apparent indifference to the integrity of the standards of soul and funk of the civil-rights era is the judgement that the form is apolitical; unlike soul, it does not have 'a dream'. For Deleuze, 'the world of judgement precisely establishes itself as in a dream' (1998: 129). Through his or her imperative to imagine, the dreamer condemns the life of the present to the quotidian prison of the everyday in relation to the promised land of the future. 'The dream erects walls, it feeds on death and creates shadows, shadows of all things and of the world, shadows of ourselves' (130). In contrast, leaving the shores of judgement involves the repudiation of the dream in favour of 'intoxication'. 'Drink, drugs, ecstasies' are an 'antidote to both the dream and judgement' (130).

In his seminal interviews with hip hop pioneers Africa Bambaataa, Grandmaster Flash and others, David Toop disclosed some of the main impulses behind the development of the form. This form developed through democratic and market principles in contradistinction to the aesthetic integrity of the art work. DJs concentrated on playing just the fragments of their records that 'were popular with the dancers … ignoring the rest of the track' (Toop, 1984: 60). Usually the most popular part of the song was the percussion break, the (non-)essential part that intensifies the rhythm and pushes the song beyond itself, beyond the appreciation of form and melody into an experience of intoxication. Toop quotes Bambaata who stresses 'that certain part of the record that everybody waits for – they just let their inner self go and get wild. The next thing you know the singer comes back in and you'd be mad' (60). The return of the singer, of melody and narrative, destroys the moment, returns the dancers back to the predictable pop dream of love and romance. To eliminate this return and sustain the intoxication, the percussion break, 'a conga or bongo solo, a timbales break or simply the drummer hammering out the beat', was isolated 'by using two copies of the record on twin turntables and playing one section over and over, flipping the needle back to the start on one while the other played through' (60). This was the beat or break-beat, the essence of the hip hop form shaped from the excessive moments of other records.

Though hip hop owes its origins to events like block parties, since the form is a development of DJing and the presentation of prerecorded music it is vulnerable to the critique of being derivative or parasitic on more original and authentic music. It is not a properly live or organic performance of music. This judgement that condemns hip hop for a lack of organisation and organic integrity is behind the observations about its fragmentary 'juxtaposition of disparate aesthetic systems' as Schloss says. Schloss is most dismissive of this claim, though his insistence that its elements are indeed fused together to form a whole – 'to say hip hop is about fragmentation because it is composed of samples is akin to saying that a brick wall is about fragmentation because it is composed of bricks' (2004: 66) – tends to restate the basis of the judgement. The image of a brick wall is a fine if workmanlike metaphor for an idea of aesthetic unity in order to judge hip hop fragmentation.

But, as Schloss says elsewhere, virtually all hip hop is based on a cyclical rather than linear form (136). Its affective loops constitute an anorganic vitality that seizes hold of the organic bodies of the dancers and coils them into the groove of a more intensive life. Hip hop is not subject to the tyranny of verse-chorus-verse-chorus which dominates most popular music and which so bored and constrained Kurt Cobain. It has no structure in that sense and can go on as long as it likes, the length being determined by the flow of the dance, through interaction with the crowd. Schloss makes an excellent (and Deleuzian) point when he draws a distinction between critics of the repetition of popular music as 'the hallmark of mass production' and hip hop's 'logic of musical repetition *as* artistic differentiation; the producer's creativity lies in the ability to harness repetition itself' (138). And just as the DJ can continue the beat indefinitely, the rapper can rap as long as he or she likes, in turn harnessing the power of repetition through the rhyme and rhythm of language.

'I fucking despise hip hop. Loathe it. Eminem is a fucking idiot and I find 50 Cent the most distasteful character I have ever crossed in my life. It's so negative' (Gallagher, 2005: 5). Noel Gallagher, guitarist in *Oasis*, speaks for many in characterising his dislike for hip hop – the often idiotic self-aggrandising, distastefully aggressive personae that populate the narratives of gangsta rap particularly; its relentless, combative negativity. As if gangstas give a fuck about the judgement of Noel Gallagher, of all people. It is 'combat that replaces judgement', for Deleuze, 'and no doubt the combat appears as a combat *against* judgement, against its authorities and personae' (Deleuze 1998: 132): 'I can't trust a cracker in a blue uniform / stick a nigga like a unicorn / Vaughn, wicked, Lawrence Powell, foul / cut his fucking throat and I smile / Go to Simi Valley and surely someone knows the address of the jury / Pay a little visit 'Who is it?' (Ice Cube, 'We Had to Tear this Muthafucka Up': 1992). Gangsta constructs a series of fictional personae to play out, in the aesthetic space of the rap, a combative relation to the judgement of state authorities. This judgement is consistent with the war that the state has stratified in institutions, economic inequalities, language, law and discipline and has harnessed outwards towards other states in wars that mobilise the poorest as its cannon fodder. Ice Cube in particular takes arms against this war and the patriotic judgement it applies to the subjects it expends in military action: 'The army is the only way out for a young black teenager … [but] I wanna kill Sam because he ain't my muthafucking Uncle' (Ice Cube, 'I Wanna Kill Sam', 1991).

'But more profoundly, it is the combatant himself who is the combat' (Deleuze, 1998: 132): 'Who's the Mack? Is it some brother in a big hat / Thinking he can get any bitch with a good rap?' (Ice Cube, 'Who's the Mack?', 1991). The multiple gangsta personae who are mobilised in the rap combat – the Stagger Lee figures, the macks, the pimps, the tricksters – are constantly engaged with each other. The constituent parts of NWA and the combat between Eazy E and Dre and Snoop, between Ice Cube and his former band members illustrate the creative and indeed commercial force of combat. Dr. Dre's seminal G-Funk classic *The Chronic* (1992) lambasts Eazy E throughout. Eazy responded with *It's On (Dr. Dre) 187um Killa* (1994) to Dre's laconic delight: 'He can make a million records about me if he wants to. He's keeping my name out there' (cited in Dimery, 2005: 688). In this regard such combat is clearly consistent with the martial modality of supercapitalism even as it contests the judgement that is on the side of (state) war. Combat is the gangsta's mode of participation in supercapitalism, his or her means of commercial survival and contestation disclosing America's own terrain as always already a field of engagement. Combat against and with this war below the threshold of domestic administrations and jurisdictions opens it to multiple powers that contest the particular relationship of power that is maintained by laws and state institutions. As that power is disclosed and disintegrated by the combatants of supercapitalism, America itself risks unravelling in a general conflagration of heterogeneous forces.

The aesthetic martial commercialism of gangsta quickly became a highly desirable and lucrative form of urban and suburban mimicry and as such a lifestyle. A simulacrum of a lifestyle, indeed, since gangsta is itself a simulation. This became especially apparent in the 'synergy' that developed in the late 1980s between sports and leisurewear companies, hip hop and the NBA. Run DMC perhaps pioneered the connection in 1986 with a song that 'turned Adidas into a hip hop brand' (Chang, 2005: 417). Two years later, Nike established a lead over rival Reebok through employing a Spike Lee character's identification with Michael Jordan in his debut movie *She's Gotta Have It*. Nike had hired the advertising agency Wieden and Kennedy and when two of their admen saw Lee's 'oddball character Mars Blackman stomp[ing] around in Air Jordans a light bulb went off'. Lee and Jordan were instantly hired to do a series of ads that propelled Nike's business beyond Reebok. Further, the success of the 'Spike and Mike' spots 'confirmed that a massive shift in tastes was occurring – from baby boomer to youth, from suburb to city, from whiteness to blackness' (417). The incorporation of blackness and gangsta's aesthetics of excess at the heart of white consumer desire needs to be addressed in order to analyse in detail its exemplary negative function in relation to supercapitalism.

# 5

# X-essence of the wigga

It always seems that I'm dreaming of something that I can never be,
I will always be that pimp that I see in all of my fantasies

(Korn, 'A.D.I.D.A.S', 1996)

$

For gangsta rappers, referring only to the experience of everyday life in the 'hood is illusory, since the records also provide the point of mediation between minority and majority cultures. Gangsta, particularly in the form of NWA, Easy E, Ice Cube, Dr. Dre and Snoop Doggy Dogg provides a commentary on the absence of a relation between these cultures, the fact that white and black are 'enemies by nature' (Chang, 2005: 337). At the same time, the gangsta commentary continually brings the status of its own speech into question: 'Why do I call myself "nigga", you ask me? / Because my mouth is so muthafucking nasty / Bitch this, bitch that / Nigga this, nigga that / In the meanwhile my pockets are gettin fat / Gettin paid to say this shit here / Makin more in a week than a doctor makes in a year' (NWA, 'Niggaz 4 Life', 1991). Snoop's million-dollar-selling album *Doggystyle* (1993), which comments extensively on the successful gangsta's life of conspicuous consumption, opens with the suggestion that its listeners get their 'pooper scooper' ready because the Dogg's about to start talking shit. The (in-)authenticity of gangsta rap, therefore, resides not in its ostensible meaning or reference, but in the power of its performance and its effects, particularly its effects on dominant white culture and the suburban mass audience.

## X-essence

On the face of it, the Gangsta nigga may seem a remote point of identification for suburban white culture. But hip hop, Nelson George argues, travels a similar trajectory to drugs and basketball into the heart of suburban America, such that 'the outlaw mystique' of Gangsta's relation to drugs and dealing is 'not so distant from the white teen experience' (George, 1998: 43). The phenomenon of the 'wigga' (white, wanna-be-nigga) is testament to this proximity, but also to its distance. Even as 'suburban dealers and addicts use urban 'hoods as drive-through windows' (43), the absence of a relation between white and black is exacerbated. That is because each term exposes the inadequacy or inauthenticity of the other. In a racially or culturally homogeneous culture, difference does not generally concern colour or ethnicity. Nationality is not marked at home as it is abroad. In traditional European communities and in parts of America, '"whiteness"' is ordinarily so taken-for-granted because its dominant status renders it invisible' (Goldman and Papson, 1998: 101). The paradox of the wigga, the white suburban teenager who mimics black speech and style, is that he or she cannot help drawing attention to an incongruous whiteness. The white-ness becomes opaque, the deathly pallor of an interior emptiness signified by the colour of the ethnic content worn on the surface. Ironically however, this ethnic content is frequently nothing other than an assemblage of brands and products of a range of American multinational corporations, brands of osten-sibly white upmarket leisurewear: Tommy Hilfiger, Ralph Lauren, Kangol, Lacoste and especially Nike. For Naomi Klein, these hitherto 'white-preppy wear labels' exploited 'the alienation at the heart of America's race relations: selling white youth on their fetishization of black style, and black youth on their fetishization of white wealth' (Klein, 2000: 76). In so doing, these companies have mobilised the spectacle of African-American expenditure in music and sport particularly, in order to evoke that which is missing in dominant Ameri-can culture.

The very simple diagram shown in Figure 5.1 means that excess is located in the interior as its essence. The diagram is there to illustrate the idea that the relationship between minority and majority cultures in the US, the non-rela-tion between black and white, is not an effect of a bipartition between inside and outside. Rather, in each case, what is interior has a quality of excess.

## Image → subject

Excess is qualitative as much as quantitative; it is no longer exterior to a stan-dard of normality. Images of excess are everywhere; they have become the norm. But how can this be possible? Common sense would insist that the very mean-ing of excess require that it be positioned outside of the standard of normality that it defines. Excess conventionally signals the inessential: something that 'is not really necessary, desirable or pleasing ... redundancy; uselessness; waste' (Bauman, 2001: 85).

Bataille, however, reverses this commonsense assumption. For him, excess poses the essential economic *problem* (see Bataille, 1988). Systems are

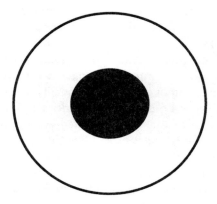

**Figure 5.1** X-essence

determined by 'the play of energy' that they struggle to utilise and contain: 'If the system can no longer grow, or if the excess cannot be completely absorbed in its growth, it must necessarily be lost without profit; it must be spent, willingly or not, gloriously or catastrophically' (Bataille, 1988: 21) Standards of normality are merely rational appropriations of the energy they utilise but which is always in excess. It is the same with the entrepreneurial energy that the US government recognises as the basis for its security; its end is war. A particular cultural symptom of this is exposed by supercapitalism: what was once the excess of a dominant culture – defining its normality through its difference – has become disclosed as interior and essential to it, especially where it provides an 'accursed' image of its essential excess.

The schema shown in Figure 5.2 implies that excess is central and also denotes that this x-essence is located culturally in the image. What does the term 'image' mean here? The term 'image' stands for the system of cultural perceptions that are determined by the range of capitalist media that articulate social relations. In the world of advertising and marketing, another word for essential is authentic. Robert Goldman and Stephen Papson note in their book *Nike Culture* (1998: 107) that time and again the authentic is located in images of the 'other'. But this 'other' is itself signified in a locus of alterity, the system of images in which there is an excess of 'others'. It is perhaps odd that anyone might suppose that the authenticity of a subject or a consumer should be locatable in or signified by a commodity or brand that is necessarily exterior to it. It is even odder that such authenticity should be identified in another race

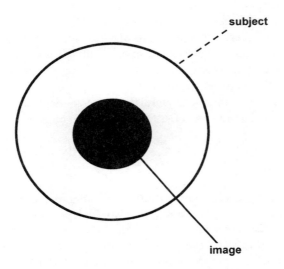

**Figure 5.2** Image → subject

or culture to which one has an embattled relation. And yet, as Papson and Goldman write,

> Once excluded from advertising's social tableaus by the politics of racism … racial and ethnic images have enjoyed a symbolic resurgence in the quest for images of difference, authenticity, and purity of experience. (107)

Authenticity, peculiarly, is an object of a 'quest' for images of the 'other'. The first oddity, then, is linked to the second in such a way as to render authenticity even more problematic. This is because the ethnic content of the image is supposed in some way to negate its status as image produced by consumer culture. Yet, it is only as an image and commodity that the 'other' can be recognised and its authenticity consumed and negated. Authenticity is thus essential to, but in excess of, advertising images; it is located as an (immaterial) object *in* the system of consumer desire but also therein still in excess of it, out of reach. Papson and Goldman suggest that

> The desire for authenticity has become tied to the quest to occupy (if only psychologically) a social space that has not been taken over by the commodity form, because commercialization (putting things into commodity form) corrupts the authentic. (104)

Even though authenticity instantly slips away from the image-commodity, to be promised in the glitter of yet another image, it is only in an analysis of images that we can discern the movements of x-essence in the subject of culture. Since x-essence is tied to the vacillation of a culture's identity with itself, the system of images and commodities disclose through the movement of their negation that which is essential to a culture. That is to say, it is precisely in the inessential, the useless and the wasteful that the essential insists; it is evident in a culture's hesitations and anxieties towards its own objects and images.

## Image ◊ X

It is necessary, then, to add another dimension to Figure 5.2 in which the image requires some 'x-factor' in excess of it that would denote its essence or authenticity. The structure is the same but this time the exterior circle is that of the image. Indeed, we can take the circle to denote the chain of substitutable images of the 'other'. In the position of x-essence to the image, then, is the 'x-factor' that would ground its authenticity.

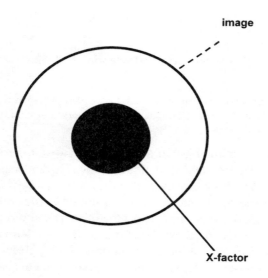

**Figure 5.3** Image ◊ X

Figure 5.3 does not replace Figure 5.2 but homes in on a particular detail in close-up, thereby revealing the same essential fractal structure. The detail is isolated in an effort to locate a particular quality in the image: its alterity. Where or what is the 'otherness' of the image? What lies in excess of the image? On the one hand, that is the subject of the image, an answer that does little more than locate the subject once again in the field of excess. On the other hand, it might be some external controlling power of the image, as if multinational corporations like Nike were in a conspiracy with African-American culture to exploit and transform the value system of white majority culture. In this case Nike would encourage the law-breaking, piracy and looting that is often associated with that culture: 'Designers like Stussy, Hilfiger, Polo, DKNY and Nike have refused to crack down on the pirating of their logos for T-Shirts and baseball caps in the inner cities and several of them have clearly backed away from serious attempts to curb rampant shoplifting' (Klein, 2000: 74). But this kind of conspiracy-theorising, however grounded in anecdotes of cynical marketing strategies, is misleading. Rather, the 'otherness' of the image must be located somewhere interior to the subject and its 'paranoia', in the intimacy of its (self-)love and hatred:

> Yeah, ha-ha, it's the nigga you love to hate / Ay yo baby, your mother warned you about me / It's the nigga you love to hate (Ice Cube, 'The Nigga You Love to Hate', 1990)

In American popular culture, the black man screens the alterity of the image as the neighbour from the 'hood that the white folks love to hate. The boys from the 'hood bear, unbearably, on the Christian commandment to 'love thy neighbour as thyself', provoking the full force of white America's self-loving enmity. The image of the gangsta, with his tales of taking 'a trip to the suburbs' for a spot of burglary, perhaps exposes the limit of the neighbour that is the basis of neighbourliness and conformity, the reference point of community. But at the same time he also confirms it, and in the images of African-American culture endorsed by brands like Nike, the black man becomes the focus of community's liberal desire to recognise 'all fellow beings'. And indeed, as long as he remains an image that can be exchanged with another in the field of capitalist media, he remains subsumed within a general principle of equivalence that determines the neoliberal parameters of conformity and equality, even peace.

However, supercapitalism thrives on war. Supercapitalism bears on that which grounds the alterity of the image in order to precipitate war as desire. But the alterity of the image cannot be grounded in another image. To authenticate the image in another image would be just to substitute one image for another, and vice versa. The alterity of the image lies in its 'x-factor', which must always be located in (the) excess of the image; that is, in the way in which it is wasteful or seems to serve no purpose, is undesirable or too desirable, useless or too useful, and in the way in which this excess affects the subject of American culture.

In its vacillations concerning the images of the nigga's excess, continually documented in the records, can be plotted the co-ordinates of the race war that supercapitalism takes as its terrain. American racism is bound up with the excess associated with the black body and what is imagined about its capacity for work, pleasure and violence. If this kind of racism is impervious to moral, economic or scientific reason, if it is beyond the limit of political persuasion, it is because in its irrationality it must be understood as generally economic. Indeed, it is an inevitable effect of the restricted, rational and moral economy of utility. Racism is another effect of the problem of excess. It is the excrescence of moral reason that bears on the 'x-essence' of its other, or of 'otherness', in Papson and Goldman's terms: 'Otherness, in the form of blackness or exotic primitivism, has acquired a frame of meaning that encompasses immediacy and pleasure' (Goldman and Papson, 1998: 105)

Positively or negatively, the x-factor that grounds the image of the 'other' always concerns excess. African Americans are more immediate, take more pleasure in life and have more fun than white folks, even in church. Or alternatively, African Americans are lazy, or overlibidinal or overendowed or excessively violent, at the same time demonstrating an excessive capacity for suffering and for joy. And of course, as slavery demonstrated, they have a natural capacity for physical work.

In the context of a restricted economy, then, such excess always implies a corresponding deficiency, so the imagined capacity for physical labour implies a diminished intelligence, or indeed it is imagined that the excess enjoyment is taken at the expense of white rational or moral seriousness. This is manifested in the suspicion that the objects of African-American enjoyment involve theft: 'Why do I call myself a nigga, you ask me? / Because police always wanna harass me / Every time that I'm rollin' / They swear up and down that the car was stolen' (NWA, 'Niggaz 4 Life', 1991).

## X ⊂ image

If the alterity of the image implies that there is some subject – the nigga – supposed to be enjoying himself in one way or another at the white man's expense, there is also the question of the object of his enjoyment and its modality. The notion of an x-factor implies that the image has something about it, some qualitative difference. What is that thing?

Ain't nuthin' but a G thang, baaaaabay!

Which is what, exactly?

It's like this and like that and like this and uh
It's like that and like this and like that and uh
It's like this
And who gives a fuck about those?
So just chill, til the next episode

(Dr. Dre, 'Nuthin' but a G Thang', 1992)

This indefinable 'thang' is not just any thing or object; it's not this or that. Rather, it is the point of excess of representation around which representation and metaphor circulates: 'It's like this and like that and like this and uh', but it's not any of those. Rather, they are defined in relation to it. It is the 'thang', the (non-)object of desire that propels the 'next episode' and then the next and then the next. As a G thang, a gangsta thang, it is the evil heart of malevolent, nihilistic shit that each record promises but holds at bay until the next episode, perhaps. As such it sustains the thrill for the listener and the consumer summoning up enjoyment and aggression and enjoyment in aggression, smacking up some bitches and putting a nigga on his back. This thang summons the excess aggression that is both immanent to the doggy-dog (dog-eat-dog, see Quinn, 2005: 146 on this pun) world of supercapitalism and the consumer, the aggression screened by the gangsta in both senses.

The wigga's mimicry circulates this thang, the ambivalent nature of which is nicely encapsulated by the term 'nigga' itself. Expropriated from the term 'nigger', that signifier obscenely loaded with hatred and suffering, nigga is an ambivalent signifier of affirmative negativity. It is a mark of recognition that is both intimate and exclusive, a word that only one nigga can use to another. At the same time, its use is by no means approved in the black community. In her discussion of the term, Eithne Quinn highlights NWA's montage at the beginning of 'Niggaz 4 Life' of quoted outrage at the use of the term. 'Why you brothers and sistas using the word "nigga"? … I ain't no "nigga", fuck that shit' (NWA, 'Niggaz 4 Life', 1991; see Quinn, 2005: 33; See also Kennedy, 2002). The appropriation of the term in gangsta rap creates a fictional persona and the world of violent cops, macks, bitches and hoes in which he operates. It is a deliberate fiction, an image – the nigga does not exist but he has powerful effects nevertheless that cut to the quick of dominant American culture.

To illustrate how the G thang operates, without existing, as the x-essence of suburban white America, I am going to introduce a thought experiment. Imagine a classroom full of suburban white kids, a classroom full of wiggas resplendent in their Nikes, their baseball caps, their designer leisure wear, their 'bling-bling'. Suddenly, outside the classroom a loud male voice shouts 'NIGGA!' Or was it 'NIGGER?' Panic strikes the white kids to the core, exposing the intimate, unfathomable violence at the heart of the consumer from which it wants to flee in horror. 'Is there a "nigga/nigger" in the school', the wiggas wonder, 'or is it us? Do we have to get our asses "ready for the lynching" (Ice Cube, 'The Nigga You Love To Hate', 1990). Or is this a gat-toting nigga come to rob the school, rob us of our "money and jewellery" (Ice Cube, 'Amerikkka's Most Wanted', 1990).' Is this the KKK or Amerikkka's Most Wanted? A specific subject of enunciation is not necessary for the nigga to strike terror into the heart of his white imitators, the same terror that compels the consumption of the records and the merchandise that might overcome it through mastering it in the imagination.

## *Quod* without *quid*

The nigga exists, then, since he has effects, but he has no substance. The nigga has no essence even though he resides as the x-essence of white neoliberal supercapitalism. He is '*quod* without *quid*', existence without essence. There is, therefore, no ontology of the nigga. It does not name the subject of African-American culture, nor does it denote its authenticity or an experience it has in common. It does not pick up the burden of African-American representation. Its thang is not articulated to the subject of African-American culture, but to its division. The thang is not of the order of representation, but inhabits the conflict that generates representations; it is the uncharacterisable figure of excess that the principle of order seeks to shape and utilise. That is why 'Real Niggaz Don't Die' (NWA, 1991). When you take aim at a nigga, you are aiming at something more than just his body or his name. Taking aim at a nigga is simply to affirm the reality of the conflict that it signifies, and in so doing engender more niggas, like the Sorcerer's Apprentice chopping up the broomstick: 'Real Niggaz don't die, they just multiply' (NWA, 'Real Niggaz Don't Die', 1991). Real niggaz don't die because, as the album title suggests, niggaz are 4 life, and while death is always present in the 'hood, it is there only to be negated. The gangsta nigga 'is he who *is*, as if death were not' (Bataille, 1991: 222)

## Image (the Nike image of African-American sporting excellence)
## 　 X 　 (the *realness* of excess)

The conflictual reality of the 'real nigga', its x-factor, is something that is capitalised on by companies like Nike but screened in the sense of projected and covered up in marketing images. Nike precisely clothe or shoe the real in *realist* images of African-American life, as Goldman and Papson extensively document:

> *Nike* both establishes itself as a 'realist' voice while at the same time representing sport as a vehicle for spiritually transcending race and class divides. *Nike* simultaneously acknowledges and denies the unequal *social and economic* realities that influence probabilities for both success and suffering. (Goldman and Papson, 1998: 94)

In their book, Goldman and Papson show how Nike's marketing strategy throughout the 1990s utilised techniques of documentary realism in order to self-consciously introduce the subject of 'the ghetto' by photographically stressing its 'realness' (102). This is a strategy that implicitly acknowledges the general unreality of advertising images. It is a formula that states that without the x-factor an image is just an image and has no other status than that of an illusion. Goldman and Papson document the success of this strategy and how it compared favourably with other brands who also attempted to mobilise the energy of African-American culture. Reebok's 'Blacktop Slam-Dunk Fest', for example, constructed a 'fantastic fiction' that did little but underscore its cynicism.

Nike has sought to transcend this kind of cynicism through appealing directly to the authenticity that is granted to African-American culture, an authenticity that is grounded in, and guaranteed by, little other than the bad conscience surrounding slavery. That bad conscience credits the authenticity and authority of African-American culture in whatever form it takes so long as it corresponds to the locus of suffering-enjoyment. Nike's goal of transcendence and universality is sought through recourse to a particular locus of sovereign authenticity: the 'soul' and the 'cool' associated historically with African-American music and style. This cool is of course exemplified by gangsta as well as basketball, elements that testify to the authenticity that Nike seeks to evoke in its images 'both positive and negative' of the ghetto (103). Nike have even been able to survive bad publicity concerning exploitative conditions of production in Vietnam and China through the utilisation of the cultural cool and authenticity of the descendants of slave labour: 'Now if you don't give a fuck like we don't give a fuck, put your muthafuckin' hands in the air' (Snoop Doggy Dogg, 'For all my Niggaz and Bitches', 1993). Picking up on the sovereign indifference of the niggas with attitude ironically played upon by Snoop Dogg on *Doggystyle* (1993), white kids, similarly indifferent to labour conditions in the East, buy anything that might be associated with the power and enjoyment of the gangsta or African-American sporting hero.

At the same time, Nike also overcome such bad publicity through their use of positive advertising which is conveyed in *concerned* images of African-American hardship and suffering. These adverts suggest that the conditions of the ghetto can be transcended through hard work and competition encapsulated in sporting achievement. Goldman and Papson argue that with these kinds of advertisements Nike 'privilege a model of the self grounded in the intensity of aggressive competition and the work ethic gone ballistic' (1998: 153). This 'inverted Protestant work ethic' 'calls not for suffering in the work place, but a suffering of one's body in an activity pursued at no one's discretion, a suffering endured willingly …[thereby proving] itself worthy of recognition through suffering' (149). Nike therefore draws a correspondence between the suffering of hard labour and the success of athletic performance. But the expenditure of labouring bodies that is harnessed in production – say the labouring bodies of young Asian women sewing and gluing Nike sneakers together in sweat shops in Guangdong Province – is supplanted by the non-productive pain and suffering of boxers, athletes and basketball players. The fantasy of the suffering black body becomes, in its support of the image, the primary site of x-essence, and an equivalence is established between work and athletic achievement that is bound up and brought together in a signifier, a logo and an imperative: 'Just Do It'. Nike, as Goldman and Papson note, 'constructs itself as a sign of performance' (52). But it is a performativity in which the excess of a body suffering in joy or pain, at the extreme limit of endurance, becomes the affective model through which heterogeneous energies are harnessed by Nike's supercapitalist modes of marketing and branded identity. Nike generates and expends (consumes) physical and mental resources – both productive and non-productive – as the energy that flows through the global supercapitalist ecosystem.

## X ◊ sovereignty (imperative form)

The 'sovereignty' that is attributed to African-American culture should not be understood in the sense of that term when it refers to the sovereignty of states as defined by international law. Rather, sovereignty should be understood economically as an immanent principle of supercapitalism which denotes economic activity that is *beyond utility* (see Bataille, 1991:198). Images of sovereign activity can take different forms, but brands like Nike seek to associate themselves with *imperative* forms of sovereignty through appealing to 'sentiments traditionally defined as *exalted* and *noble* and tends to constitute authority as an unconditional principle, situated above any utilitarian judgement' (Bataille, 1985: 145). With Nike's pre-eminent figure of the early 1990s, Michael Jordan, that judgement was even situated above the highly circumscribed notion of utility associated with his sport. Goldman and Papson cite Philip Martin from 1995 commenting, 'Jordan long ago ceased to be a mere athlete. He transcended his sport and became a global figure, an avatar of cool integrity, and exemplar of masculine confidence and grace', adding that this is because Nike 'constructed him that way' (50). This image of transcendence was constructed as early as 1985 in the 'Jordan Flight' commercial in which Jordan literally takes flight, leaving the confines of his sport to the sound of jet engines: 'The theme of human transcendence conveyed by the image of Jordan in flight became fused with the Nike *swoosh* reinforced by the "Just do it" tagline' (49).

Since the value of brands is highly uncertain and contingent, it becomes crucial for a successful brand to associate itself with a value that is imagined as transcendent, sovereign, indifferent to the market values established by consumer capitalism even as it is a direct differential effect of them. In a secular society, sovereignty must also be an effect of chance or an absolute risk. The risk that stakes all on success establishes a sovereign value and the element of chance confers the unworldly grace of fortune's blessing.

This element was emphasised in Nike's Play campaign (1994) that featured Michael Jordan, Jackie Joyner-Kersee and Charles Barkley. Employing once again a realist documentary style 'with ads that had the subdued feel of public service spots' (109), Nike addressed the debilitated state of black neighbourhoods by focusing on the sports and fitness programmes that were being axed and the playgrounds that had been rendered unsafe. In 'sombre black and white images of an impoverished landscape' Nike highlighted the contingent conditions of sporting excellence. In the commercial, Jordan poses a series of questions: 'What if there were no sports? If you couldn't join a team, what would you join? … What if there were no sports? Would I still be your hero?' (110).

If black kids can no longer join basketball teams, what are they going to join? The implication is obvious: street gangs; if not a sports star then a gangsta. But gangstas have their own mode of sovereignty, which remains the subtext of this and many of the commercials. The nigga 'who lives by the trigger' embodies in his own way the risk of desire and the 'doggy-dog' world of supercapitalism. For Bataille, the risk of death is what differentiates sovereignty from mastery and slavery in Hegelian terms where those positions are established precisely by the refusal of that risk. Sovereignty involves the refusal of that refusal. It 'is essentially the refusal to accept the limits that the fear of death would have us respect in order to ensure, in a general way, the laboriously peaceful life of individuals. Killing is not the only way to regain sovereign life, but sovereignty is always linked to a denial of the sentiments that death controls' (Bataille, 1991: 221–2).

For Hegel, of course, recognition beyond all judgement of utility is inscribed in the state and in state law that recognises its citizens as equals. But as the state withdraws its recognition, its opportunity and its laws from the 'no go areas' as a consequence of neoliberal economics, then the law is replaced by the sovereign imperative of the risk of desire.

## Brand Image

This formula suggests that the authenticity of the brand is established in an image of 'otherness' that is supported by the x-factor in the form of a sovereign imperative that goes beyond any judgement of utility: 'Just do it'. There is no reason given, nor an end required or supposed. This imperative and the risk of all in an act of pure performativity, elevates the brand image to a position of transcendence. From this exceptional position, the image can then determine the rule that establishes a universal set. It becomes sovereign, an image of the truth.

In the late 1990s Michael Jordan's position of pre-eminence was usurped by another black sporting hero, Tiger Woods. For Goldman and Papson it is not just Woods's talent as a golfer that makes him significant. Just as important is his 'multiracial background', which Nike presents 'as a signifier of universality … a signifier of Humanity itself' (1998: 114). But even as Woods's multicultural credentials provide a unifying metaphor for global capitalism which renders all signifiers of race and ethnicity exchangeable, he still requires an x-factor to propel him beyond a position of simple equivalence. This is signalled in the famous 'I am Tiger Woods' commercial that features a series of boys declaring, 'I am Tiger Woods.' This sequence deliberately echoes the closing scene of Spike Lee's film *Malcolm X*. In this scene a series of African-American schoolchildren are encouraged by their teacher to declare, on Malcolm X's birthday, 'I am Malcolm X'. Goldman and Papson argue that in this move Malcolm's x-factor is incorporated into Tiger Woods as politics is displaced by sport. Woods transcends the reality of conflict, the Malcolm x-factor that is nevertheless essential to his image. But, further, this factor becomes universalised in speech as 'the utterance itself becomes an action', establishing each child as a hero of the brand in the image of Woods. This action is driven by the imperative that affirms, 'I am desirable'; 'I am universal'; 'I am truth.'

## Image
## sovereignty (abject form)

The transcendence of the image can also be supported by the authenticity of abject failure. Here the purity of the sovereign imperative is linked to the impurity from which it severs itself: 'If the heterogeneous nature of the slave is akin to that of the filth in which his material situation condemns him to live, that of the master is formed by an act excluding all filth' (Bataille, 1985: 146). The mastery of Michael Jordan or Tiger Woods involves the transcendence of both a slavish condition and the sovereign abjection of the gangsta who ruins his life in crime and violence.

This formula is illustrated by one of a series of Nike commercials from 1995 featuring first-person narratives of black athletes. The most famous, entitled 'Work', is narrated by Penny Hardaway. Hardaway, a basketball player for Orlando Magic, debunks the myth of natural black athleticism, 'some believe we come out dunking once we are conceived', and cites Public Enemy, 'Don't Believe the Hype' (1988). Rather, a maternal imperative, 'Mom and Grandma', instilled a work ethic that enabled their boy to be great (Goldman and Papson, 1998: 97–8).

Another commercial in the series has a less uplifting story to tell. It is told by Peewee Kirkland, an unknown ex-basketball player – the 'guy who could have made it, but walked away'. Once drafted by the Chicago Bulls, a guy who scored

135 points in one game, Kirkland gets seduced away from his sport, to be dragged into 'every kid's worse nightmare': 'The streets, the life of crime, takes lives and that needs to be remembered' (98). As Goldman and Papson note, the only thing to identify this narrative as a Nike ad is the *swoosh* sign, the 'Just do it' slogan having been omitted. Peewee is no longer capable of doing it, but his impotence guarantees the potency of stars like Jordan and Woods, and authenticates the fecundity of the *swoosh*.

## X-essence of supercapitalism

While the x-essence of gangsta is traceable in the marketing strategies of companies like Nike, the heterogeneity of the figure cannot be utilised or controlled in any unproblematic way. The excess of this form and figure produces other effects.

John Walker Lindh, the American suburbanite who turned up for the battle of Mazar-i-Sharif, sporting an AK–47 and calling himself Abdul Hamid, took a circuitous route to radical Islam. At 14 he was just another wigga with a passion for hip hop, hanging out in shopping malls, looking for the latest gangsta rap records to add to his large collection. At 16 he had already dropped out of Tamiscal High School, an apparently elite 'alternative' school paid for by his wealthy, liberal parents. Walker Lindh's decision to become a Muslim initially had nothing to do with the Koran, sympathy with the plight of Palestinians or enamoration with Osama bin Laden. Hip hop drew the young white American to *The Autobiography of Malcolm X* and the Nation of Islam. From the modest anti-establishment beginning represented by NWA, Air Jordans and Malcolm X books, Walker Lindh sought out a different form of authenticity in the Koran and the religious instruction afforded by the local mosque. Then he got his parents to pay his way to Yemen so he could learn to speak 'pure' Arabic. From there he headed to Pakistan to join a *madrassah* in a region known to be a stronghold of Islamist extremists.

Many American commentators have puzzled over the enigma that, as *Newsweek* commented, Walker Lindh 'grew up in possibly the most liberal, tolerant place in America [yet] was drawn to the most illiberal, intolerant sect in Islam'. For Hoover Institution scholar Shelby Steele, Walker Lindh, 'was prepared for this seduction not just by the wispy relativism of Marin County, but also by a much broader post-60s cultural liberalism that gave his every step toward treason a feel of authenticity and authority'. Jeff Jacoby of the *Boston Globe* concurs, stating that 'there is nothing perplexing' about Walker Lindh's journey to Islamic jihad.:'He craved standards and discipline. Mom and Dad didn't offer any. The Taliban did. But his road to treason and jihad didn't begin in Afghanistan. It began in Marin County, with parents who never said "No".' Steve Chapman, in *Capitalism Magazine*, points out how this form of reasoning ironically brings Walker Lindh close to being a paragon of right-wing virtue, as a God-fearing soldier serving a strict code of morality who went off to fight what he believed to be a just war. Chapman notes that if he had become 'a born-again Christian and joined up with rebels in Iraq – John Walker might be a conservative hero'. Chapman also dismisses the idea that Walker Lindh's treason was a product of liberal decadence, by pointing to the conservative backgrounds of Timothy McVeigh and Theodore Kaczynski, the Unabomber (for the above quotes and other articles on the case see www.capitalismmagazine. com, 2001).

Walker Lindh and McVeigh perhaps have little in common other than a desire to reject corporate America. The force of this negative desire could be said to be in direct proportion to the relentless positivity of an American liberalism that, apparently like the Walker-Lindh parents, says 'yes' to everything. America says 'yes' to everything to do with itself in a nihilistic self-loving enmity.

The desire of McVeigh and Walker Lindh, however, cuts across the federal and economic ideals of US control and cultural saturation that are both directed by and towards goals of efficiency (Lyotard, 1993: 147). While it is difficult to imagine a direct alliance between the anti-federalist, anti-corporate anti-semitism of the US white suprematicist and survivalist movements and the anti-Jewish and anti-American force of extremist Islam, there are nevertheless signs that a strange schizoid alliance might be emerging. In November 1999, as Slavoj •i•ek comments, 'a strange thing took place in New York politics … Lenora Fulani, the Black activist from Harlem endorsed Patrick Buchanan's Reform Party presidential candidacy, declaring that she will try to bring him Harlem and mobilize the voters on his behalf" (•i•ek, 2000: 65). This is the same Pat Buchanan who said that the 11 September 2001 attack was divine retribution for the sins of homosexuality, promiscuity and abortion tolerated by liberal America, New York in particular.

In the same essay, •i•ek argues that 'the only "serious" political force today' that addresses people with an anti-capitalist rhetoric is that which speaks in the name of extreme nationalism, racism and religious fundamentalism (•i•ek, 2000: 64). Similarly, the only European government since the end of the cold war to oppose and confront the Western alliance and American military power did so in the name of national independence and racial and religious purity. In the process it undertook a domestic policy of internment, expatriation and extermination that introduced the phrase 'ethnic cleansing' into the lexicon of international politics. The phrase 'ethnic cleansing' is the correlate of 'ethnic marketing' not just in the employment of the same euphemism 'ethnic' for 'race'. They correlate precisely in so far as ethnic cleansing is the radically negative reply to the homogenising effect of a global capitalism that reconfigures ethnicity in the language of consumable differences. •i•ek argues that the left fails to understand 'the dynamic of today's ethnic-religious "fundamentalisms"' to the degree to which they confuse these forces with fascism and compare their violence and antagonism with the Nazi persecution of the Jews. It is more likely, however, that the fascist legacy of world war two, and its aftermath, has very much to do with current extreme resistance to capitalism, perhaps not in any specific political ideology or content but precisely as a symptom of the Anglo-American obsession with the Nazis, and the perpetual use that is made of their evil as a foil to set off the goodness and generosity of liberal democracy and capitalism. 'Ethnic-religious fundamentalisms' therefore can most powerfully affirm their difference from the Western liberal consensus through the violent negation of others' difference, rejecting absolutely the notion of a multicultural society. The relationship is symbiotic since, in turn, the evil glamour of Hitler becomes the lamp by which any object or scene of the West's displeasure is presented, illuminated and condemned.

In his essay 'Welcome to the Desert of the Real' (published before 11 September 2001), •i•ek seemed to be on the verge of diagnosing the fascism inherent to the West. That is, an American supercapitalism that mobilises work forces in secret labour camps (export processing zones) in a constant war of economic domination. But •i•ek fails to see anything in the West other than an irresponsible postmodern liberalism run rampant. And yet his powerful unconscious succeeds in producing a symptomatic desire adequate to the stakes involved in his call for a powerful and 'charismatic, antiliberal, populist Leader' to save the world from the cynical alliance he sees between multiculturalism and multinationalism (72). Such a figure he locates in anti-capitalist nationalist leaders of the extreme left and right:

> In democracy, individuals DO tend to remain stuck at the level of 'servicing the goods' – often, one DOES need a Leader in order to be able to 'do the impossible'. The authentic Leader is literally the One who enables me to effectively choose myself – the subordination to him is the highest act of freedom (72).

•i•ek here reveals his uncanny proximity to the American neoconservatives. His desire for a charismatic leader, predicated on his rejection of the creature comforts of democracy, is exactly the same as Leo Strauss or Allan Bloom. Fortunately for •i•ek, the neoconservative policy for the new American century that found favour in the White House has precipitated American leadership in a more authoritarian direction since 11 September 2001. It is the most vivid political manifestation of the sovereign imperative immanent to supercapitalism, precipitating the world into the post-democratic era.

## Notes

1    The diagrams in this chapter have been 'sampled' from an article by Jacques-Alain Miller (1988). They illustrate certain aspects of the Lacanian concept of '*extimité*'. In this chapter this concept has been adapted in such a way that they demonstrate how much Bataillean concepts are 'extimate' to those of Lacan.

2    See the fierce criticism to which Quentin Tarantino was subject over the use of this
     word in *Jackie Brown*, particularly from fellow film-maker Spike Lee.

# 6

# Big Momma Thang

We gangstas bitch / Even more dangerous now we're filthy rich
(Lil' Kim, 'Notorious K.I.M.', 2000)

## Ain't nuthin' but a G string

The opening track to Lil' Kim's debut album *Hardcore* (1996), 'Intro In A-Minor' begins with the sound of a car pulling up on a busy New York street, reminiscent of the famous dramatic section at the climax of Stevie Wonder's 'Living in the City' (1973). A sharp exchange between the taxi driver and his ride at the derisory tip, gives way to the latter being heard purchasing a ticket for Lil' Kim's *Hardcore*. But he's not going to a concert. As the box-office girl hands back the change, whispering 'fuckin' weirdo' under her breath, it becomes clear that this is a patron of an XXX adult movie cinema featuring hard-core pornography.

The patron enters the movie theatre and what we will later recognise as Lil' Kim's first musical track, 'Big Momma Thang', is audible as he purchases a small order of popcorn, a large order of butter and a load of napkins. Moving into the auditorium, various groans, gasps and thwacks greet him from the screen. The patron settles down and there is the sound of a zip being unfastened … Hard on the heels of the zip, exaggerated, comedy sounds of masturbation are heard as the patron starts groaning at the action on screen, calling out Kim's name: 'Yeah. Come on. Kim. Kim. Yeah. Work it, bitch!' He comes and the next track, 'Big Momma Thang', kicks in.

It is an explicit, vulgar and disarming beginning to an album, even a hip hop album. It is disarming because one would suppose it to be a risky way of characterising a typical consumer of the album. Immediately upon putting the CD on for the first time, the scene of purchasing the album is replayed as the act of entering a sleazy fleapit – a very retro scene, furthermore, that recalls the 1970s when hip hop was just emerging as a form of entertainment in a few clubs and block parties in and around New York and hardcore pornography could only be viewed in a few XXX movie theatres. By 1996 when *Hardcore* was released, pornography was rarely consumed in the cinema, film having given way to home video, cable TV shows like the Playboy Channel and of course the internet as the favoured medium. Indeed, Lil' Kim's record is itself an indication that pornography has migrated well beyond the red-light margins downtown to become almost mainstream. Perhaps the retro effect acknowledges that pornography is not as transgressive as it once was and the record attempts to evoke the frisson of the dirty-mac cinema in order to sustain it. Does the opening imply solidarity for the porn punters or contempt, as the patron's comically abject performance would suggest? If Kim's the hoe, then we, with our sweaty hands on her CD, are the john.

'They say it's pornographic', says Lil' Kim on 'Custom Made' from *Notorious K.I.M* (2000), as she comments on how people like to have sex and masturbate to her records. On the same album, 'How Many Licks' (2000) 'goes out to my niggaz in jail / Beating they dicks to the double X-L', while 'Suck My Dick' (2000) supposes that she's 'even got some of these straight chicks rubbing their tits'. 'Kitty Box', on *The Naked Truth* (2005), invites its listeners to picture Lil' Kim as a *Playboy* centrefold adopting various standard pornographic poses: masturbating, appearing topless on a yacht, sucking on some candy, in a shirt and no panties, skinny dipping, pole dancing … the phrase '*Playboy* centrefold' being repeated four times up to the chorus.

While it is possible that people purchase Lil' Kim's CDs as if they were blue movies or porno mags, it is unlikely. In fact, Lil' Kim's constant drawing attention to the scene of consumption of her image and the specific medium of the exchange continually deflates the fantasy. The listener is not invited through some narrative device to imagine making love to Lil' Kim on a yacht he or she is invited to imagine purchasing *Playboy*. And while it is one thing to masturbate to a picture in a magazine, it is perhaps more challenging to masturbate while *imagining* that you are looking at a picture in a magazine. Lil' Kim's records are not about sex so much as about the consumption of sex, that is to say the production, exchange and consumption of images. Further, they provide a very funny, ironic and critical commentary on hip hop's participation in the de-eroticisation of sex in the general eroticisation of the economy. The generally erotic economy evacuates sex of all of its transgressive singularity and it becomes the 'sex-essence' of supercapitalism, opening desire on to an unlimited terrain for the consumption of more and more luxurious goods and images, brand names … Prada, Gabbana, Versace, Ferrari, Maserati, Cristal, Nike, Playboy are the most frequent brands and labels name-checked on Lil' Kim's records. It is why the words '*Playboy* centrefold' are repeated at the climax of Lil' Kim's litany of erotic poses. It is not her body that provides the most erotic image, but the label itself.

Lil' Kim came to hip hop prominence in 1995 as part of the Junior MAFIA (short for Masters At Finding Intelligent Attitudes). This was a collective of young talent from the neighbourhood of Bed-Stuy (Short for Bedford-

Stuyvesant) in Brooklyn, New York brought together by Biggie Smalls (Christopher Wallace AKA Notorious BIG) who knew them during his days as a drug dealer. Apparently ejected from her home at the age of fifteen by her father, Kim struggled to survive on the streets as a drug courier. It was in this capacity that she met Biggie Smalls, who subsequently encouraged her to follow in his footsteps into the world of rap. They became part of the Bad Boy Entertainment family run by P-Diddy (Sean 'Puffy' Combs).

At the time, Bad Boy was enjoying an intense East-Coast–West-Coast rivalry with Death Row Records, run by Marian 'Suge' Knight, home of ex-NWA producer Dr. Dre, Snoop Dogg and the Dogg Pound, Nate Dogg and Tupac Shakur among others.[1] As is well known, it was in the context of this mafia-style corporate rivalry that both Tupac Shakur and Biggie Smalls were gunned down in separate incidents on 7 September 1996 and 8 March 1997 respectively.

The revival of the East-Coast rap scene came in response to the development of Californian gangsta rap into 'G-funk'. As Eithne Quinn writes, 'P-Diddy's trademark "hip-hop soul" sound … was an outgrowth of G-Funk's melodious beats' (2005: 186). The album conventionally credited with the move from the harsher sound of early gangsta rap to G-funk is Dr. Dre's *The Chronic* (1992), which featured a number of Death Row artists, Snoop Dogg and the Dogg Pound, including Nate Dogg. Alongside Nirvana's *Nevermind*, it has been hailed as the most influential album of the 1990s. The style is very distinctive and somewhat paradoxical in terms of style and content. As Quinn notes, the album presents 'ever more vulgar topics coupled with highly produced and highly commercial beats' (143). Given that *The Chronic* features the song that she gives as the title of her book, 'Nuthin But a G Thang', it is not surprising that Quinn gives an excellent reading of this album and the album that followed and consolidated the 'G-Funk' style (see chapter 7). This was Snoop Dogg's *Doggystyle* (1993), also produced by Dre, that became an instant bestseller, making millionaires of Snoop, Dre and Suge Knight. The highly commercial style is linked to equally provocative content, as before, but in a different way. Quinn suggests that these albums are 'flagrantly antipolitical', but that is indeed part of their provocation, and in that sense they sustain a relation to the political domain.

The mode of engagement, however, changes: gangsta's documentary-esque uses of social commentary, politicised media statements, and the righteous anger of NWA and Ice Cube gives way to G-Funk's 'laid-back low metabolism sounds and lifestyle images'. For Quinn, these communicate 'a posture of increasing alienated complacency' (144). The alienation and complacency are perhaps an effect of the fact that they are also beginning to be marketed more explicitly to a cross-over white audience and therefore appeal to a certain fantasy-scene of black enjoyment. The albums offer a celebration of 'negative, exploitative images' of black men and women luxuriating in every kind of profanity and bad taste. They introduce the era of bling-bling, million dollar cribs and pimped-up rides. The signature track usually cited to sum up the cruising G-lifestyle is Snoop's 'Gin and Juice' with its chorus:

> Rollin' down the street
> Smoking indo,
> sippin' on gin and juice
> laaaid back
> with my mind on my money and my money on my mind.
> (Snoop Doggy Dogg, 'Gin and Juice', 1993)

The complacency, however, is somewhat undercut by Snoop's often taunting delivery. He presents a cold-eyed, sardonic pursuit of the pleasure principle that is beautifully and chillingly conveyed by his distinctive voice, according to Robin Kelley 'the coolest, slickest Calabama [California meets Alabama] voice I've ever heard' (cited in Quinn, 2005: 146). Quinn calls it 'soft-spoken, languid, half-sung' (146), to which could be added sweetly sinister and slightly camp, an almost perpetually ironic performance of chilled-out misogyny. From the very first it taunts liberal America with the debased reality of the American dream, which is invoked directly at the beginning of the album as its main character is blackmailed back into drug-dealing and pimping.

While the language and imagery is still violent (Snoop represents himself as being shot halfway through the album), it has become more cartoon-like and comical in its brutal indestructibility (he survives to put more bitches and niggas on their backs). But, more fundamentally, there is a change of emphasis in the 'badman-mack' composite that provides the template for the generic gangsta persona. Instead of the gangsta-cum-guerilla, surviving in the 'hood through whatever means possible, Amerikkka's most wanted, the nigga you love to hate, transmutes into the fantasy pimp figure that white adolescent boys envy and want to emulate. For those middle-class students dreaming of a stable of foxy little whores (see Lou Reed's 'I Wanna Be Black'), *Doggystyle* is custom-made to exploit the blaxploitation image of the black pimp as master of enjoyment.

The pimp's flamboyant image and lifestyle becomes the model and metaphor for the presentation and marketing of a life of conspicuous consumption. As an image of potent masculinity, however, the pimp is an ambiguous figure. If he is the 'daddy' of his family of hoes, the top dog of his stable of bitches, he is a daddy who eschews any role of paternal responsibility. Quinn notes that 'part of the pimp's style and image involves the eschewing of the role of responsible breadwinner. Down payments on flashy cars, expensive clothes, and pricey jewelry all proclaim the fact that money is not being invested forebearingly in family and future' (122). Indeed, in this emphasis on shopping, the pimp's interests are conventionally more feminine than masculine. Ice-T, who claims to have been a pimp, emphasises this aspect when he comments on key errors made by would-be pimps in an interview for a TV documentary:

If you really listen to these guys that say they are pimps, they've got it backwards. (*puts on a high-pitched voice*) 'I'm a pimp, I'll take you shopping and buy you clothes. I'm a pimp, we're goin' go spend all my money. That's not pimping. (*laughs sneeringly*) Pimping is when bitches take ME shopping and buy ME something. (Ice-T in Upshal, 2005)

Revealingly, the pimp is perfectly equivalent to the hoe in the interests that define him; it is simply a question of who is working and who is buying. He may live off the labour of women, but his enjoyment is 'feminine' in its dedication to the masquerade; the daddy is really nothing more than a wanna-be Queen Bitch. Lil' Kim's 'Big Momma Thang' hits the spot with its chorus that discloses the camp desires of the G-funk persona who has given up on the 'badman' image in so far as its violence no longer appeals to the 'X' of the paternal principle: 'Killas be quiet … Tough talk, tough walk shit is tired', and that what they really want is to be someone like her. The 'G' Thang has become the Big Momma Thang: 'You wanna be this Queen B, but ya can't be / That's why you're mad at me' ('Big Momma Thang', 1996). The pimp persona is just as much a whore to the image as his hoes, particularly when his persona is being put to *work* in the narratives of G-funk rappers. In this figure, the surplus value of female labour is put back into circulation, reinvested in the production and marketing of gangsta rap. Who is the figure who negotiates and transcends this diamond-encrusted treadmill?

## Work ethic gone bootilicious

Lil' Kim's *Hardcore* (1996) introduces and develops the Queen Bitch persona, Lil' Kim's alter ego, who features in all her records to date. *Hardcore* essentially tells the tale of Queen B's rise to wealth and fame in a music business that for a woman is virtually no different from the sex business. The first music track, 'Big Momma Thang', begins 'I used to be scared of the dick / Now I throw lips to the shit / Handle it like a real bitch', matching her sexual capacity with her capacity to earn success in the business, counting the number of times she 'cums' by the number of diamonds in her rings ('twenty-one / And another one, and another one, and another one / 24 carats nigga'). Sex is always both an economic and a martial figure in which production, consumption and expenditure are indeterminate: 'Beretta inside of beretta / nobody do it better / Bet I wet cha [shoot you/cum on you] like hurricanes and typhoons / Got buffoons eatin' my pussy while I watch cartoons' ('Queen Bitch', 1996). But while she gets 'down and dirty for the dough' ('Big Momma Thang'), she's not a hoe: 'That's the difference between me and other bitches, they fuck to get they riches / I fuck to bust a nut, Lil' Kim not a slut / I gotta reputation to look out for' ('Fuck You', 1996).

'I ain't a prostitute, I just tell the truth' ('Off the Wall', 2000). The truth concerns the reality of the situation in which she is placed as a woman in the business. As such, Queen B must draw a fine but crucial line between hustling as a purely commercial and relatively degraded practice – 'You broke hoes need to throw in the towel' ('You Can't Win', 2000) – and hustling as a mode of sumptuous expenditure in the context of a generally eroticised economy. It is a distinction that Georges Bataille notes in his discussion of prostitution in his book *Eroticism: Death and Sensuality* (1986). Historically, prostitution took women out of the domestic sphere of work and duty into direct contact with male desire in whose 'close embrace nothing remained but only a convulsive continuity' (132). But this general economic aspect of pure loss became over-shadowed by the commercialism of the modern period and, since the seventeenth and eighteenth century, prostitution has functioned as the negative image of capitalism as it developed against the backdrop of feudalism. No longer tied to the land and the paternal authority of a feudal lord, freemen found their value subject to the laws of the market and the capitalist mode of production. The prostitute, freed from family ties, selling her labour to whoever is willing to pay, became a negative metaphor for the whole system. For Bataille, how-ever, the commercial aspect of prostitution is secondary even though it is es-sential that she (or he) be paid:

> If the prostitute received sums of money or precious articles, these were originally gifts, gifts which she would use for extravagant expenditure and ornaments that made her more desirable. Thus she increased the power she had had from the first to attract gifts from the richest men. This exchange of gifts was not a commercial transaction. What a woman can give outside marriage cannot be put to any productive use, and similarly with the gifts that dedicate her to the luxurious life of eroticism. This sort of exchange led to all sorts of extravagance rather than to the regularity of commerce. Desire was a fiery thing; it could burn up a man's wealth to the last penny, it could burn out the life of the man in whom it was aroused. (133).

If it can be argued that the gangsta pimp and hoe represent negative, mirror-images of supercapitalism, then the general economic aspect of prostitution needs also to be considered. Since supercapitalism is a system based more on financial speculation, war and consumption than on capital investment and industrial production, in which everything is sold as if it served no purpose other than enjoyment, where there is the prospect of the satisfaction of every desire and in which huge fortunes may be amassed and lost, prostitution (and pornography) can again be reclassified and regraded along with other high-performance, high-earning professions such as in the sports and music busi-ness. So while it is certainly the case that for Queen Bitch, if 'Niggaz wanna get laid; I gotta get paid' ('Custom Made', 1996), this payment comes in excessive amounts of money and the most luxurious commodities: 'I'm a diamond clus-ter hustler' (Queen Bitch', 1996); 'niggaz buy me glass slippers and diamond fingernails' ('Custom Made', 1996), riches destined for further acts of expenditure: 'Like ashes in the urn, more money to burn / Damn my ass is firm' ('You Can't Win', 2000). Ultimately, it is not just the money that is burned but the men who give it as she continues to bust nuts and further enhance her reputation and high market value: 'Niggaz do anything for a Lil' Kim poster' (How Many Licks', 2000); 'Niggaz give they life to be with me for one night' ('She Don't Love You', 2000).

Of course, the Queen Bitch persona is not a representation of a pre-modern, high-class whore like an Ancient Greek *hetairae* or Roman *delicata, famosa* and *venerii* (the latter harlot-priestesses) whose wealth, status, independence, lack of social stigma and social desirability put them in a different discursive category to modern commercial prostitutes. But, like the sports star, she is exemplary in that prostitution is no longer the purely negative image of a bourgeois commerce supposed to be restricted, rational and moral in its emphasis on production and utility. In contrast, the postmodern economy, according to Jean-Joseph Goux's critique of Bataille's economic categories, is defined by the inability to distinguish between, on the one hand, useful production based on a rational measurement of human needs and, on the other hand, extravagant, luxurious expenditure which wastes time, goods and resources without profit or return. The erosion of the possibility of differentiation allows previously unimaginable levels of expenditure to emerge, useful and useless activity entwined to the extent that the restricted economy of production incorporates the excesses once expended in a symbolic, ritualistic and sumptuary general realm, including premodern prostitution (see Goux,1998a). Prostitution then no longer remains the purely negative mirror-image of commercialism, but is transvalued as an affirmation of the negativity of desire and consumption and as such becomes a privileged figure for supercapitalism.

The Queen Bitch personae does not service her consorts; she busts their nuts and burns them out, inveighing ever greater performance: 'I'm a picky one I like my dicks rock hard' ('Queen Bitch Pt II', 2000). The dicks have to be harder, rock hard, harder than that, they have to keep coming longer and longer, working later and later. Indeed, Queen B establishes a new Olympic standard for sexual performance: longer, later, harder. 'I like a nigga to put his back in it', she says in 'We Don't Need It' (1996). While Nike 'privilege a model of the self grounded in the intensity of aggressive competition and the work ethic gone ballistic' (Goldman and Papson, 1998: 153), Queen B introduces a work ethic gone bootilicious in which the goal is to 'sex you continuously' ('Big Momma Thang', 1996) with a continuous flow of images, 'a good ass shot ... to keep a nigga dick rock', in order to increase (general) economic performance ('Queen Bitch', 1996). By *Notorious K.I.M* (2000) the Queen B persona has become a successful entrepreneur in her own right: 'P-Diddy introduced me to the business side' ('You Can't Win', 2000); 'I'm a business woman now so I'm not concerned' ('Notorious K.I.M', 2000). As entrepreneur, Kim can fully exploit the continuity between commercialism and continuous sexing-up.

Lil' Kim's *Hardcore* (1996) anticipates the general direction towards pornography taken by hip hop and gangsta rap at the end of the 1990s. This is evident not just in the albums of course, but especially in the videos, cable TV shows and movies. While hip hop videos have always been sexy, 2Live Crew's successful defence of their video 'Me So Horny' (1996) opened the door to more explicit content. Sir Mixalot's 'Put 'em on a Glass' (1994) was the first video to feature bare breasts, soaped up and applied to various screens, windscreens, windows and cameras. The notoriety and success of this video meant that Sir Mixalot subsequently hosted his own show on Playboy TV. However, it wasn't until 2001 that hip hop went properly hardcore.

Appropriately, Snoop Dogg revisited *Doggystyle* and produced in conjunction with Larry Flynt's *Hustler* an adult movie that combined hardcore sex with previously unreleased music. It was 'a monumental achievement', according to Sean Carney, head of marketing and publicity of *Hustler*, not simply because of its artistic merit (whatever that may be) but because it went on to sell more copies than any previous adult movie and it was the first hardcore film to be featured in the mainstream video chart. This achievement is monumental, then, because it indicates a decisive mainstreaming of hardcore pornography in America.

This mainstreaming effect of hip hop's involvement with hardcore was the topic of a TV documentary by David Upshal, 'Porn With Attitude', aired on Channel 4 in 2005. The reference to NWA is appropriate because the documentary features DJ Yella, ex-member of NWA, who retired from rapping after he discovered that porn offered him 'far richer pickings than hip hop ever did'. As if confirming Queen B's work ethic gone bootilicious, the male hip hop stars past and present involved in the porn industry all stressed its economic dimension and the hard work involved. Interviewed in the documentary alongside his collaborator Big Man, DJ Yella emphasised the hard work, but also characterised the business in terms characteristic of supercapitalism. It requires total identification with oneself as an economic being, always flexible, always potentially at work, always mobilised, always at war in the market: 'I am porn', DJ Yella affirms in the documentary, 'I live it 24 hours a day. I'm editing, shooting all the pictures, filming. I'm in the trenches. If porn is a war, I'm in the trenches.' His colleague Big Man concurred, but remarked that this didn't mean that they didn't enjoy it: 'We both like to fuck. If you don't wanna fuck, you don't need to be here. It's his fucking job.' Staring resolutely into the camera, DJ Yella confirmed, 'Gonna fuck today. One of my work days, a regular work day.'

Of course such statements emphasising sex as a day job may have the effect of arousing envy in those with more mundane jobs or no job at all. But for the latter at least sex may retain its singularity as a heterogeneous event. When sex becomes work it necessarily becomes a banal, repetitive, daily activity, absorbed here not only in the automatism of repetitive work, but also the minimal narrative and relentless predictability of porn. Sex, work, pleasure become homogenised into the same process in which production and expenditure coalesce on the same plane of consistency driven by the demand for greater efficiency and performance, ultimately determined by the flows of finance and communication systems. The subject (artist–performer–worker) becomes absorbed by and in a particular sex-image that functions, like Coca-Cola or Nike, as a brand imperative that the products must continually reaffirm and reinforce. Commenting on 50 Cent's explicit video 'Groupie Love', Money B from Digital Underground notes that 'you expect 50 Cent to have a houseful of bitches. He walks in the kitchen and he gets his dick sucked while he's pouring orange juice. That's what you think. [This video] just reinforces what the image already is' (quoted in Upshal, 2005). 50 Cent's level of performance is so intense that he has to be at work having his dick sucked before he's even had his breakfast orange juice. When sex becomes work and when pleasure is absorbed by the repetitive and automatic insistence of a media ecosystem, everything accedes to a new order that absorbs the intensities and energy previously associated with eroticism. Luxurious expenditures, transgressive pleasures, wasteful consumption and extreme enjoyments, once part of the general economy beyond production and use-value, are incorporated as the new rules and imperatives of supercapitalism and its corporate system of social relations. Deregulated sex and violence, the stables of an industry worth billions of dollars, become bound up with an imperative that pushes way beyond human fantasy, a programmed imperative that is the pure expression of the machinic violence of supercapitalism.

## Ain't nuthin' but a G spot

If production is driven by an imperative traditionally associated with violent modes of non-productive expenditure, Lil' Kim's follow-up albums to *Hardcore* frequently highlight that consumption is commanded by a work ethic that is driven by a similar imperative. This begins, in *Hardcore*, with an all-too-common feminine complaint about the inconsiderate incompetence of her male lovers: 'Niggas cum too fast for me / I wanna wake him up to do his duty / Nigga use that tongue, click the booty, click the booty' ('We Don't Need It', 1996). From *Notorious K.I.M* (2000) on, however, this complaint becomes an all-consuming command and metaphor for consumption generally: 'Lick it right first time or you gotta do it over / Like it's rehearsal for a Tootsie commercial' ('How Many Licks', 2000).

The complaint also touches on a symbolic point of contention in racial and sexual politics, reinforced in the pop misogyny of gangsta rap/G-funk, where the command 'Suck my dick!' plays out the relation of male sexual dominance. The chorus to Lil' Kim's track 'We Don't Need It' (1996) stages a sexual standoff in which that relation is contested in the form of a symbolic exchange. Lil'

Kim and her fellow Junior MAFIA member Lil' Caesar exchange a series of escalating demands:

> If you ain't suckin' no dick, we don't need it, we don't need it
> If you ain't lickin' no clits, we don't want it, we don't want it
> If you ain't drinkin' no nut, we don't need it, we don't need it
> If you ain't lickin' no butts, we don't want it, we don't want it.
> ('We Don't Need It', 1996).

That such a stand-off betrays a tension in the sexual mores between black men and women is iterated by a character in the Quentin Tarantino screenplay for *True Romance* (1995). In a scene excised from the movie directed by Tony Scott (but included as an out-take in the DVD), three pimps forcefully debate the importance of providing women with oral service (for a discussion of this scene in the context of the rest of Tarantino's *oeuvre* see Botting and Wilson, 2001a: 124–31). A character called Big D debunks the misogynist gangsta rhetoric deployed by black men: 'Shit, any nigger say he don't eat pussy is lyin' his ass off' (Tarantino, 1995a: 8). His colleague Floyd is nonplussed: 'Hold on a second Big D. You sayin' you eat pussy?' Big D not only confirms that this is the case but testifies that his appetite is all-American in its capacity: 'Nigger, I eat everything. I eat the pussy. I eat the butt. I eat every motherfuckin' thang' (8). The boast fails to impress Floyd, however, who sees it as yet another sign of black male humiliation. Indeed, taking a historical view, he lays the blame on white men. Addressing Floyd and another (white) pimp, the wigga Drexl, Floyd makes the following speech:

> There used to be a time when sisters didn't know shit about getting their pussy licked. Then the sixties came an' they started fuckin' around with white boys. And white boys are freaks for that shit ... then after a while sisters get used to getting their little pussy eat. And because you white boys had to make pigs of yourselves, you fucked it up for every nigger in the world everywhere ... Now if a nigger wants to get his dick sucked he's got to do a bunch of fucked-up shit. (8–9)

The conflict represented by the stand-off over oral sex is the main theme of Lil' Kim's track 'Suck My Dick' in which the male domination implied by the title is undermined, ridiculed and contemptuously returned. Exclaiming that she is interested in just one thing, 'All I wanna do is get my pussy sucked (Nigga!)', she demonstrates her dominance by leaving her partner high and dry: 'All they can do for me is suck my clit / I'm jumpin' up and up after I cum / Thinkin' they goin' get some pussy but they gets none'. She reserves further humiliation for later by recording the whole process for the enjoyment of her girl friends: 'Got the camcord layin' in the drawer where he can't see / Can't wait to show my girls he sucked the piss out of my pussy' ('Suck My Dick', 2000).

If Lil' Kim's 'Suck My Dick' confirms the conflictual basis of Floyd's analysis, the subsequent track, 'How Many Licks', adds a racial dimension, in the process raising it to a more general economic level that articulates and conjoins all forms of oral service in the system of supercapitalist consumption. The track begins with Lil' Kim commenting on her cosmopolitanism such that she has seen a lot of different faces and even 'fuck[ed] with different races', listing a white dude called John, a certain Italian called Tony whom she particularly favoured because 'he ate my pussy from dark till the mornin', a Puerto Rican who used to be a deacon ('but now he be sucking me off on the weekend') and an African-American called King Kong who had 'a big ass dick and a hurricane tongue'. But if the highly generic nature of these conquests does not immediately disclose this multiculturalism as a deliberate parody of ethnic marketing and the global mall in the form of self-advertisement, the chorus makes it unequivocal. It is taken from a well-known 30-second commercial for Tootsie Roll industries in which various cute cartoon characters question how many licks it takes to get to the Tootsie Roll centre of a Tootsie Pop.[2] While it is now commonplace for advertising agencies to use popular songs in their commercials in various ways, it is less usual to reverse the process. With the former the complaint is usually that the (future) memory of some deathless pop classic is being destroyed through its re-contextualisation and indelible association with a debased product. Hip hop has no scruples about such recontextualisation of course, and Lil' Kim's use of a commercial riff scandalously turns a jingle aimed at children into a song about cunnilingus. The repeated chorus line, 'how many licks does it take till you get to the centre of the...' leaves off the name of the product so that the association Tootsie Pop/pussy can be made silently in the imagination of the listener.

In the following verses, the song builds on the equivalence, Lil' Kim becoming paper-thin as she refers to herself as simply an image in a magazine, a poster, a character in a gangsta narrative, a luxury item and a bling accessory:

> Some niggaz even put me on their grocery lists
> Right next to the whip cream and box of chocolates
> Designer pussy, my shit comes in flavours
> High-class niggaz got to spend paper
> Lick it right the first time or you gotta do it over
> Like it's a rehearsal for a Tootsie commercial
> ('How Many Licks', 2000).

This song nonchalantly conflates ethnic and individual identity to commodity form, reducing them to popular market brands and products while recognising and realising their maximum potential through the metaphor of oral pleasure and its degrees of intensity. Identity, desire, sex are no longer remotely defined by paternal prohibition and law, but are driven nevertheless by an implacable imperative: 'Just Lick It', just lick Big Momma's thang. And therein lies the point of integral excess and impossibility at the heart of the systemic demand. Not only have you got to lick it, but you've got to lick it right. Otherwise 'you gotta do it over' and over and over, unendingly on and on. Lick, lick, lick, lick, lick, lick, lick, lick, lick, lick, lick. How many licks is that?

## Notes

1   See Quinn, 2005, for an account of the enormous significance of the 'black entre-
    preneurship' that Knight, Combs and others represent, its 'ghettocentrism' and
    rejection of assimilation and bourgeois aspiration. Quinn quotes Jay Berman, CEO
    of the music industry's lobby group the Recording Industry Association of America,
    stating in 1994: 'Rap music has empowered an entire new generation of successful
    young black entrepreneurs. I think some people are more afraid of that than the
    music' (164).
2   A Tootsie Pop is a lollipop with a soft Tootsie Roll filling produced by Tootsie Roll
    Industries.

# 7

# Mom and pop rage

'Pain is God'

(Korn, 'Kill You', 1996)

## Children of the Korn

By associating cunnilingus with a Tootsie commercial aimed at children, Lil' Kim's 'How Many Licks' mischievously risks broaching one of the biggest taboos in American culture. From the prohibition on stem cell research and the struggle over abortion, to the Parent Music Resource Center and moral panics about paedophilia and internet child pornography, childhood innocence provides the last sacred object for the sustained erection of paternal law in America. Medical science, First Amendment rights, the rights of women, and the continual growth of America's multibillion-dollar entertainment industry all founder on the imagined sensitivities of a child, sensitivities all the more powerful when the child is actually unborn or a point of pure cellular potential.

Except that, as 'How Many Licks' suggests, it is not so much paternal as maternal enjoyment that is implied by the law protecting childhood innocence. Indeed, the American music business first became subject to this law in 1985 when Mary Elizabeth Gore (known as 'Tipper'), wife of Democrat senator and later Vice-President Al Gore, came across her 11-year-old daughter listening to a song by Prince. Upon reading the lyrics of 'Darlin Nikki' from *Purple Rain* (1984), Gore was appalled to discover that it appeared to be about a girl masturbating with a magazine (*Washington Post*, 19 June 1985). Alerting the wives of other senators like Susan Baker, wife of Republican Treasury Secretary James Baker, and Nancy Thurmond, wife of Senator Strom Thurmond, Gore set up a committee and pressure group called the Parent Music Resource Center (PMRC) aimed at the censorship and regulation of popular music. The PMRC's first major success was the introduction of the 'Tipper Sticker' in 1985, the Parental Advisory Label that currently adorns most rap and metal CDs. While some stores like Wal-Mart refused to stock records bearing the label, the label actually functions like a trademark guaranteeing a certain standard of transgressive authenticity, thereby increasing sales. Faced with the choice of a marked or unmarked CD, most children interested in rap or metal will unquestionably opt for the 'harder' record authenticated by Tipper's sticker. In the context of supercapitalism, therefore, maternal law operates not so much as prohibition or censorship but as an imperative that directs consumer choice. Rap and metal have been overwhelmingly targeted by the PMRC, thereby directing choice towards the music of anti-Oedipal violence that provides further support for maternal law. It is a virtuous spiral.

Korn's self-named debut album, credited with inaugurating the nu metal or white hip hop subgenre, occupies this ambivalent space perfectly. Released in 1994, *Кояn*'s cover depicts the apprehensive gaze of a small girl on a swing looking up out of the frame, shielding her eyes as if staring into the sun, or indeed into the face of the purchaser of the CD. The large dark shadow that stretches across the bottom half of the cover, however, indicates that she is looking fearfully up at a threatening male figure. The back cover, meanwhile, depicts the same scene but with the swing now empty, a number of large boot prints below the swing suggesting a struggle and abduction. The cover therefore evokes childhood innocence threatened by a sinister male figure even as his position is occupied virtually by the consumer looking at it. The picture constructs a position of paternal violence that is empty but can be occupied by anyone. This space is vacant yet it structures the relation between subject and object, consumer and product. Only the dark shadow cast by this empty space evokes the unspeakable, incestuous, paedophiliac pleasures that are substituted by the act of consumption, buying a CD. Which is to say that the consumer of the CD cover is situated in such a way that a viewer's identification flickers between the fear in the eyes of the girl and the frisson of violence that they summon up by directly addressing the consumer's gaze.

Sacrifice constitutes the sacred, of course, and the continual evocation of the corruption of childhood innocence sustains the romantic origins of American liberal consciousness. *Кояn*'s cover further integrates it with supercapitalism by articulating the banality of consumption (buying a CD) with the transgression of the last taboo in American culture (incest/paedophilia). The ancient purpose of sacrifice was to establish and sustain a community through a gift to the gods or the spirit world. For Georges Bataille, this amounts to the ritual destruction of a useful object – the first fruits of the harvest, a domestic animal or a slave. The sacrifice of utility breaks open the object of restricted economy on to the sacred realm of general economy. The violence of the sacrifice withdraws the victim from the world in which it was reduced to the condition of a thing and calls it 'back to the *intimacy* of the divine world, of the profound immanence of all that is' (Bataille, 1992b: 43). It is this order of intimacy opened by violence and eroticism which religion tries to reconstitute and control in its laws and rituals.

In Christianity the meaning of sacrifice takes a singular form in the crucifixion. Here the ultimate good, the son of God, is sacrificed in an act of sublime evil. God the Father is an ambivalent figure in this scene, beyond good and evil, since he allows evil to occur in order to expiate the sins of humanity. Humanity's sins are correlated to the pain endured on the cross binding the Christian community together in apprehension of the spectacle. For the religious, the Passion of Christ is an occasion simultaneously for agony and ecstasy.

> In the elevation upon a cross, humankind attains a summit of evil. But it's exactly from having attained it that humanity ceases being separate from God. So clearly the 'communication' of human beings is guaranteed by evil. Without evil, human existence would turn in on itself, would be enclosed as a zone of independence: and indeed an absence of 'communication' – empty loneliness – would certainly be the greater evil. (Bataille, 1992a: 18)

Notwithstanding the cynical alliance of neoconservative and evangelical America, neoliberal America is secular and committed to the eradication of evil in all its forms. While superficially there is reference to the 'axis of evil' and 'evil doers' generally who are enemies of 'freedom' where the meaning of that term is determined by the economic ideology of supercapitalism, the pursuit of evil goes further than neoconservative rhetoric and foreign policy. From serial killers to rogue genes, psychological disorders to physical imperfection, evil is no longer a metaphysical or moral principle but has materialised as an objective reality. And hence it can be materially pursued right down to the genetic or biochemical level and eradicated. For Jean Baudrillard this 'universal process of the eradication of evil' (2005: 17) that accompanies the 'total operationalization of the world' (29) constitutes the 'transparency of evil' (1993). While bureaucratic processes of transparency are designed to expose and eradicate signs of evil, evil 'shines through' (*transparaît*) in the very process of exposure and operationalisation.

While an interest in the occult and 'running with the devil' is a traditional element of heavy metal (see Walser, 1993), evident in names like Black Sabbath, Judas Priest and Blue Oyster Cult, it does little but betray a nostalgia for the lost metaphysical and moral principle of evil. Ozzy Osbourne, self-styled Prince of Darkness, ironically presents in his own reality sitcom one of the few reassuring paternal images in American popular culture. In contrast, nu metal bands address the transparency of evil, that is the 'greater evil' of the 'empty loneliness' that is an effect of its operational eradication. They do this in various ways hinting at the overexposure of childhood, the evacuation of all excitement from the sanitised malls and desolate towns that provide the general background from which the music irrupts. Nu metal, as a kind of white hip-hop, differs from traditional heavy metal not just because its lyrics are frequently rapped rather than sung, or because drum machines, samples and scratching are added to the power chords, but also because elements of funk, punk and industrial are included in the mix. Further, 'nu skool' metal replaces the 'old school' metal fantasy of evil (with its repertoire of warlords, hell's angels, satanism, debauchery, wizards and dragons) with the evil of an excess reality. The albums locate themselves in evil's transparent glare as both its object and illumination in the form of corrupted innocence, abused and abandoned by paternal authority. Above all with Korn, the acknowledged originators of nu metal, it is the abused and bullied child who becomes exposed as the object of sacrifice, the 'accursed share' that bears the burden of communal negativity. Bataille defines the accursed share as 'a surplus taken from the mass of *useful* wealth ... destined for violent consumption' that 'radiates intimacy, anguish, the profundity of living beings' (Bataille, 1988: 59).

Childhood, as a sacred place of uncorrupted innocence, is largely an invention of romanticism, popularly resonant in the writings of Jean-Jacques Rousseau and in William Blake's 'Songs of Innocence' for example. Liberal protests against chimney sweepers, other forms of child labour and workhouses largely succeeded in taking childhood out of the use-circuit as a force of production and set it aside as a surplus special place of creativity, imagination, idleness and play. A certain romantic wildness thus also became associated with childhood, heightened precisely by the schooling that sought to educate and regulate it. James Kincaid, in his book *Erotic Innocence* (1998) argues that the romantic child 'was largely figured as an inversion of Enlightenment virtues and was thus strangely hollow right from the start: *un*corrupted, *un*sophisticated, *un*enlightened ... oddly dispossessed and eviscerated, without much substance' (53). A sacred yet negative space, then, both in the sense of being an inversion of rational and productive principles and also as a site of playful 'otherness'. Above all it is established as a period of special innocence and vulnerability, formative and deformative of adult life, its memory radiating retroactive anguish, intimacy, horror and joy.

As such, childhood becomes a screen for the projection of adult fears and fantasies, an ever-mobile threshold of prohibition and normalisation. All mainstream media productions in the US must be suitable for 'family viewing', the benchmark for which is determined by a notional six-year-old child. The banality that mainstream America inflicts upon itself and the rest of the world provides reassurance against the 'transgressive' margins that it sustains as the 'cutting edge' of supercapitalism. The blank screen of the romantic child becomes the ubiquitous space of entertainment's banal projections, locus of all interactivity, all work and all play, establishing a plane of consistency for all aesthetic and economic activity, but evacuated of all content. The romantic child is sustained in supercapitalism as the vacuole around which its commodities, its toys, its luxuries, its candy and its pornography circulate and expand. Everything is sold as if it were a toy, an object of play or pleasure. Fun, even adult fun, is continually assimilated and mainstreamed through the law of banality operating in the name of childhood innocence. The vacuole is an absolute *moral* void marking the threshold of eroticism that opens on to an abyss of paedophilia, at the edge of which structures of parental authority and control tremble. (See Botting and Wilson, 2004: 68 on how social and economic life becomes determined by a highly ambivalent toy law that is continuous with an obscene toy joy that it promises. 'The children of the Korn was born from your porn ass twisted ass way' (Korn, 'Children of the Korn', 1998).

'Blind', the first track on *Korn* (1994), seems to reiterate the cover in its description of the effects of staring directly into the violence of the paternal sun. It is a song predominantly about pain that hollows out a deep interior space of fear, foreboding and always-already-therapised anguish: 'My inner self-esteem is low / How deep can I go'. The songs proceed in a similar vein, the album constituting almost a case study of an abused abuser, victim turned self-loathing executioner: 'My life is ripping your heart out and destroying my pain' ('Lies', 1994). The songs move through stages familiar in rock 'n' roll – high school, dating, loneliness – but with rage rather than joy or nostalgia. 'Ball Tongue' hurls a torrent of verbal abuse at someone stuck at home buried in self-pity, who is clearly a mirror image of the singer. 'Need To' directs similar ambivalence towards a potential partner: 'You pull me closer, I push you away / You tell me its okay, I can't help but feel the pain / I hate you'. 'Clown' and 'Faget' detail the nightmare of high-school bullying: 'Why did you tease me? Made me feel upset / Fucking stereotypes feeding their heads / I am ugly. Please just go away'. Reference to 'low self-esteem' and 'stereotypes' betray the presence of therapy and progressive schooling that prepares a place, a language and even a mode of subjectivity for the victim of abuse. 'Shooters and Looters' even supports educators anxious to protect children from traditional nursery rhymes: 'Nursery rhymes are said, verses in my head / Into my childhood they're spoonfed / Hidden violence revealed, darkness that seems real / Look at the pages that cause all this evil' (1994).

While these lyrics are clearly remarkable in the context of the heavy metal tradition, they are amplified by an equally remarkable vocal performance that is supported by a hammer-thumb funk bass powering an atonal seven-string twin-guitar attack. But, as Tommy Udo suggests, it was Davis's voice that was the band's 'unique selling-point', a voice that 'goes from agonising suffering to ultra-violent threat and pleading in the space of a few bars' (Udo, 2002: 60). Indeed, this facility is put to use in order to convey the schizoid duality of abused and abuser, different voices threatening and pleading, raging and whining from the same dark interior. The 'primal scene' of the album's catalogue of therapised horrors is 'Daddy', an epic account of incest and child rape. Characteristically, Davis vocalises both parts in such a way that it is not always clear whether the act is past or present (or even both), the son re-enacting his own abuse: 'Little child, looking so pretty / Come out and play, I'll be your daddy / Innocent child, looking so sweet / Rape in my eyes … I feel dirty / It hurt / As a child / Tied down / That's a good boy / And fucked your own child / I scream / No one hears me' ('Daddy', 1994).

The song apparently has an indirect biographical reference. Udo quotes Jonathan Davis correcting misperceptions about the track. 'Daddy' was not written 'because my dad fucked me up the ass', rather it was because Davis's mother and father were incredulous about his claims to being abused by someone else and were apparently indifferent to them: 'They thought I was lying and joking around, so they never did shit about it' (Udo: 2002: 61). Perceived lack of attention and childhood trauma are frequently cited as the impetus behind a career as a performer. But conventionally the flawed past that determines the tragic trajectory of the star remains hidden, part of his or her seductive enigma. Mythically, the unavowable pain that is the cost of the heightened sensibility of the artist establishes the necessary distance for art even as it testifies to its humanity. With 'Daddy', however, all distance is abolished as trauma is obscenely acted out in and as a performance. A self-enactment of paternal violence, the terrible rage of a terrible song about nothing but itself, echoes in the silence of paternal indifference.

Its reverberations spawned a generation of imitators, bands formed by a 'new generation of post-grunge teenagers [who] liked the aggression of the music and identified with what Davis talked about in the songs' (Udo, 2002: 58). Korn's success was also aided by aggressive marketing and self-promotion. 'They established themselves as a great brand as well as a great band', affirms Udo, 'their readily identifiable logo is as recognisable as the Nike swoosh or the McDonald's golden arches' (52). That may be something of an exaggeration, but the name and logo Korn, designed and drawn by Davis himself, has a number of interesting myths surrounding it that perhaps help to indicate how the brand might profitably articulate mainstream and margin.

## Hardcorn branding

The Korn logo first appears most prominently at the top left-hand corner of the cover of their first album. It is part of the network of dark shadow that spreads over sand beneath the feet of the girl on a swing. Stretching out behind her, the logo seems to grow out of the shadow of the girl's head, rather than form part of the giant shadow of the menacing man in the foreground. Perhaps 'Korn' therefore can be seen to be on the side of the potential victim. On the other hand, since the sign-shadow is rendered in perspective as if it were part of the world of the picture, the logo itself must be positioned somewhere in the virtual space outside of the frame in the eye line of the girl's anxious gaze. The logo is therefore undecidably situated in the space between abused and abuser, like most of the songs on the album.

There are a number of interesting stories about the origin of the name. In his book *Brave Nu World* (2002), the journalist Tommy Udo retells the most familiar story that circulates about the choice and design of the logo:

> the name Korn was inspired by Jonathan overhearing two gay men at a party
> talking about 'rimming' (oral sex performed on the anus of another). One of
> them said that he had diarrhoea and excreted on his partner's face; when the
> partner opened his mouth, he found a corn kernel on his tongue. From then on,
> whenever he said the word *corn* to anyone, he would get close to puking. Hence
> the altered spelling, Korn with the reversed capital letter R in the middle, the way
> a child might spell it. (Udo, 2002: 59).[1]

The story has all the hallmarks of an urban myth, but its retelling here produces a *non sequitur*. It is difficult to see how the unsavoury tale justifies Udo's
'hence'. It is not clear whether it is the gay man in the story or Jonathan Davis
himself who subsequently feels like vomiting at the sound of the word corn,
but it is somewhat perverse for a singer to choose a name the sound of which is
associated with nausea. It might make audience introductions uncomfortable
if not eventful. Changing the C to a K and reversing the R clearly does not alter
the sound of the word. And what does the story have to do with the childlike
topography? Udo clearly believes that the elements are linked because of an
apparent discomfort or ambivalence concerning homosexuality evident in some
of the songs on the first album. He mentions 'Faget' particularly. Udo suggests
that the preferred reading of this song is autobiographical. It is a protest against
homophobic bullying. Davis, a 'skinny, bookish and nerdy' kid whose first band
nicknamed him 'HIV', draws on his teasing by high-school 'jocks'. The song
climaxes with Davis screaming: 'I'm just a faget / I'm a faget / faget / I'm not a
faget / what am I? / faget / you mother fucking queers'. Udo notes however that
the song has been occasionally misconstrued as a homophobic statement, and
indeed 'in fact has become so for the bonehead element who rarely look beyond titles' (59).

While this information provides a context for the anecdote's resonance, it
still doesn't really offer any explanation about the choice or what that choice
might mean to Davis, his band and his army of fans and followers who wear
the T-shirts and hoodies and buy the branded merchandise. If Korn's songs
aren't homophobic, the anecdote would certainly seem to be, particularly when
repeated outside of its supposed original telling in a private conversation. The
idea of rimming is somewhat unsavoury outside the specific site of erotic sublimation, but even this is challenged by the sudden eruption of diarrhoea. The
incongruous presence of the indigestible piece of corn is not just a disgusting
detail, it also adds an element of the uncanny for an American, given the iconic
place of corn in the Midwestern home of the jolly green giant. The corn kernel
was clearly not at home in that specifically gay part of America.

In order to discern the meaning of these sorts of short myths and narratives,
it is often instructive to apply a structural analysis. A. J. Greimas's semiotic
square is helpful in organising the main narrative elements in order to disclose
the major anxieties and deadlocks that determine their structure. For Greimas,

narrative is organised initially into pairs of oppositions that undergo a nega-tion. The semiotic square does not itself concern meaning but the 'deep se-mantic structure' that organises the relations of signifying elements. Narrative begins with the positing of one element (S1) with its opposite (S2) and subse-quently their negation (-S1) and (-S2). Meaning generally concerns drawing correspondences: S1 is to S2 as -S1 is to -S2. According to Greimas, this simple structure provides the condition for the production and apprehension of any narrative or semiotic unit, however minimal. The relations are drawn diagram-matically in Figure 7.1.

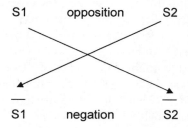

**Figure 7.1**  Greimas's semiotic square

The key elements of Udo's account of the Korn myth can thus be broken down accordingly to the same very simple skeletal form and perceived as shown in Figure 7.2.

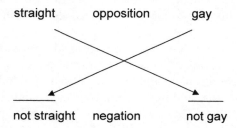

**Figure 7.2**  Not straight/not gay

The initial opposition concerns Davis who is established as 'straight' through the designation 'gay' of the two men whose conversation he overhears. The intimacy of their private conversation is heightened by the subject matter con-cerning the sexual activities of one of the men. The specific detail concerning the corn kernel captures Davis's attention significantly since he will later name his band 'Korn'. Whether or not it is he or the gay man who is nauseated by the sound of the word is not clear in the story. Assuming it is the gay man, Davis's naming of his band will clearly have the effect of alienating the man in the story. Either way, the corn should be placed in the position of the negation (-S2) of 'gay' (S2) for two reasons. First, in the story it is the part that remains undigested, inassimilable to the gay men, even as it provides a link between them through its involuntary exchange. The corn is violently voided from the gay man, as if it caused the bodily disruption that negated their sexual activity. Subsequently, even the sound of the word will bring him 'close to puking'. Second, while it would be an error to categorise a commodity in terms of sexuality, corn connotes a certain Midwest mainstream American culture that is clearly associated with heterosexuality and 'family values'. Davis's identification with the gay abjection of the corn is thus explained narratively and culturally. His position is parallel to the corn in his estrangement from the gay milieu of the two men at the party. But, further, his family background is associated with 'straight' agricultural America, the 'Oakies' who migrated to Bakersfield in Northern California. Udo reports Davis stating that 'Bakersfield, it's the other home of country music ... it's called Nashville West. I did some of my tracks in Buck Owens' studio. I don't know, we got a weird upbringing. We're inbred Oakie guys' (Udo, 2002: 55). Again, there is an interesting inversion of normal expectations here. The upbringing is only weird, perhaps, from the point of view of rock music which is usually associated with metropolitan centres like New York, Los Angeles, Chicago and so on. Oklahoma is a major corn-producing state (though by no means the biggest), and Davis's family background would no doubt have determined that his childhood was marked by the regular consumption of corn cobs, corn bread, grits and polenta. Indeed, the unfashionable origins of bands is a consistent theme in nu metal. Slipknot, for example hail from Iowa, the name of their most renowned album, also known as the corn state.

Following the logic of the self-perceived weirdness of this straight upbringing of his childhood, then, Davis perverts 'corn' into 'Koяn', a 'not straight' version of the 'not gay' object. It is important to remember that 'not straight' does not necessarily mean 'gay'. Any more than 'not white' means 'black', although a certain racist fundamentalism might assume that. The semiotic square shown in Figure 7.3, then, resembles a chiasmus in which the 'two gay men story' produces the name of the band through Davis's ambivalent identification with corn. Davis is to the gay men, what Koяn is to corn.

Further, Koяn introduces the idea of a childlike or innocent form of perversion of straight America as a means of protecting it from gay America. Perhaps this is the 'answer' to the problem of Davis's bullying at high school. The 'skinny, bookish and nerdy' Davis was not gay, but he clearly wasn't straight either in the eyes of the cornbread, beefcake jocks who called him faggot. Davis's answer 'Koяn', then, manages to produce the name of a band and ultimately a brand that positions its albums and products outside of the restricted moral economy represented by the traditional commodity corn. But, at the same time, it does

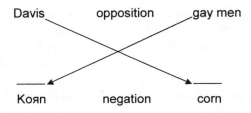

**Figure 7.3**  Коян/corn

not generalise it totally into the purely non-productive forms of expenditure represented by rimming, diarrhoea and vomiting that open up the body's integrity to heterogeneous forces of excretion that Slipknot will later broach with their own marketing tag line, 'people=shit'. The logic that produces the brand name Коян, therefore, can be applied to an account of the emergence of supercapitalism as a non-dialectical negation of Bataille's opposition between restricted and general economy (see Figure 7.4).

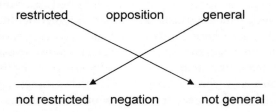

**Figure 7.4**  Not restricted/not general

Supercapitalism involves a negation of the opposition that defined traditional capitalism. American capitalism, as an expression of the puritan work ethic, involves the useful reinvestment of the surplus for the purpose of the generation of further profit rather than its wasteful expenditure. Nevertheless, the domain of moral and rational utility to which capitalism is confined means that there is a sacred and profane dimension in relation to which it is restricted. The domain of childhood, for example, is exterior to American capitalism because, on the one hand, morality insists, its innocence should not be exploited, while, on the other, its ignorance and play require that it be excluded from the rational order of political economy. Nevertheless, restricted economy regards childhood as a sovereign good. The meaning of the terms 'restricted' and 'general', therefore, is an effect of their opposition.

To understand supercapitalism means negating this basic opposition. It is possible to illustrate this by returning to the Коян anecdote. Here corn can be taken as a symbol of the goodness of traditional American economy: moral in

its wholesome, nutritious utility. This quality is precisely negated in the anecdote where the corn takes on a sinister quality destructive of the good order of
the human body, causing its own violent evacuation. This might be read, in the
context of the gay sexual activity, to be an operation of auto-immunity on
behalf of the corn. It takes itself out of the use-circuit, turning itself into the
demonic, hardcore corn-kernel of straight American mainstream negativity in
order to protect itself from the contamination of gay marginality. The corn
negates its purely functional role in restricted economy to become a figure of
dysfunction. But this is in order to protect the restricted domain from that of
the general by deploying heterogeneous forces, thereby paradoxically making
them useful. The corn is no longer an element of restricted economy, but it is
not general either.

Correspondingly, on the basis of this negation, Koяn is devised in a childlike
gesture apparently drawn by Davis with a crayon held in his left hand, the misspelling and reversed letter emphasising childlike ignorance, play and indifference to good order. The brand thereby negates the restricted meaning of corn
in a more poetic way. The signifier is no longer functioning with reference to
an obvious signified or commodity, but is invoking a range of heterogeneous
emotions and memories concerned with childhood which designates some kind
of dysfunction of the rational economic order underpinned by sound education. Is this a good example for children struggling to learn to spell?[2]

The misspelling potentially summons up bad schooling, bad parenting, childhood disaffection or trauma later confirmed by the lyrics and performance of
the band. In so far as it provides a point of identification on this basis of
intergenerational antagonism, it thereby successfully homogenises a disparate
group of disaffected teenagers into a market. It is a classic supercapitalist ma-
noeuvre which proved extremely profitable. Subsequently Korn's
entrepreneurial activities have been entirely consistent with the ruthlessly competitive imperative that has characterised deregulated, unrestricted
supercapitalism. Indifferent to the restricted/general logic that orders traditional rock-band anxieties about artistic integrity or 'selling out', Korn em-
braced corporate sponsorship, first sporting Adidas leisurewear, then
'mercilessly' dumping them 'a few months later for a more advantageous deal
with rival sportswear company Puma' (Udo, 2002: 62).

By Korn's third album *Follow the Leader* (1998), the nu metal subgenre had
been defined and their leadership was being acknowledged and celebrated not
only in the title of that album but in their setting up their own 'Family Values'
tour franchise. The first tour in 1998 featured Korn protégés Orgy and Limp
Bizkit, the former involving a previous collaborator with Davis, the latter discovered by Davis. The tour included Ice Cube (who also features prominently
on 'Children of the Korn' from *Follow the Leader*), an endorsement that secured the rap credentials of nu metal, to the delight of their predominantly
white audience. Contemporary and subsequent acts like the Deftones, Staind,

Papa Roach, Dry Kill Logic, Linkin Park, Static-X, Coal Chamber, Slipknot and System of a Down, among many others, became associated with the subgenre and all benefited when it became the music fashion of choice for teenagers and, increasingly, pre-teenagers in the late 1990s and early 2000s. The nature of the merchandising followed suit, to the point where, by the beginning of the twenty-first century, nu metal exerted 'total economic and artistic domination of the music industry', surpassing even hip hop in ubiquity, to the alarm of some of the participants. Udo reports Slipknot's drummer and spokesman Joey Jordison (aka #1) noting, 'the next thing I knew you were seeing Slipknot on lunchboxes … I know we're a band for kids, but all of that stuff in the stores made us look like a kiddie-shit band' (Udo, 2002: 21). If it was disconcerting for the musicians, what about the parents? Their pre-teen children were suddenly listening to hard rapcore and nu metal rants about serial killing, hatred, self-loathing, self-harming, suicide and sexual violence in a torrent of F and C words. It was not so much kiddie porn as porn for kiddies. But, unlike Tipper Gore, and her distress at Prince, the parents of nu metal kids were buying them Slipknot lunch boxes whose satanic imagery and tag lines includes the equation people=shit. They were relaxed about the routine marketing transgressions of rock, or completely indifferent, one brand being after all equivalent to another: Power Rangers, Marilyn Manson, Power Puff Girls, Korn, Hello Kitty, Slipknot …

At the same time, kids were beginning to brand themselves, pubescent and prepubescent children piercing and tattooing ever more parts of their body in order to keep up with the demands of a fashion industry apparently transfixed, in the 1990s, by gay and lesbian S&M culture. Or so it has been suggested, just as it is suggested that the tattooing, piercing and branding was a gesture of anti-Oedipal rebellion, nu metal kids presenting a visual spectacle precisely in order to appeal to a paternal gaze that has apparently closed its eyes.

## Piercing rage

The white hip hop or nu metal 'look' cuts across a number of subcultural fashions. On the one hand, there is the identification with and mimicry of the African-American appropriation of branded leisurewear. A good example would be Korn's adoption of Adidas, which also resulted in a lucrative sponsorship deal. On the other hand, in sharp contrast to designer labels and bling, the nu metal look was continuous with skateboarders. As Udo comments, the skateboarders' 'fob chains, incredibly baggy jeans, inverted baseball caps, training shoes, dreadlocks, body and facial piercings – dovetailed neatly with that of most of the nu metal bands. Look at early pictures of Limp Bizkit, the Deftones or Korn and it looks like they've come straight from the skate park' (Udo, 2002: 59).

Piercings and tattoos became almost epidemic in the 1990s, not just in heavy metal (where tattoos had always been *de rigueur)*, but across the spectrum.

Inspiration for the multiple piercings that suburban kids queued up to receive came from a variety of ethnic practices, body art and gay and lesbian subcultures. Whether or not it caused disquiet among parents, it attracted the attention of academics and therapists. In her essay 'Cut in the Body: From Clitoridectomy to Body Art' (1998), Renata Salecl considers the phenomenon from a psychoanalytical point of view. While it is highly debatable that her reading is strictly applicable to the whole range of different practices (from clitoridectomy to body art) that she appears to homogenise into one cultural symptom, some of the points she makes do chime with concerns raised by nu metal bands like Korn. Salecl argues that piercings and body modifications are not 'the repetition of or the return to premodern forms of initiation; they should rather be understood as a way in which the contemporary subject deals with the deadlocks of so-called postmodern society' (28). Whereas, in premodern societies, piercings and body modifications such as circumcision and scarification mark the entry of a subject into a particular symbolic order usually at the point of puberty or adolescence, 'post-modern' piercings are an effect of hyperindividuation in which subjects are attempting to 'mark' and locate themselves in the absence of a credible symbolic order. Piercers are 'trying to find some stability in today's disintegrating social universe' (31). Postmodern inscriptions on the body are not the answer of 'the big Other' to the question of existence, but 'the subject's answer to the non-existence of the big Other' (32). The provocative piercings disclose the 'impotence of authority' even as they mimic the harsher practices of its premodern manifestations. Salecl also perceives, in the self-harm and mutilation that such practices represent, a perverse protest against the big Other who is perceived to have somehow 'betrayed the subject' (35). Using Lacan's three categories of imaginary, symbolic and real, Salecl sees in the eclipse of the symbolic father and disbelief in the authority bound up with the father's name and law, the emergence of the father in the register of the real: 'Today's disbelief in the fictional character of the father's authority caused a return of the father as real – the father who is a harasser, abuses children, has insatiable sexual desires' (36).

It is important to note that the 'real' father in Lacanian terms is not the actual or biological father. Rather confusingly, the actual father is imaginary. This is because he is the one who gets the blame for all the subject's self-perceived faults. The imaginary father is the one who, to paraphrase the poet Philip Larkin, fucks you up. The real father, on the other hand, is a phantasmatic manifestation of the disgust associated with the father's sexual enjoyment of the mother. He is the obscene father of jouissance, whose pleasure is monstrous and who threatens everyone around him.

In the generic mom and pop rage that characterises many lyrics in nu metal, Korn's in particular, the father tends to vacillate between the imaginary and the real registers, sometimes in alarming ways where, as with 'Daddy' (1994), he is both and there is an almost psychotic identification with paternal enjoyment that goes beyond the perverse in which the father's voice is vocalised by the son. Salecl's argument would suggest that without the symbolic to hold them apart, the real bursts through the imaginary in moments of grotesque obscenity. 'Mr Rogers' from *Life is Peachy* (1996) reprises 'Daddy's' theme of paternal abuse: 'This child's mind you terrorized … old man / My childhood is gone because I loved you'. 'Dead Bodies Everywhere', from *Follow the Leader* (1998), rehearses a standard adolescent complaint: 'You really want me to be a good son, so why do you make me feel like no one'. 'Kill You' (1996) places teenage angst on a traditional stage that plays out Oedipal rivalry in a fantasy death-fuck with the wicked stepmom. 'You were my step-mom who always wanted me out of your sight' / I would come walkin' in and I'd say hello, but you slap me and you make some fucked up comment about my clothes … the visions in my head, were with you with a knife in your ass, laying dead / All I wanna do is kill you'.

Salecl further correlates the phenomenon of piercing, again problematically, with masochism, or at least with its mimicry. Masochism is diagnosed as a perversion because, Salecl suggests, it constitutes a mocking denial of symbolic castration that through its very mockery of the rituals of castration attempts 'to find a law that would complete it' (39). Piercing and tattooing are not 'clinical forms of perversion', but are a neurotic 'imitation of perversion' staged by subjects in order to 'try to show how they are not essentially marked by the law, since they can openly play with the castration rituals' (39). Nevertheless, the pain that piercing and tattooing imply is essential because it is a search for 'the real' behind the paternal fiction: 'The cut in the body thus appears as an escape from the imaginary simulacra that dominate our society' (39).

Reference to pain and even masochistic fantasy constantly feature in Korn's lyrics: 'I feel the pain of your needles / As they shit into my mind' / I scream without a sound … [you] left me a fuckin' slave' ('Good God', 1996); 'In my eyes you kinda rape me' ('No Place to Hide', 1996); 'Pain is God' ('Kill You', 1996). But God is dead and accordingly the reference to pain becomes so pervasive and non-specific that it is disclosed as ultimately vacuous, numb, dead, becoming subject through repetition to the same logic of the simulacrum in abolishing all reference. As the opening song 'Dead' from *Issues* (1999) states, everyone and everything is hated for no specific reason other than 'All I want in life is to be happy' ('Dead', 1999), its opening line. By this album, Korn's mom and pop rage has spiralled off into a fictional world of its own devising, with Davis's rantings reverberating into an echo chamber hollowed out by the vacuity of the therapeutic discourse that he increasingly deploys: 'Why can't I relate? … Been hating all the faces of everything that I could find' ('Hating', 1999).

An irony of Salecl's argument is that psychoanalysis has been one of the most powerful forces undermining paternal authority by exposing it as a fiction. Furthermore, as Korn's lyrics demonstrate, the discourse of therapy in general, if not Lacanian psychoanalysis in particular, shapes the phantasmatic scenarios that provide the basis of the complaints and their symptoms. In a similar way, psychoanalysis is doing nothing other than diagnosing its own cultural effects in a completely circular fashion, while appealing for the resurrection of some paternal principle that someone somewhere can believe in for the rest of us.

Even as it appeals to lost authority, therapy exercises its own through transforming and neutralising all conflict in the production of therapeutic discourse. An amusing example occurs in the documentary *Metallica: Some Kind of Monster* (2004) by Joe Berlinger and Bruce Sinofsky, which provides an intimate insight 'into the psyches' of the megastar thrash metal band. In the film the band employ a therapist to resolve conflict between the individual members but also, they hope, to help get them back in touch with the negative emotions that provided the impetus for the aggressive rock of their heyday. Jaded by family life and the millionaire comforts that come with success, they are nevertheless discontented, not least because the rage has gone. Their therapist succeeds in two ways. First, because the band members start to become subjects of his discourse, and begin to speak, think and relate to his terms, many of which they are in any case already familiar with because of their general cultural currency. Secondly, while therapy provides a way of thinking and reflecting on negativity, the therapist gets the band practically back in touch with their negative emotions not because of any specific advice he gives, but just through his annoying ubiquitous presence. Their rage returning, the group suspect him of wanting to be regarded as a member of the band, and they fire him. The resulting album is a return to form, however, and a huge success. One way or another, then, therapy succeeded in simulating and generating through the friction of its discourse the negativity of Metallica's rock 'n' roll psychodrama. It became a product of therapy itself.

Perhaps a similar process can be seen in the 'play' to which multiple piercing subjects traditional castration rituals according to Salecl. In so far as these practices are drawn from gay and lesbian subcultures, they are clearly not about subjection to an austere heterosexual order predicated upon the organisation and control of normal genital sexuality. Here, the logic of male and female circumcision, the primary castration rituals, is to pay the debt of entry into the symbolic order by giving up a part of jouissance. Circumcision implies a repression of some part of sexual pleasure, particularly for the woman who has undergone full clitoridectomy. The purpose of piercing in gay and lesbian subculture, however, is quite the contrary. Multiple piercings are aimed at the maximisation of pleasure through the eroticisation and stimulation of multiple parts of the body. It is a moving beyond the genital maturity that is recommended and promised by traditional psychoanalysis as the result of successful Oedipalisation towards the activation of the drive in its determination of multiple erogenous zones. Piercings popularly occur not just in the clitoris, penis, nipples, navel and tongue, but also along various other margins or borders of the body like the lips, nostrils, eyebrows and all along the horn-shaped aperture of the ear. In moving away from the traditional symbolic role of ornamentation, jewellery's role in the masquerade becomes secondary to its role as a practical implement of bodily pleasure. As a consequence, it becomes excessive and ugly in relation to the usual norms of fashion. Salecl does not take seriously the account that, according to her, 'young people' usually give to explain their so-called obsession with piercing as a way of escaping 'the pressures of the dominant fashion industry' (1998: 39). Or at least she regards it as contradictory since it leaves them to 'randomly follow fashion rituals' in the absence of 'strong national or religious beliefs' (39).

And yet, for Bruce Fink in his commentary on Lacan, this kind of 'living out of the drive', exemplified by the practice of multiple piercing, involves satisfaction or enjoyment that is indifferent to the gaze of the Other: 'The subject pursues satisfaction without holding the Other responsible for it and without granting the Other the preeminent status of being the only one who can provide it' (Fink, 2004: 127). And it makes sense that gay and lesbian ornamentation be regarded as a practical means to enjoyment rather than simply a demand that the paternal big Other straighten that enjoyment out.

The so-called mimicry of gay and lesbian practical ornamentation by suburban teenagers no doubt affords them similar erotogenic pleasure but presumably also risks invoking parental disapproval. Certainly it provokes Salecl's disapproval. However, perhaps even here this kind of piercing is not, as she suggests, an attempt to appeal to the impotence of the paternal fiction and provoke it into existence and consistency. On the contrary, perhaps it is a sign of indifference to the therapised space of the Other that has taken over the paternal role in its absence. Perhaps it is the very mirror of the indifference of kids in a highly mediatised therapy industry whose interest is solely in generating, simulating and eroticising adolescent deviance for the purposes of its own visibility and expansion. As such, therapy mimics the fashion industry itself in that it requires localised examples of 'deviance' to provide the reference and market for the next innovation. And it is powerfully exposed in the trajectory of Korn's lyrical content of therapised pain and its significant role in the band's commercial success.

It is not just the logic of prohibition and loss, or more particularly the loss of prohibition itself, that is at stake here. Rather, it is a question of 'excess control' where excess is a modality of systems of control that are themselves excessive. The inter-dependent relationship between excess and control has superseded law and transgression as the governing opposition, or dominant paradigm, of supercapitalism. With relation to enjoyment and consumption, the main question is no longer one of prohibition or taboo, but of economic maximisation. Such maximisation, however, both depends on, and implies, an erotics of marking and recording, stimulating, generating, anticipating, speculating on, and so on: in short, managing excess consumption as a means of facilitating and sustaining it profitably. In place of law and the desire that it instantiates, control emerges in the midst of an overproduced and unregulated supply of goods. Or rather, control and excess emerge together, each directly implying the other. Beyond useful, rational or moral purpose, control is itself excessive. Excess is an effect of control, then, even as further control is demanded in response to greater excess. This is evident across the board, from the social problems of obesity, eating disorders and addiction to the technological concern to control the unpredictability of events, the political concern to control the threat of the heterogeneous forces that are both interior and exterior to it. And indeed the possibility of assimilating and maximising on the differences denoted by such heterogeneity.

To explore this further, I want to look at another symptom of adolescent rage that seems to be more radical than therapised mom and pop rage. Apparently indifferent to mom, pop and their surrogates at school, the target of this destructive rage is American adolescence itself, as a symbol of the American way of life. The next chapter broaches the school shootings that occurred in the 1990s and culminated in the event at Columbine High School in Colorado.

## Notes

1    Udo also notes a number of other versions which suggest that it is short for kid porn, or that it is a play on Kern County where Davis is from, or that it is an abbreviation of coroner, Davis's job at the time (Udo, 2002: 60). Yet another version is that it stands for Keep On Running Nigger.

2    In 1998 a student wearing a Korn T-shirt was suspended from his school in the Midwestern town of Zeeland, Michigan. Korn's response was characteristically supercapitalist in its combative deployment of the 'gift', a major figure of general economy for Bataille. Udo notes that the band responded to the principal's action 'by giving away free T-shirts outside the school [which] got the principal to overturn his position and got a lot of publicity for themselves' (2002: 64).

# 8

# Columbine

I'll never live in the past
Let freedom ring with a shotgun blast.

('Davidian', Machine Head, 1994)

## 20 April 1999

On 20 April 1999 Eric Harris and Dylan Klebold turned up at their school at around 11a.m. armed with two shotguns, a 9-mm Hi-Point carbine semi-automatic rifle and a TEC-DC9 handgun. Ammunition and $CO_2$ bombs were packed into utility belts and the pockets of their cargo pants. Their backpacks were crammed with bombs. In addition they carried two duffel bags filled with pipe bombs, $CO_2$ canisters and propane tank bombs. They were intent on causing as much havoc and killing as many people as possible, especially their fellow students. Indeed, they seemed intent on blowing up the whole school. By the time they had turned their guns on themselves, nearly an hour later, they had succeeded in killing twelve students and one teacher; twenty-four others were wounded, many very seriously.

Although this attack was preceded by others at Springfield, Oregon, Paducah, Kentucky and Jonesboro, Arkansas, the event at Columbine was by far the most deadly and traumatic, causing recriminations in the national press. Liberal America called for greater gun control – as in the Michael Moore documentary film *Bowling for Columbine* (2002) – while more right-wing America supportive of the pro-National Rifle Association blamed lack of parental authority, absence of discipline and respect. Both sides roundly condemned what they perceived as the violent culture of film, video games and music. In the wake of the shootings, both 'left' and 'right' converged on the 'predatory' nature of popular culture that apparently turns children and adolescents into killers (see McLaren, 1995).

In a thoughtful and important book, Julie Webber remarks that while left and right converge and switch positions in their attempt to be more righteous, 'neither wants to admit that school shootings are a problem whose roots lie far beyond any simple causality related to cultural artifacts' (Webber, 2005: 18). Rather than the effects of 'predatory' culture, the availability of weapons or 'some privation peculiar to the individual shooter', Webber sees the roots of the shootings 'embedded in social practices and the environment of the school and the society' (18). In particular, Webber considers the 'hidden curriculum' that orders and directs the schools themselves. 'At present', she writes, 'school's objectives (educational, instructional, social or otherwise) are dictated by the demands of unrestrained consumerist culture', what I have been calling in this book supercapitalism. The hidden curriculum is the implementation of the dual imperative of supercapitalism that is, on the one hand, to be competitive, to produce and to consume to excess and, on the other hand, to control and conform to 'the hidden curriculum's production of nihilistic norms' (10).

The school shootings are 'unintended consequences' of the 'heightened competitiveness, consumerism, and militarization' of supercapitalism 'as it reproduces itself and its own rationale in schools' (5). The shootings are its purest expression in so far as supercapitalism is driven by an inhuman principle of expenditure rather than production. The 'production of nihilistic norms' provides the system with its most efficient vehicles of consumption and expenditure. To examine this claim more closely, I want to read the Columbine event in the light of both Webber's analysis and the Bataillean concepts deployed elsewhere in this book. Since Webber herself concentrates on the school shootings leading up to 20 April 1999, I want to concentrate on Columbine in order to plot out the co-ordinates of the terrain both shaped and traversed by the forces of supercapitalism as it informs institutional practices and produces subjectivities. That is to say that if there is a psychological structure at stake here, it not so much that of Eric Harris or Dylan Klebold but of supercapitalism itself as it applies to the production of subjectivity in schools. In this context, popular cultural artefacts become important not because they cause students to kill but, on the contrary, because they provide compensatory fantasies that enable belief and therefore participation in the system. After D. W. Winnicott, Webber calls popular cultural artefacts 'secondary gains' that 'allow students to sublimate the desire for revenge (against their parents, the school and society)' that allow them to 'play' safely with reality (6).

Using the statements of Eric Harris, the following argument plots the co-ordinates of the supercapitalist production of student subjectivity. These statements are *not caused by* but are nevertheless *consistent with* much of the lyrical content and obsessive fixations of the nu and other metal bands. Harris had his own favourites, though they tended to be German or German-American examples of the industrial metal genre, particularly Rammstein and KMFDM. In order to describe the field of forces that determine this psychological structure, I am appropriating an old topological schema from Jacques Lacan (see Lacan, 1986: 197). This topology of an essentially paranoid structure of subjectivity is expanded and adapted according to Bataille's terms drawn from his essay, 'The Psychological Structure of Fascism' (Botting and Wilson, 1997: 122–46) to provide an understanding of the power of supercapitalism.

In redrawing this topology, virtually all of Lacan's terms have been replaced but the relationality remains the same. This is for the purposes of explication, to plot the forces at stake topographically and perhaps to emphasise the proximity as well as the differences between the thought of Lacan and Bataille.

## The psychological structure of supercapitalism

Figure 8.1 is divided up into three interlocking and overlapping segments. In the top left-hand corner the triangle self–joy–normativity containing the term *ideology* denotes the space of the school and its official curriculum. In so far as it has educative and cultural goals aimed at reproducing the model citizen or 'self', American education still has a residual ideological function. In America, as Allan Bloom complains, this ideology is predominantly liberal and directed towards openness and multiculturalism to the degree to which that term affirms American values. In its presentation of these values of inclusivity and sharing the good life available to those who work hard, the curriculum is geared around the avoidance of conflict in two ways. First, it presents a conflict-free model of culture about which there can be no argument. Allan Bloom takes a Nietzschean line in denouncing the paradoxical openness of the liberal

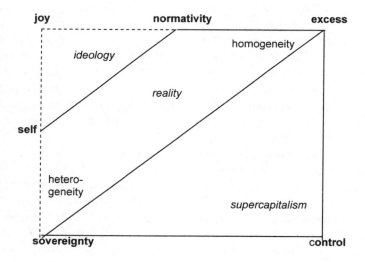

**Figure 8.1**    The psychological structure of supercapitalism

curriculum as nihilistic because its rationalism and reasonableness precludes passionate belief in anything, even in itself. Bloom's illiberal view is supported by the liberal Michael W. Apple, but from another perspective, since the latter suggests that this conflict-free model is actually the violent effect of a hidden curriculum:

> The hidden curriculum of schools serves to reinforce basic rules surrounding the nature of conflict and its uses. It posits a network of assumptions that, when internalized by students, establishes the boundaries of legitimacy. This process is accomplished not so much by explicit instances showing the negative value of conflict, but by the nearly total absence of showing the importance of conflict in subject areas. The fact is that these assumptions are obligatory for students, since at no time are the assumptions articulated or questioned. (Apple, 1975: 95–119)

Julie Webber cites this passage in support of her argument that the containment of conflict 'is detrimental to students'' development of the necessary skills that will enable them to function in a democratic society (Webber, 2005: 2). This is another way of saying that it operates to circumscribe and contain any possible threat to the dominant system that is ideologically justified by reference to democracy. Resistance to this educative model immediately positions a student in the position of radical evil since it must necessarily challenge the very basis and goodness of the American way of life as embodied by the school. Students who question or demonstrate discontent or frustration resist the basic assumptions of the school curriculum and are therefore structurally placed, in the uncomplicated rhetoric of George W. Bush, in the same position as the 'evil doers' who are enemies of freedom. The production of a curriculum devoid of conflict is therefore a violent act of radical exclusion in the name of openness, inclusivity and democracy, the very basis of which cannot be challenged. It is an act of violence that is recognised by the students precisely when they embrace the fantasy of radical evil in which they are located and contemplate attacking the school and its products. As a fellow student of Eric Harris and Dylan Klebold put it, 'everyone talks about violence. Everyone contemplates blowing up the school' (Ord, 2005).

Student violence is exposed in fantasy outside of the curriculum in the space denoted by the quadrangle self–normativity–excess–sovereignty that contains the word 'reality'. This term is not meant to be synonymous with Lacan's notion of the real as that which resists symbolisation absolutely, but rather denotes the sense of reality that is produced by both ideology and the vision machines of supercapitalism. It is, on the one hand, the space of 'real life' as opposed to school, and, on the other, the 'reality' that is both heightened by the excitement of popular culture and left lacking in its absence. It also denotes the spaces where the school shootings take place. While conflict or disagreement is expunged from the formal curriculum, students, Webber suggests, 'needing to express the disagreement they experience … channel this frustration into the spaces where the teacher is no longer in control: the hallways, the cafeteria, or the library' (Webber, 2005: 3). These are precisely the places where Harris and Klebold did their shooting; they began in the cafeteria hoping to blow it up at one of the busiest times of the day, and ended their own day in the library killing or wounding twenty-two out of its fifty-six occupants before killing themselves. They also killed as they stalked the school hallways, but studiously avoided the classrooms, the latter becoming unlikely sites of refuge for the wounded and their aids.

For Webber, 'that this violence occurs in these "free" spaces and not in the classroom should alert us to the idea that it is directed against publicity itself' (9): that is to say, the 'commons', the symbol of 'one of the important hallmarks of democracy: freedom of assembly' (9). But the attack on this space is also one of the highest affirmations of publicity in its contemporary sense, and indeed democracy. Here we should also understand the term *reality* as in the sense of 'reality TV' since these 'free' spaces are almost always under surveillance. One of the most famous images of Harris and Klebold is the one where they are captured on CCTV in the cafeteria. One of the effects of this kind of television is to provide publicity images and thereby enhance the celebrity that notoriety instantly affords in the news and entertainment media. A website dedicated to Harris and Klebold notes that while their acts should not be commended, they have nevertheless become the 'poster boys for evil', 'icons for the degeneration of society, and icons for misfits who see their own fantasies of revenge in the Columbine High School shootings' (Ord, 2005). Reality TV shows like Endemol's *Big Brother* are built around and assume a general acceptance of CCTV as not only a means of regulation but more importantly as an essential threshold of visibility that provides a means of self-promotion and therefore economic survival. While no one has yet killed themselves on a reality TV show, the shows' format is organised around the tension produced through the stage-managed excitement of unpredictable events. A real killing would provide such a show with its apotheosis, of course. In the meantime, Harris and Klebold's status as poster boys for evil should assure that they remain pre-eminent in some notional vote or TV-lists show of the all-time-greatest school shooters.

This space that is both inside and outside the school is mediatised not only by the presence of CCTV cameras, but also by the cultural images, objects and brands that articulate relations between groups of school students. This is the space of the school cliques: the jocks, the skateboarders, the drama kids and, notoriously in Columbine, the goths also known as the 'trenchcoat mafia'. These so-called subcultural groupings are homogenised, of course, in relation to their heterogeneous margins, a relation that becomes most intense in the spaces outside the control of the formal curriculum. As Webber writes, these are the areas 'where the cliques exercise their greatest power, and students who do not find a group identity in them, much less a positive one, are doomed to play the role of outcast' (2005: 9). Current fashions in popular culture provide the signifiers through which difference can be marked, the system of differentiation itself providing the means of identification and opposition. In Columbine, the goths were opposed to the jocks who baptised them with their name after the goth fashion for wearing long, black trenchcoats, a fashion that was given further cultural resonance by the *Matrix* films. But the opposition is formal and as stylised as the position of a baseball hat on the head. The jocks would wear theirs with the peaks to the front, and carefully rounded non-jocks, the majority of high school boys, would wear it backwards. If the jocks represented the elite to the degree that athletic prowess is privileged in the American high school system, the non-athletic goths would strike a more negative pose, revelling in the idea that 'the Goths represent the nihilism in modern society' (Murphy, 2001: 127, 138).

Popular culture thrives on images of cultural heterogeneity, aggression, violence, sex and the seduction of transgression. Indeed, through their appeal to such subjects, these cultural forms and images give a phantasmatic consistency to a system of value and belief that is actually lacking in everyday life in American society. As such they provide a useful vehicle for sublimating frustrated desires and discontents, whatever the ostensible moral purpose of a particular fiction. 'Students may ... take revenge', writes Webber, in the fantasy scenarios provided by novels, films, journals, websites, music, video games, computers, and so on (2005: 6). In so doing, the conflict of desire, value and belief takes place in another scene in place of the students themselves. The students are thus rendered *passive* by these entertainments (rather than stirred to violence) precisely through their identification with them. Webber writes, 'these objects believe in our place, and it is more comforting to know that others believe than it is to imagine what it might take to maintain our own beliefs while living amid nihilism' (7). Ironically, the goth nihilist masquerade with its black lips, white skin, black trenchcoat and deathhead buttons actually sustains, minimally, an idea of life in the midst of the shopping-mall nihilism of the economic bottom line. The space of *reality* then is essentially a fantasy space in which real violence irrupts only when the fantasy collapses. When cultural artefacts and objects fail to sustain identification, desire defaults directly to the force of non-productive expenditure generating the hidden curriculum's 'nihilistic norms' (10), and 'the lack of anything to affirm is rendered positive only by becoming an active will to annihilate' (Wernick, 1999: 8).

The triangle sovereignty–excess–control at the right-hand base of the square demarcates the space of *supercapitalism* that supports and determines the spaces above. The principle of excess drives supercapitalist overproduction which provides the economic conditions for normativity against the backdrop of a landscape of waste. Excess is located in the 'maternal' position of the primordial object of demand (see Lacan, 1986: 197), a demand that is rendered infinite. Like Madame Edwarda, Bataille's figure of feminine excess, demand just goes 'on and on, weirdly, unendingly', demanding a 'stream of luxury' (Bataille, 1989: 158). But the generalised infinite demand of supercapitalist excess nullifies any specific demand that requires speech and therefore generates desire. There is no necessity for the consumer to articulate his or her demands in speech (thereby alienating demand in and as desire) because the demand is already encoded and required, indeed is itself demanded.

In this way, the principle of excess also becomes one of control that radically negates the possibility of conflict. Control in turn relies on the spectacle of excess in order to ensure its violent proliferation in the form of homeland security. This logic did not require the generation of media spectaculars by enemies of American power, but was already ubiquitous, not least in schools. As Webber notes,

> In their effort to make schools 'safe', policymakers and schoolworkers have rationalized an atmosphere of fear and mistrust among students by subjecting them to routine forms of monitoring and discipline, such as metal detectors, locker searches, dress codes, censorship of virtually any suspect media and popular culture, profiling, expulsion, and incarceration. (Webber, 2005: 13).

Eric Harris anticipates the correlation between formal and hidden curriculum in one of his statements prior to the shooting.

> Don't blame my family ... they brought me up just fucking fine, don't blame toy stores or any other stores ... I don't want no fucking laws on buying fucking PVC pipes ... don't blame the school, don't fucking put cops all over the place ... the admin is doing a fine job as it is. (1999a)

Supercapitalism, as a combination of unregulated commerce and militarisation, thereby reproduces and justifies itself as a kind of 'protection racket' in which it terrorises its subjects with its own excess, currently in the name of the war on terror. Since it has evacuated the position of symbolic authority, it has to literalise the 'gaze in the Other' through its systems of security and surveillance. These systems are indeed a symptom of the 'post-authority' world, but that does not mean that power is not exercised violently over subjects on the contrary. The third term in this triad, sovereignty, should be understood in a way that is both more and less than the sovereignty of states. First, in so far as it presides over the field of *reality* in the diagram, it should be regarded as sovereignty in a state of suspension. The work of Giorgio Agamben has of course emphasised this side of sovereignty, arguing that the rule of law which states are supposed to instantiate are in certain key respects always in a state of exception or emergency: 'The state of exception establishes a hidden but fundamental relationship between law and the absence of law. It is a void, a blank and this empty space is constitutive of the legal system' (Agamben, 2004b). The place of symbolic authority is filled by decree, technobureaucratic forms of regulation and administration, and more and more by the dictates of raw power.

'My belief is that if I say something, it goes. I am the law, if you don't like it you die.' Eric Harris's statement of his philosophy on his website (1999a) draws attention to the powerful fantasy of such absolute sovereign power that the unregulated space of the 'commons' generates. The statement negates 'the formal equality and ideology of American democracy' (1999b) that fails to govern the reality of everyday school life, but in so doing gives voice to the unavowable force immanent to the hidden curriculum of supercapitalism. His many statements on his website, in his videos where he and Dylan tell how they want to kill the 'niggers, spics, Jews, gays, fucking whites', and in his colleague's yearbook such as 'you know what I hate? MANKIND!!!! ... kill everything ... kill everything', in so far as they are public or semi-public pronouncements are perhaps simply provocation (Murphy, 2001: 155). In so far as they are provocation, they constitute an appeal to symbolic authority (or the 'gaze in the Other', as Lacan describes the ego-ideal) not in order to appear likeable, but to appear unlikeable (Lacan, 1986: 197). This also seems to be the attraction of the signs and symbols of Nazism that the goth trenchcoat mafia introduced to Harris and Klebold and that also determined the date of the attack, 20 April, the anniversary of Adolf Hitler's birth. The trenchcoat mafia enjoyed, according to Murphy, 'dressing up like the Nazi SS cult and goose-stepping around Columbine High in defiance of the Jocks' (Murphy, 2001: 140–1). The Nazi provocation perhaps also accounts tangentially for Harris's particular interest in music which focused on the German industrial-metal group Rammstein and the German-American metal band KMFDM, which Harris took to be an acronym for 'kein Mehrheit fur die Mitlied' (no mercy for the majority) (88). There is absolutely no suggestion that either Rammstein or KMFDM is a neo-Nazi group, and both issued trenchant public denials when Harris's interest in them became evident in the wake of the killings. Nor is it necessary to believe that Harris was a neo-Nazi himself. The attraction of Nazism lies in its frisson of absolute taboo, the newsreels of Hitler that Harris and Klebold also liked to watch perhaps evoked by the guttural German voice of Rammstein's singer precipitated by the power chords of their form of industrial metal.

Nazi Germany is the pre-eminent symbol of anti-democracy for the West, every 'rogue' leader or state who meets its displeasure being compared inevitably to Hitler or fascism at some point. The all-purpose utility of the Nazi slur suggests that its ideology has lost all specificity. Having been decisively defeated in world war two, its ideology did not pose the same threat to America nor did it warrant the same attention as Soviet communism. Indeed, Nazi military technology and techniques were quickly adopted in the name of the Soviet threat. Eventually Nazism became purely spectral, as a style and a pantomime provocation, being endlessly rerun as entertainment on the History Channel.

Hitler and his Nazis are placed on a plane of entertainment or infotainment that offers up a whole range of fictional and quasi-fictional figures, 'role models' of good and evil with whom to identify in fantasy. Endlessly exchangeable, the authority of these paternal figures gives way to the supercapitalist system itself, which renders them all equivalent and selects them on the basis of ratings, or on yet another lists show of all-time greatest Americans, musicians, sports heroes, dictators. In Lacanian terms, then, the 'paternal identification of the ego-ideal' (Lacan, 1986: 197) (occupied by sovereignty here) would not be marked by any figure of media authority or anti-authority like Hitler, Bill Clinton, Michael Jordan, Charles Manson or even Marilyn Manson. So-called amoral Hollywood villains and action heroes are frequently cited as examples of a 'predatory culture' that glorifies violence and thereby causes anti-social behaviour (McLaren, 1995). But it is these figures themselves who are the imaginary prey of the virtual position of ultimate predator which is established by the supercapitalist system itself, as Gillian Rose suggests. Whether it be Hollywood or the Discovery Channel or even the History Channel – a viewer is invited to identify with the fly as prey of the spider or the spider as prey of the rodent, or the Shia'a Iraqis as prey of the Sunni or the Sunni as prey to the Iranians. The ultimate predator can be made to identify exclusively and yet consecutively with one link or other in the life cycle, because she can destroy the whole cycle, and, of course, herself. Since she is the ultimate predator, she can be sentimental about the victimhood of other predators while overlooking that victim's own violent predation (Rose, 1996: 47–8).

It is this virtual, sovereign position of absolute predation that perhaps informs the Columbine action, rather than any specific appeal to a paternal figure. The violence of Harris and Klebold was not Oedipal in the sense of being directed by or against an obvious paternal figure. As Webber notes, both Harris and Klebold had this in common with many of the other school shooters: 'Avoiding the typical urban myth that students will express anger at a hated authority figure, like a principal or teacher, student shooters aim for their peers' (Webber, 2005: 2). Andrew Wernick, in his article on the shootings, also emphasises this (Wernick, 1999: 2). Although Harris and Klebold were 'fag-baited and pushed around in the halls and food lines for being physically weak and socially marginal ... the action both under and overshot any motive of revenge'. There was no hit list and not even jocks were especially singled out or seriously pursued.[1] The victims were randomly selected, simply ordinary and vulnerable students, much like Harris and Klebold themselves outside their fantasies.

A Lacanian reading, therefore, might suggest that the killings were the result of a classic paranoiac confusion between ego-ideal and ideal-ego in which they enacted an extensive suicide through murdering their mirror image in other students and each other. Harris and Klebold's violence was not anti-authority, but perhaps its pure expression against the (self-)image of weakness that it wished to purge. That is to say, it was the negative affirmation of the ultimate predator who wishes to destroy 'the whole cycle and herself' through blowing up the whole school.

## Joy

Indeed, for Andrew Wernick, the significance of the Columbine event lies not in the success Harris and Klebold had in killing fellow students but in what they actually failed to accomplish. They failed to blow up the whole school. Wernick stresses that in attempting to blow up the cafeteria at peak time, 'the idea was to kill everyone in the school' (1999: 5). Their main goal was extermination. Symbolically, he argues, their intention was 'to immolate the *community* of Columbine High – themselves included – *as a whole*' (7). In reflecting on this goal, he makes three points. First, the attack was directed not just at a specific community, but at the very idea of community itself. Wernick takes this to disclose the 'aporia' of an imposed idea of community 'on a jungle of anomic and power-and-money-mediated competitiveness' that precludes the possibility of imagining any other kind of community (7). Second, as 'the hateful negation of a hateful world', the shootings were the direct identification 'with the negating impulse itself' that is made 'manifest in real and fictional moral monsters' and can be taken 'as a signature of the times' (8). Third, the act radically negated the idea of the American good life, positing it as 'hideous beyond redemption' and issued a challenge, in a way that was impossible to ignore, that there is an authentic basis for hating everything (8). Therein something of a revolutionary impulse stirs for Wernick, even though it could not help but fail symbolically since the reaction from the media and social commentators 'swallowed up' its meaning.

Perhaps, following Deleuze, it could be argued that a revolutionary impulse remains virtual to the event even though it failed to become actualised. Such an impulse nevertheless remains real as a consistently ominous promise and threat. For Deleuze, while the event can promise a genuine future in the inauguration of something radically new, every event is also 'a kind of plague, war, or death' (Deleuze, 1993: 80). Each genuine event is revolutionary nevertheless, and there is no revolutionary act that is not joyful however ugly its effects (2003: 251). The event is actualised in revolutionary joy, but for that to be figured in the event at Columbine, then a different understanding of sovereignty in relation to joy needs to be brought into play. In a Bataillean sense, the sovereign joy of an event can never be actualised in the project that develops from it, not even a revolutionary project.

The second reference to the meaning of sovereignty, therefore, is that which is 'opposed to the servile and the subordinate' (Bataille, 1991: 197). According to Bataille, 'what is sovereign in fact is to enjoy the present time without having anything in view but this present time' (199). Sovereignty is the joyful negation of all forms of servile and systemic modes of existence determined by work, utility and production in an ecstatic affirmation of the moment. Such sovereignty is related to, but surpasses, the mastery that is produced in the Hegelian dialectic. Hegelian mastery is an effect of the slave's refusal to risk death. The idleness and consumption of the master is both the condition and the effect of the slave's labour; indeed the enjoyment of the master is the end and meaning of the slave's work. The Bataillean sovereign, on the other hand, is not determined by the slave, and his joy is of a different order to the enjoyment of the master. The sovereign does not put the slave to work and therefore does not partake of any dialectical movement or labour of the negative. On the contrary, the sovereign's negativity is directed towards his slavish nature which becomes the object of sacrifice. 'In a fundamental way', writes Bataille, 'the impetus of the sovereign man makes a killer of him' (220). Sovereignty is always linked to 'a denial of the sentiments that death controls' (221). So while sovereign life calls for the risk of death, of the necessity of pushing oneself to the limit of the deferral and avoidance of death, that is not in order to become master, but in order to dissolve into the moment and 'become NOTHING', because in 'ceasing to be useful, or subordinate, it becomes *sovereign* in ceasing to be' (204). This is the moment of joy, in the zone beyond the cares of life and death, completely indifferent to wealth and power. In an affirmation of life's immensity and exuberance, the sovereign acquires a genuine luxury in his or her contempt for riches. 'Beyond a military exploitation and a religious mystification and a capitalist misappropriation', Bataille's sovereign rediscovers the meaning of wealth 'in the splendour of rags and the sombre challenge of indifference', exposing the lie that 'destines life's exuberance to revolt' (Botting and Wilson, 1997: 208).

On his website, Eric Harris poured similar scorn on the American mode of servile existence: 'most of you fuckheads out there in society, going to your everyday fucking jobs and doing your everyday routine shitty things, I say fuck you and die' (Harris, 1999a). Harris and Klebold, it seems, sacrificed everything servile in themselves and in the image of other students, thereby giving themselves up to death for the joy of violent expenditure. In his account of the Columbine event, John F. Murphy Jr cites eye-witness reports that Harris and Klebold 'were ecstatic in their happiness' (2001: 222). One witness heard either Harris or Klebold cry out, 'This is what we always wanted to do! This is awesome!' (208). Another said, 'They were laughing after they shot. It was like they were having the time of their life' (225).

There are two possibilities then suggested by the axis sovereignty–joy depending on the meaning of sovereignty. On the one hand, there is the possibility that in breaking with all modes of servile existence the event announces a break with all of its determining conditions and opens on to a future that cannot be foreseen. It is the expression of a desire to break the whole chain of existence and begin again. On the other hand, such an action is consistent with the sovereignty of American power which situates its ideal subject in the position of ultimate predator. Anything revolutionary about the act of Harris and Klebold in that instance would be the double of American power, an unintended consequence or manifestation of its latent death drive. On his website,

Eric Harris identifies specifically with symbols of American power even as he rejects the government in statements that ground his violence in a patriotism that belies even his racist provocations. On America, he states:

> Love it or leave it motherfuckers. All you racist (and if you think I'm a hypocrite come here so I can kill you) motherfucking assholes in America who burn our flags and disgrace my land, GET OUT! And to all you assholes in Iraq and all those other little piece of shit desert lands that hate us, we will kick your ass if you try to fuck with us or at least I will. (1999b)

Harris's fantasy is to be the instrument of raw American power in a patriotic fervour that transcends multicultural difference since it regards all difference as equivalent (white American racists are the same as Iraqis). Harris's 'equal opportunity hatred' (Wernick, 1999: 6) has the same logic as that which prevailed in the second Gulf War where the exercise of raw American power was justified by the assertion of 'universal' American values in which the terrifying ('shock and awe') imposition of 'freedom and democracy' brooked no opposition other than the terror it generated to define itself. And it is the same logic that perceives enemies of America everywhere, both inside and outside of its national boundaries, homogenised as evil-doers on the side of terror.

Harris's idea of raw American power takes the 'sovereign form of sovereignty'; it provides the imperative that negates even as it taps into the pair's 'revolutionary effervescence' (Botting and Wilson, 1997: 139). This, Bataille argues, is the characteristic tactic of fascism. However, in spite of Harris's patriotism and his penchant for black trenchcoats, the American sovereign imperative does not take the sacralised military form of the Nazis. Unlike Nazism, it is not a question of the militarised internal domination of the militia – the American white supremacists and some of their survivalist fellow travellers are quite marginal to the US military machine, often having been rejected or ejected from it.[2] Rather, the imperative of the sovereign form of sovereignty mobilises the whole socius on a general technological plane in the name of efficiency. Yet this is precisely the Western legacy of Nazism for Jean-Francois Lyotard. The imperative of 'the techno-economico-scientific megalopolis in which we live (or survive)' is consistent with Nazism since it 'employs the same ideals of control and saturation of memory, directed towards goals of efficiency' (Lyotard, 1993: 147). It is this imperative that organises and directs energies as much as any aesthetic, ideological or political mobilisation since it establishes them all on the same plane of consistency.

The main weapons used by Harris and Klebold can be seen as a metonymy linking up aesthetic, ideological and political fields, particularly the two shotguns,[3] and the Hi-Point Model 996 Carbine and TEC-DC9 semi-automatic hand gun. As Murphy suggests, 'the shotgun plays a unique role in the history of death and destruction in the [American] West', being the iconic weapon of the gunfight at the OK Corral and of outlaws robbing stagecoaches and deputies 'riding shotgun' (2001: 200). 'Firing an explosive shell full of pellets', the shotgun, writes Fred Botting, 'kills through excess' and thus becomes the obvious weapon of choice for a 'natural born killer' (Botting and Wilson, 2001a: 111). Discussing Mickey Knox, the hero of Quentin Tarantino's screenplay, Botting shows how the weapon retrospectively locates the naturality of Mickey's destiny: 'Holding a shotgun, it all became clear ... I'm a natural born killer' (Tarantino, 1995b: 89–90). In his union with the ideal image of the gun, Mickey 'accedes to the sovereignty of the shotgun, of himself as shotgun' (Botting and Wilson, 2001a: 111–12), 'presenting the extremity of fullness which comes of pure negativity, of the sovereign expenditure that, beyond all systems and control, can only act to destroy them, to shatter their closure' (112).

But with Harris and Klebold, the pure negativity represented by Mickey Knox's shotgun is but one element in an arsenal so technologically enhanced and hyperefficient that it goes way beyond the limit of even a natural born killer. The magazine capacity of the TEC-DC9, for example, exceeds that of the M16, the main US Armed Forces battle rifle, the classic Soviet Russian AK–47, and the Uzi, the Israeli Defense Force battle rifle and favourite of the US Secret Service. When Harris and Klebold confronted the terrified teenagers in the cafeteria and library of Columbine High they had with the TEC-DC9 'more firepower ... than an American soldier had fighting the Viet Cong at Hamburger Hill in South Vietnam, or an Israeli paratrooper attacking the Jordanians near the Wailing Wall in Jerusalem in 1967' (Murphy, 2001: 191). It is not a question of a single gun, then, not even a shotgun, but of a certain technological tendency that moves beyond human proportion as it takes lethality to a level of pure abstraction. Even as human bodies suffer the consequences of the abstraction of this technological plane, it establishes a site of becoming: becoming-weapon or becoming-bullet.

> I am your unconsciousness
> I am unrestrained excess
> metamorphic restlessness
> I am your unexpectedness
> I am your apocalypse.

(cited in Ord, 2005)

In his web essay on the shootings at Columbine, 'From Absolute Other to Eric and Dylan', Douglas Ord cites a poem from Harris's website that builds powerfully from, as Ord says, an 'incantatory' 'self-referential' beginning that promises 'what I don't like I waste' through 'a kind of annunciation' (part of which is quoted above) that culminates in the following lines:

> Shockwave
> Massive Attack
> Atomic Blast
> Son of a Gun is back ...
> Born to kill

All are equal
No discrimination
Son of a gun
A simple equation
Son of a gun
Master of fate
Bows to no God, kingdom or state
Watch out
Son of a gun
Superhero number 1

The 'poem' builds through affirmations of multiple forms of non-productive expenditure, linking sovereign and systemic violence in a provocative, parodic and incendiary litany of threats. However, none of these lines were originally written by Eric Harris. They were assembled by him from the lyrics of three KMFDM songs, 'Waste' (1997), 'Stray Bullet' (1997) and 'Son of a Gun' (1996).[4] All three songs thematise in interesting ways the paradox which determines that the sovereign form of sovereignty can only be characterised though an identification with weaponry, waste and laying waste. The lines from 'Waste' suggest that the speaker is the waste that lays waste. 'Stray Bullet' explicitly figures this as a random projectile, the speaker becoming the unconscious subjectile of an 'unrestrained excess'. Fired without aim, at random, or having overshot its purpose, the stray bullet finds its unconscious destination through tracing the destiny of the unintended consequence: 'I am your unexpectedness … your apocalypse.' 'Son of a Gun' expands the trope to nuclear dimensions, the sovereign subjectile of martial technology bowing to 'no God, kingdom or state' as it threatens 'shockwave … massive attack'.

The lyrics to these songs from the albums *Symbols* (1997) and *Xtort* (1996) are powerful in themselves, but Harris's simple bricolage, as Ord Suggests, 'exponentially increases' his poem's impact as it builds and 'enlarges the dimensions, both semantically and symbolically, of the event he and Klebold were planning' (Ord, 2005). Except that there are three supplementary lines written by Harris at the end that seem to comment on their predecessors: 'If you don't like it, well … / You know what to do / Anything I don't like – SUCKS!' The brattish ineptitude of these lines in the context of those that came before, cannot help but undercut the hyperbole of KMFDM, hinting at a discordance in the joy of becoming-weapon, and hinting also at the essential servitude of the subjectile son of a gun. This is not just in the gap opened up by mimicry – the inevitable effect of the mediation of language and cultural artefacts that alienate such identification even as they enlarge it. More, it is as if Harris realises that there is something in him that remains in excess of the 'unrestrained excess' of the stray bullet.

One of the curiosities of Harris and Klebold's action in the library and elsewhere at Columbine is that technological objects became their targets as well as students. Members of the first generation to grow up with the personal computer, Harris and Klebold were 'techies' and fans of computer games, particularly *Doom* and *Wolfenstein 3D*. Harris even created and customised *Doom* scenarios, adding his own graphics and sounds which were available for internet users to download. These are known as the 'Harris levels' (see www.snopes.com/horrors/madmen/doom.asp). Klebold was an even more adept software engineer than Harris, and yet computer and television screens became targets of their weaponry as well as students, perhaps hinting at an oscillating identification. J. F. Murphy Jr describes how, sparing one student, 'Dylan shot and killed a television set instead. In another gesture of rage against the machine, Dylan then picked up a chair and threw it at a computer monitor up on the table' under which was hiding a terrified student (2001: 231). Another account has Harris slamming a chair down on top of a computer terminal on the library counter, his last violent act before leaving the library only to return to kill himself some minutes later.

## Becoming-machine

In an interesting comment on the other school shooters, Julie Webber notes that 'we find students "triggered" into aggressivity when the technology that they have used to "believe" for them lets them down' (2005: 7). For Wernick, in spite of the numbers of students killed, the action at Columbine was an abject failure, 'the initial mystery for the police was why (given all the armament and opportunity) so *few* were actually shot' (1999: 7). Their two main propane bombs, lodged in the cafeteria, failed to go off, as did a number of others. Towards the end of the shooting, Harris's shotgun recoiled and broke his nose. The relation between Harris, Klebold and the technology that defined them seems to have been agonistic as well as enhancing. It is not clear whether the young men were let down by their technology or vice versa, but it is in the locus of this (in-)operativity that the relation becomes eventful.

Technology here should be understood not just as a set of tools or prostheses, but as the means of relationality itself that shapes and affects the character of the subject and object in the relation, whether it be video games, personal computers, the internet or gun-collecting. In this sense everyone surviving in the West's 'techno-economico-scientific megalopolis' is engaged in an equally agonistic process of becoming-technical or becoming-machine. Becoming-weapon is simply another form of becoming on a plane rendered consistent by technological in/operativity.

Becoming-machine should be understood not in the sense of human bodies becoming like machines, or of minds becoming like computers through imitation, metaphor or control, or of computers becoming like human minds. Rather, it should be understood, in the sense introduced by Deleuze and

Guattari, as a form of symbiotic sympathy and interdependence (1988: 232–9). Though there is no reason why such interdependence should not also include antagonism. For Deleuze and Guattari, becoming does not involve a process of imitation, resemblance or identification. Nor does it imply an evolution in the sense of evolution by filiation or descent. It is not a question of humans evolving into computers, or of computers displacing human beings on some evolutionary ladder. Rather, 'becoming is always of a different order than affiliation. It concerns alliance. If evolution includes any veritable becomings, it is in the domain of the *symbioses* that bring into play beings of totally different scales and kingdoms, with no possible filiation. There is a block of becoming that snaps up the wasp and the orchid, but from which no wasp-orchid can descend' (238). Becoming involves an alliance with some other thing that draws the subject beyond itself into a domain of new experiences and new forms of subjectification. The interactive mode of web-user follows the initial relation between computers and the original hackers who developed them. Hackers benefit the machine by developing it, ironing out the bugs in its systems, designing better software, facilitating changes in hardware, adapting it to new tasks and new environments, increasing its efficiency, making it faster, more powerful. In return, the hackers experience the thrill, the rush, the joy in the speed of each successful response, a joy that takes the machine-hacker assemblage on a journey towards new modes of symbiotic existence.

While there is a significant difference between hackers, operators and the interactivity of end-users, all involve a process of becoming in the sense of an alliance with some other thing that draws one element beyond itself into a domain of new experiences and new forms of technicity. Becoming-machine enables an element to do more things, or do them differently – to actualise the virtual potential of bodies as technical elements. This process also, necessarily in the case of the people-parts of any assemblage, involves new forms of subjectification. As Guattari argues, heterogeneous elements constitute a machine 'through *recurrence and communications*' (1995: 121).

However, with supercapitalism, recurrence always takes the form of the new (another new computer, another new video game) that constantly modifies the mode of interactivity, demanding new skills. In supercapitalism the process of becoming is also bound up with the production of the new as a modality of forgetting, obsolescence and death. An object loses its economic technicity the moment it fails to operate within new blocks of becoming – becomings that must always work at the 'cutting edge' of each machine assemblage. When it fails to work in new ways, fails to actualise its potential, fails to enter into a new form of subjectification, its technicity disappears. The object is then inoperative, obsolescent; it becomes junk. For example, the technicity of a computer programmer is sustained to the degree to which he/she can operate as the addressee and enunciating vehicle of a multiplicity of different machine-languages, so long as he/she can operate, and be operated by, different interfaces, networks, environments according to the very high tempo that is determined by the rate of technologised consumption. Each different mode of becoming implies the obsolescence and uselessness of the former, and a rapid emptying-out and reformulation of subjectivities.

As Ellen Ullman writes in *Close to the Machine: Technophilia and its Discontents* (1997), 'knowing an IBM mainframe – knowing it as you would a person, with all its good qualities and deficiencies, knowledge gained in years of slow anxious probing – is no use at all when you sit down for the first time in front of a UNIX machine' (1997: 101). Everything has to be re-learnt, a whole new relationship with the machine must be established and adapted in order for the machine to operate effectively in and as an assemblage. The first rule is to forget everything one once knew, to empty out one's subjectivity, and be prepared to be spoken to, and by, the machine. You must 'bow your head, let go of the idea that you know anything, and ask politely of this new machine: "How do you wish to be operated?" If you accept your ignorance, if you really admit to yourself that everything you know is now useless, the new machine will be good to you and tell you: here is how to operate me' (101–2). Total dysfunction is always around the corner, however, when the object wears out its capacity for further becoming: 'It had to happen to me sometime: sooner or later I would lose sight of the cutting edge. That moment every technical person fears – the fall into knowledge exhaustion, obsolescence' (95). Each element of machinic becoming must forget each previous mode of existence, but the machine itself remembers, unconsciously, in so far as it retains an archive of systems, bodies and machinic parts that have become 'blocked' and rendered useless through exhaustion or perverse libidinal attachment to bits of obsolete machinery and code (118–21).

For most end-users the space of technical experience becomes fetishistic, quasi-sacred in multiple ways (more 'animistic, magical, mystical' (Derrida, 2002: 91)). In the growing disproportion between knowledge and know-how, the relation becomes affective rather than rational or instrumental. Identification and dependency becomes more intense, as does the rage and violence when the machine refuses to operate, or renders its operator inoperative, junk, burnt-out. It is this inherent antagonism in the oscillation between operativity and waste in the process of becoming-machine that is the subject of the next section.

## Notes

1   Though Webber notes that 'faggot' is a common 'trigger word' in a number of the other shootings (34–5).
2   As was indeed the case with Eric Harris and Timothy McVeigh.
3   A Stevens 12-gauge double barrel shotgun and a Savage-Springfield 12-gauge pump action shotgun.
4   Perhaps significantly, Harris omits the line 'shit for brains' before the line 'born to kill'.

# 9

# Rage of the machine

Changing into something less than human
No longer part of this machine

(Static-X 'Machine', 2001)

## Mecanosphere

An episode of MTV's *Celebrity Death Match* illustrates one of the many misconceptions concerning the relation between rage and the machine. In this episode, pioneering rap-metal band Rage Against the Machine were pitched against 'the machine', a giant robot. Singer/rapper Zack de la Rocha, bassist Tim Commerford, drummer Brad Wilk and guitarist Tom Morello proved to be no match for the machine, and the MTV audience were treated to the machine mashing up the drummer and bassist before they could flee, while the singer and guitarist suffered mutilation and arm amputation before all their guts were crammed into four mayonnaise pots.

Rage Against the Machine (also known as Rage or RATM) don't normally have problems with machines, indeed their music and living depend upon them. Rather, the 'machine' is for Rage another word for the new world order of global capitalism that both dominates America and is dominated by American corporations, businesses and bureaucracies. In their rap attacking the hidden curriculum, 'Take the Power Back' (1992), the machine is the 'system' that 'disses us' from the moment that it 'teaches us to read and write'. It is an ideology machine linked to a corporate machine that exploits 'the planet's poorer nations as cattle for profit, while soothing the fat, rich West into a dull manipulable stupor' (McIver, 2002: 103). Rage's goal is to wake up the West, in solidarity with those poorer nations, 'with a ferocious mixture of rapping and riffing' (McIver, 2002: 103). In so doing, Rage was one of the first bands to synthesise rap and metal into a form that provided the 'blueprint' that Korn and nu metal would follow.

While Rage's understanding of the machine is informed by a socialist critique of capitalism, American imperialism ('I warm my hands on the flames of the flag', 'Bombtrack', 1992), new-left activism and identity politics attacking both the hidden and formal curriculum of schools: 'the present curriculums / I put my fist in 'em / Eurocentric every last one of em' ('Take the Power back', 1992). this is not the case with the subsequent nu metal bands whose rage is just as intense, though less informed by Marxism. Biohazard, another metal band whose early use of rap can be credited with pioneering the nu metal genre, addressed similar themes to Rage, often (as their name would suggest) emphasising the environmental damage caused by capitalist exploitation and the waste of natural resources. Formed in 1988, their first major-label album, *State of the World Address* (1994), combined rap and metal with political rage directed at nuclear power, pollution, greed, violence and rage itself which becomes the object of self-reflection: 'We live our lives full of rage … negative emotions project zero / Worryin' and hating, you'll never be a hero' ('Down for Life', 1994). Their fourth album, *New World Disorder* (1999) concludes with the title track, an ensemble rap raging before a desolate urban landscape ravaged by nuclear and chemical warfare, populated by genetic mutants and branded cyborgs: 'I woke up, bar codes on my forehead, it's a living nightmare, my family's all dead', and clones: 'there's no sun, they put a fucking chip in me / I'm a clone, matta fact it's a different me', that culminates in 'the grand finale, strap my body with TNT, take the president and his bitch with me' ('New World Disorder', 1999).

It is concern with new technology, particularly information technology, that seems to provoke most identifications of supercapitalism with the metaphor of the machine. The machine of supercapitalism is perceived as especially invasive, transformative and controlling: 'Corporate society prints out your thoughts spiritually sold and bought … Connect your soul now get online, / Mind control taking your life' (Biohazard, 'Control, 1999). Further, digital technology is seen as reformatting existence, leaving nothing outside this basic process of computer mechanisation: 'Zeros and ones are everything – execute me' (Slipknot, 'New Abortion', 1999). Ironically, this rage against the machine comes from bands belonging to the first computer-literate generation, the first generation of bands to develop websites and to benefit from internet marketing and online communities and fanzones. Part of the anxiety seems to be drawn precisely from the proximity to and dependence on the machine. But the reduction of music to digital information not only threatens its specificity, it also extinguishes it as a form of representation. As Baudrillard affirms, 'the whole universe of the digital, where binarism of 0 and 1 leaves room only for an operational universe of figures … ushers in the twilight of the sign and of representation' (Baudrillard, 2005: 69). And with the sign and representation, the sun sets on humanity also, as it has been hitherto understood.

There is of course something automatic, knee-jerk and therefore machinic about invoking the machine as a metaphor for supercapitalism, especially when

using machines to amplify, in every sense, the message. The very opposition
and relation between the form of the machine, mechanisation, automisation,
machination and the rage that rises righteously in the name of living sponta-
neity is itself automatic and mechanical, not least as an effect of language as the
primary engine of difference and differentiation. While rage rages against the
machine, it repeats and multiplies, becomes subject to the logic of the automa-
ton as it becomes *all the rage* to rage: 'rage, it's the fashion these days' (Biohazard, 'What Makes Us Tick', 1994). There is the sense that rage is part of the
violence of the machine; its uncontrollable excess essence: It is precisely because 'I'm a high tech kid, [that] you get a bomb in the mail' (Biohazard, 'New
World Disorder', 1999).

These concerns about the relation between human and machine, in the context of the transformative effect of new technology, chime perfectly with similar academic concerns in the 1990s. In particular the opposition between 'man
and machine' was deconstructed following the method introduced by Jacques
Derrida, resulting in the suggestion that the human species should be considered originarily prosthetic, the effect of an originary 'technicity' (see Stiegler,
1998: 1–81; Beardsworth, 1995).[1] This suggestion was contested by followers
of Gilles Deleuze and Félix Guattari, however, as not going far enough. For
Keith Ansell-Pearson, the problem with the notion of originary technicity is
that it sustains the human as supplement, therefore privileging 'man and machines as the medium of negentropic complexification' (1997: 224). Originary
technicity remains residually humanist since 'man', even as a supplementary
effect of his own prostheses, heads the hierarchy of complex beings and a (post-
)evolutionary telos. Instead, following Deleuze and Guattari, and scientists like
Lynn Margulis, Ansell-Pearson argues that it is necessary to think 'in the more
involuted terms of an originary mechanism. It is a question neither of man nor
of machines but solely of nonhuman becomings' (224).

Deleuze and Guattari reject the commonsense assumption that considers
the machine to be a subset of technology. As Guattari argues, 'we … consider
the problematic of technology as dependent on machines, and not the inverse.
The machine would become the prerequisite for technology rather than its
expression' (1992: 33). What Bernard Stiegler calls 'technics' is not, for Deleuze
and Guattari, the condition of 'man'; rather, social machines create different
modes of technics, different technical systems. These social machines are not
to be understood in a metaphorical way, as if societies operated like a machine;
rather, heterogeneous elements, people, animals and things, are determined to
constitute a machine through the existence of what Guattari calls a machinic
phylum (1995: 121). Here we move from machine (little m) to Machine (big
M): what Deleuze and Guattari call the Mecanosphere (1988: 69). The question now concerns different kinds of machine, or machinic assemblages, and
how they inter-relate, how they work, and what they can do in the context of a
generally economic machinism. But is it not the case that the use of the term

'machine' determines that heterogeneous elements are homogenised, at the very least, into an order of operativity establishing, as Baudrillard suggests, a 'purely operational universe'? That is, the Machine deploys and homogenises all forms of heterogeneity according to a machinic determinism that would orchestrate and conduct the interrelations, the transformations, and so on, even if it did not reformat the universe into digital information. Perhaps not a general machinism then, in Bataille's terms, but an unrestricted one, unrestricted by the opposition of a pure humanity or organicism.

For Deleuze and Guattari, the machine is not defined by that which is real or not-real, actual or virtual, symbol or non-symbol; the machine is concerned only with what works, and as such it is productive. But the machine is not interested in whether its products, or its operativity as such, is useful or not useful in so far as those categories refer to ideas of human need. The machine generates new forms of subject and subjectification as a by-product of its 'non-human becomings'. Deleuze and Guattari's interest in developing a machinic conception of the world in *Anti-Oedipus* (1984) was partly in order to liberate thought from the 'despotism' that psychoanalysis both diagnoses and institutionalises in a therapeutic form. Furthermore, they argue that psycho-analysis rediscovers and retraces the death instinct in capitalism, which pro-duces a 'paranoiac' subject. In contrast, they substitute a 'schizoanalysis' that draws on what they perceive to be liberating aspects of schizophrenia: 'Schizo-phrenia is the universe of productive and reproductive desiring machines' (5). It seems to me, however, that *Anti-Oedipus* offers a way of transforming psy-choanalysis into an analysis more adequate to the deterritorialising flows of supercapitalism that can be understood as a kind of 'schizocapitalism'. Pre-cisely through their reworking, they produce a mode of conceptualisation that provides one way of analysing the psychic economy of supercapitalism, where the hitherto 'paranoiac' subject bursts through the limits of its subjectivation into the sovereign joy of multiple becomings.

Deleuze and Guattari note the similarity between their schizoid machines and the mechanical flows of capital, but insist that it is 'a serious error to con-sider the capitalist flows and the schizophrenic flows to be identical' (245).[2] Whatever the non-identity between the two flows, one certainly provides a conceptual model for the other, which is helpful in perceiving what is at stake in twenty-first-century supercapitalism. Essentially, schizoanalysis differs from (Lacanian) psychoanalysis by dropping structure, the symbolic and the signi-fier. This is not because these things no longer exist, or do not function as concepts, but because Deleuze and Guattari took the view that the essential importance that psychoanalysis placed on them blocked any escape from the 'imperialism of Oedipus' and the 'despotism' of the signifier. Desire remained blocked in an always-Oedipalised triangulated structure. The unconscious was conceived always in literary terms as a form of classic theatre in which endless versions of the family romance are played out. For Deleuze and Guattari, on

the other hand, it was more productive, more liberating, to regard the unconscious as a factory (a dream factory, perhaps) rather than a theatre. Later, of
course, it becomes networked. The unconscious [is] an acentred system, in other
words a machinic network of finite automata (a rhizome), and thus arrives at
an entirely different state of the unconscious. The unconscious is both produced (it is not a result of repression) and becomes wholly productive, expunged of all negativity. Or, rather, Bataillean negativity is appropriated as part
of the 'production of consumption' (4).

Schizoid desiring machines inhabit 'the technical social machine' and frequently involve 'the perverse use or adaptation of a technical social machine'
(Guattari, 1995: 124).[3] 'Desiring machines are the same as technical and social
machines, but they are their unconscious' (144), they 'constitute the non-oedipal
life of the unconscious' (125). Guattari develops his notion of a desiring machine in a large part through adapting Lacan's concept of the *objet petit a*. Lacan
opens up the series of partial objects beyond the breast and the faeces, to the
voice and the gaze. For Guattari, precisely because of his 'refusal to close them
off and reduce them to the body ... The voice and gaze escape the body, for
example, by becoming more and more adjacent to audio-visual machines' (104).
Desiring machines consist in the assemblage of part objects that can break free
of the unity of the body and the structure of the family. 'The breast is a machine that produces milk, and the mouth a machine coupled to it', write Deleuze
and Guattari at the beginning of *Anti-Oedipus* (1984: 1). But, in the context of
supercapitalism's own 'dream factory', it is also perfectly possible for the orality
of such an assemblage to be hardwired to a scopic drive in which all breasts are
silicone, milkless and locked into a desiring assemblage with a camera. The
assemblage breast–silicone–camera occurs in the conjunction between 'o' (or
*a*) as the little machine and 'O' as the big Machine of supercapitalism in which
the human–non-human elements of sex are re-articulated and reorganised on
screen.

Along with structure, Deleuze and Guattari also do away with the symbolic
order in *Anti-Oedipus*. This is not because families and kinship relations have
ceased to exist, but because it is the logical consequence of thinking outside an
Oedipal structure. In this regard, schizoanalysis is again both ahead of and in
tune with developments introduced by supercapitalism since the 1980s.
Supercapitalism is indeed in the process of dismantling the main familial structure of the symbolic order, leaving its spectral law to float across a range of
disparate institutions, corporations and economic practices. Families are no
longer the means by which wealth is exchanged and maintained. Indeed, families do not make economic sense and hinder the establishment of a really flexible labour market. Families are not maintained on the basis of the fundamental symbolic ties of kinship but by extremely fragile, narcissistic investments
and increasingly by contract. It is apparently already possible in America to
divorce one's parents; soon perhaps it will be possible to divorce one's children.

Even the incest taboo is dissolving, as it must, in an age of sperm banks, in vitro fertilisation and genetic manipulation. Replacing paternity and the taboo on incest, however, is a general sacralisation and eroticisation of the child. As we have seen, the 'mom and pop rage' of the post-baby-boomer generation, evident in the lyrics of Korn and other nu metal bands, has almost established child abuse as a necessary formative condition (see also Kincaid, 1998).

But if the symbolic order is less and less effective as an analytical concept, symbolisation itself is clearly still essential, as is the role of the signifier within it. However, symbolisation is nothing without its technical support; it cannot be simply a question of signifiers in isolation. Deleuze and Guattari complain about the signifier as 'a sort of catch-all that projects everything back onto an obsolete writing-machine' (Deleuze, 1995: 21). But there are very many different technologies of writing, different writing machines whose technicity is effective in different spatial and temporal networks. Discussing creative or artistic production in the context of supercapitalism, addressing the rage that is integral to the machine, requires developing a concept of econopoiesis.

## Econopoiesis

> Money is a kind of poetry ... [but] if money is a kind of poetry, 'poetry' in the broad sense of cultural forms generally in various media is also a    kind    of money. (J. Hillis Miller, 1995: 128)

> People=Shit (Slipknot, 2001)

The poetry of paradoxical equivalence: money equals poetry; poetry equals money. Beauty equals efficiency. Commerce equals war. War equals desire. Desire equals machine. Machine equals rage. People equal shit.

That people equal shit, however, is as incontrovertible as it should be uncontroversial. Hence all those toilets. But the presence of all those toilets also indicates that shit presents a problem of waste disposal: 'Occupying an uncertain and troubling space between a nature that is never surpassed and a culture that is never closed off, shit defines civilization' (Botting and Wilson, 2001b: 189). And civilization now produces more self-defining shit than ever before in human history. As fast as waste products are flushed out to sea, buried, burnt, stacked up in landfills and recycled, more waste is generated. Obsolescence is not only built into the products of contemporary capitalism, its speed increases as each new generation of technological products renders the previous ones junk. Waste is essential; it is wealth-creating. Shit is the definitive human product; waste defines what people are.

As heterogeneous matter, shit also announces a moral and spiritual dimension. Where shit is regarded as bad, it negatively defines what is good, pure and sacred. That people equal shit was acknowledged 500 years ago in Martin

Luther's message to his medieval parishioners, whom he considered to be wallowing in the profane world of putrefying flesh: 'you are the waste matter which falls into the world from the devil's anus' (cited in Lacan, 1992: 97). Luther was, of course, the leader of the Protestant Reformation, a profound international religious movement that transformed Christianity and, among many other things, led to the founding of America broadly according to the Protestant, Puritan principles of the Pilgrim Fathers.

'Contagion – I'm sittin' at the side of Satan' ('People=Shit', 2001). Though the genealogy may be long and complex, Slipknot are authentically Luther's heirs, and have taken up his equation as one of their characteristic slogans that appears as part of a signifying assemblage that features on much of their merchandise: posters, T-shirts, hoodies. 'People=Shit' is the title of the second track of *Iowa* (2001), the band's second album. Acclaimed by Tommy Udo as 'the Sgt Pepper of negativity' (2002, 126), it makes 'nearly everything else in modern doom rock sound banal, the empty yap of mall gangstas' (127).

This piece of Slipknot merchandise, with its arresting equation, is not a poem or a piece of literature, although it might be. It might be, if literature were regarded not as a privileged mode of discourse but as *a particular manner of reading and deciphering signs*' (Ehrmann, 1981: 248). Slipknot's signifying assemblage with its provocative equation, people=shit, is emblematic of a paradoxical poetic principle immanent to supercapitalism. Emblems were forms produced in the Middle Ages. A medieval emblem was generally comprised of an image, a statement or motto, and a name, often emblazoned on armour shields and such like. The emblem for the House of Slipknot is comprised of a large bar code and a motto, 'People=Shit'. As archaic as such an assemblage is in one way, in another way it is a profound comment on, and instance of, the subject of econopoiesis in the context of supercapitalism, which is driven by the conjunction of new technology and consumerism.

While, for Luther, people equal shit because they have fallen into sin and the profane world of fleshly appetite, for Slipknot the equation is superimposed over a representation of a large bar code that surrounds and transcends it, and floats above the band's logo. This juxtaposition of elements would seem to suggest that people equal shit in the context of supercapitalism that is in some sense purified of the human needs and appetites that result in the shit that defines them. Indeed, in relation to the bar code, perhaps people *are* shit, are supercapitalism's shit, the waste of its waste. Supercapitalism exists primarily for itself, driven by a principle of (in-)operativity and excess-control, symbolised by the machine-readable binary code.

The bar code is a product 'fingerprint' that contains information concerning the identity, price and so on of particular products. Bar codes enable manufacturers and retailers to keep track of their products, through accessing information stored in a network of data banks and corporate computers, providing information about the identity and quantity of products consumed and their consumers. However, as a form of read-only technology, the bar code is itself already obsolescent and is being replaced by the 'smart label'. This is a bar code with a radio-frequency identification tag (RFID) that enables a product to 'speak' as well as to be read and is therefore capable of being tracked from its point of production to its consumption and ultimate disposal – or from birth to death. The smart labels are tracked by 'readers' embedded everywhere, in factories and stores, in doorways, on walls and in home appliances and gadgets. Purchase and payment occur instantaneously as the product, be it another ready meal, CD or slim volume of verse, makes itself known to the computers in one's bank. Manufacturers and corporations can track the whole history of the product and, on the basis of this information, anticipate, determine and resupply the 'needs' that they have already generated. The bar code/smart label gives a product its existence in the network; it enables it to speak, to tell the tale of its life and destiny. In many ways it replaces the consumer as the subject of capitalism. Its speech may be simple and banal, or 'dumb', as the new economists say, but collectively the chips in these smart labels enable a network machine assemblage to function as if it were endowed with a 'fabulous intelligence'.

The piece of Slipknot merchandise has two bar codes, of course: an operative one and an inoperative one. The latter effaces the former even as it draws attention to bar codes generally in a gesture of anti-capitalism. Part of the mechanism of the semiotics of the marketing of cultural products is, of course, to generate images and statements that invite identification and desire, promising pleasure and happiness. The statement 'people=shit' repeats this process in a mechanical but also perverse way. Pleasure is taken in the identification with abjection and in the aggressive negativity that the recognition implies and excites. In this instance, the machine of supercapitalism finds its most effective means of operativity through exciting resistance and generating a fantasy of anti-capitalism.

The bar code operates in the same perverse way. It does not function as a bar code, as a piece of binary code, but is taken out of that use-circuit and given a new function as a signifier of supercapitalism itself. And to the degree to which it does that, it can be employed as a signifier of anti-capitalism. But then again, it can be redeployed as a key signifier in a campaign of corporate marketing. Detached from its purely technological function, the bar code has been deployed in many different areas as a tattoo, as an accompaniment to anti-capitalist slogans, as an image on a T-shirt, as part of the logo of one of the most popular music television channels, and so on. The bar code accrues a poetic excess of meaning that ultimately renders it meaningless, simply generating different effects, opening up new markets, suturing different communities together, positively and negatively, as subjects (or subjectiles) of supercapitalism.

The third term in the assemblage is the brand, the name of the band Slipknot, in the form of a recognisable logo. It is the name of the artist, that which functions as a point of differentiation in the system of commodity signification and brand recognition. A brand name has an author function in the way in which it provides a signature and a means of delimiting an oeuvre of products, however small or large: Slipknot, Korn, Arsenal, Bret Easton Ellis, Quentin Tarantino, Disney, FCUK, Will Self. But these brand names are not simply the names of individual authors or subjects. They mark products and signify little clusters of cultural and commercial production.

The transformation of the author function to include brands and corporations is part of a process in which a creative understanding and practice has been generalised throughout the economy to inform all aspects of life, even those not commonly associated with culture. This poetic principle must be understood outside of a narrow conception of the culture that usually provides the object of cultural theory and analysis. Literature, for example, no longer operates most effectively in literature, but everywhere else. The life that once animated literature as an effect of its poiesis (the source of its creativity) has departed the heritage museum of literary study. At the same time, the language of creativity, beauty, poetic originality and vision, as well as the language of poetic rage, negativity and indignation, has become integral to general economic, commercial and technological thinking. A literary imagination bound up with a certain idea of human experience and potential has quietly, but no less powerfully, informed the creation, implementation and presentation of diverse enterprises. A form of textual play, reading, writing and deciphering signs, has become an integral part of non-literary, scientific and technological discourses, both in their theory and in their commercial applications.

It is not simply that literature has declined in importance, just as reading and writing appear to have ceded to film, pop music, television and video games. These new forms produce a more powerful poietic effect in the context of a capitalism that thrives on technological innovation. At the same time, literary pleasure and study seem to have lost their value in the face of emphases on the vocational and practical usefulness of education. Yet elements of a literary imagination have permeated cultural and economic assumptions everywhere. Commerce increasingly requires the creation, rather than the simple exploitation, of demands and markets; industry looks to creative solutions to the point that the entrepreneurs who provide them become romantic figures. In the recent history of technological advances, too, key designers and innovators are romanticised as much for their vision as for their technical ability to imagine and realise new, virtual worlds, to render experience palpable in new spaces.

The unrestricted economy of supercapitalism is generated by those marginal differences, produced by artistic, technological innovation that can be quickly reproduced and supplied on a mass scale. New forms of identification and individualism are simulated as instances of differentiation, frequently authenticated by self-authorising assertions of avant-gardism, political radicalism, outrage, anti-capitalism, etc. that anyone can speculate upon in the market.

Supercapitalism demands a rethinking of the relationship between aesthetics and economics. Aestheticisation has been generalised through supercapitalism's automated medium of exchange and in the process representation has given way to presentation, the contours of which are shaped by techno-economic imperatives. In the place of the unpresentable, presentation overwrites and creates the new and the now, performatively, in a process of econopoiesis. Econopoietic presentations engender performance in both quasi-theatrical and techno-economic senses. Just as presentation is not subservient to a reality principle, it is also indifferent to moral, utilitarian or rational economic thinking: it takes its bearings from simulation and the imperatives of supercapitalism in which consumption, waste and luxury are pre-eminent features rather than heterogeneous by-products. Supercapitalism is characterised by the precedence that supply enjoys over demand, by its creation of desire over need, its delivery of commodities that people did not know they wanted to consume. Thus, the entrepreneur becomes gift-giver, gambler, visionary, assuming the role of avant-garde artist by making the new and making the news. Like an inventor or an entrepreneur, poetry must introduce something new into the circulation of discourses and commodities; artistic successes just as much as commercial successes depend on innovation, the introduction of something surprising that disturbs the familiar. Art and literature have thus become transversal and operate as the paradoxical poetic principle of supercapitalism.

Econopoiesis is a general principle, operative everywhere. Indeed, it is the very principle of life, where technically embodied, econopoietic creation precipitates life in a fictional direction, its selection dependent upon the performance of its fitness functions in the context of the 'bionomic' ecosystem. Here, econopoiesis broaches auto- and bio-poiesis as the poetic principle of emergence, consistency and transformation within complex systems.

Perhaps this has always been the case, and cultural history might discern a phylogeny or evolution which predates the modern disciplines of art and literature and which involves the collocation of three categories that comprise a writing machine in an expanded sense, which is 'techne': the technique or mechanism (organic or inorganic) that conveys and shapes the form of the exchange of information. As vehicle, as practice and technique, techne also sustains the continuity and memory of the life or 'bios' that it materially supports; there would be no bios, however, without an effect of 'poiesis' that occurs in the machine's operations with its outside. Pure mechanism would simply go on producing the same things over and over again, and would never result in the generation of life in a sense that traverses the opposition organic or inorganic. It is not just a question of autopoiesis (self-production and reproduction), but also of an allopoiesis in which the life of the mechanism depends upon interaction with components outside itself. Life requires a point of creation or poiesis – in fact, it requires a continual process of creation – that is the effect of the machine's complex interactions and exchanges with its environment, with other machines and other forms of life, exchanges that introduce change, mutation, adaptation, and so on.

Politicised analysis in the humanities thus becomes a practice both critical and clinical that differs significantly from the role of the cultural critic, for example, where the cultural correctness of a work correlates to its political correctness, as it does for a critic like Walter Benjamin. Politicised analysis must acknowledge that culture cannot operate outside of the systems of mediatised exchange in which it emerges and is presented. At the same time, without a poetic principle, supercapitalism cannot create the new, cannot generate the desire necessary for its current growth. Instead, it is a question of evaluating the affects and effects of the heteroeconopoietic movements immanent to the life of systems.

Where econopoiesis generates homeostatic forms within a generally restricted bionomic ecosystem, heteroeconopoiesis traces the emergence and disappearance of singular poietic irruptions of negativity and difference. Poietic life is singular, in the sense that creation requires death. Heteroeconopoietic forces traverse even as they inscribe, transcribe and generate a life that can only be the effect of an interaction, or exchange, but which generates an excess that is not exchanged, that is lost without profit or return. In the midst of a continual process of complex yet ultimately mechanical exchanges and repetitions, poietic life, paradoxically, is the effect of singular non-returnable, non-exchangeable expenditures of energy that die and disappear, that are not recorded and do not return. Politicised cultural analysis here, then, would be interested in the traces of a singular, sovereign form of expenditure that correlates to its poetic affects, in its refusal to be subordinated to any form of value or economic utility.

For Bataille, while literature has always been associated with a form of utility as either an aesthetic or commercial product, or a form of moral or political instruction, there is also an irreducible part of literature that 'will not serve'. Literature is evil, but it is precisely in this way that literature can achieve political significance. This is because by its refusal of the aesthetic, political and moral configurations of the good that inform its production, literature exposes the limitations of these systems. Poetic elements, there ostensibly to provide the occasion for the triumph of moral good, break closed systems as they take possession through the poetic affectivity of their excess, their sovereignty. In so doing, they disclose and represent the forms of heterogeneity by and through which political formations establish order and exercise power.

In 'People=Shit' Slipknot affirm that like John Milton and William Blake (and Bataille), they are also 'sittin' at the side of Satan', and indeed advertise the fact in all the Judaeo-satanic visuals that adorn their stage set, album covers and merchandise. In spite of this, as Udo notes, in their lyrical imagery they generally 'avoid all the old occult cliches' that are associated with heavy metal, death and black metal in particular. Rather, Slipknot's imagery evokes 'the grittier world of mass murderers and serial-killers, the real-life monsters who stalk America [the] white trash demons' (Udo, 2002: 131). Most notably, on *Iowa's* title track, a fifteen-minute exploration of the mind of a man who kills women in order to reshape them in his own image. For Udo, this is 'one of the darkest rock and roll songs ever because there wasn't even the hint of pretension that it served some moral purpose. It was evil, in a real sense' (137).

'Good is the passive that obeys Reason. Evil is the active springing from Energy', writes William Blake (1984: 149). Bataille concurs and draws from the Gnostics a conception of evil as base matter, 'as an *active* principle having its own autonomous existence as darkness (which would not simply be the absence of light, but the monstrous archontes revealed by this absence), and as evil (which would not be the absence of good but, a creative action)' (Botting and Wilson, 1997: 162). Slipknot's evocation of evil as a monstrous creative principle is consistent with Bataille's association of evil with heterogeneous base matter and excess – corpses, waste, pollution and shit, as well as the passionate energy of rage and hatred.

Slipknot's ambivalent use of the universal product or bar code in their brand imagery is consistent with this. It is introduced on *Slipknot* (1999), their first complete album, on the opening track '742617000027', which was the bar code number of their debut EP *Mate. Feed. Kill. Repeat* (1998). Above a cacophony of throbbing generator sounds and squeaking electronic noises, runs a tape loop of a voice saying, 'The whole thing I think is sick' over and over again at different speeds. The sound clip is sampled from a documentary on the mass murderer Charles Manson. This introductory noise-collage, then, presents a (mal)functioning machine's apparently self-reflexive commentary in the voice of (or on) a serial killer. Since the voice is mechanically distorted through being played at different speeds, it is not immediately clear if this is the voice of Manson or a voice describing Manson, but it makes no difference. The juxtaposition of Manson and the bar code accentuates the value of the life that is effaced and encoded by the machine of supercapitalism. The value of that life can only be affirmed in evil through the image of its sacrifice, which becomes a metaphor for the life that is rendered shit by the machine.

The bar code connects the branded product – the subject or object – to the network of supercapitalism as a piece of information. The subject-brand is a piece of digital code that becomes a mobile nodal point in an assemblage or meshwork of points of interconnection. Through drawing attention to its status as a machined brand, Slipknot accentuate the other aspect of their imagery, the heterogeneous life of the masses, the rage and joy of the 'maggots' as they call their fans, that is immanent to the machine. They are the rage of the machine. The energy of the rage is directed towards this machine that defines everything, every utterance, according to its (in-)operativity as a form of information exchange. The machine constitutes an electronic ecosphere that supports and sustains life only in so far as it is economic, which is to say as long as it consumes productively. Rage therefore emanates from a point heterogeneous to the machine: an impossible point of authenticity that is constantly referred to by these bands, but which is nowhere locatable and barred – barred, coded and branded. The authenticity of any utterance is of course instantly erased the moment that it signifies as an element in the network of the machine that produces it as a new product and object of consumption. Always attempting to bump up against the limits of the consumable, therefore, authentic utterances lie at the vanguard of capitalisable innovations. Authenticity is a continually mobile, lost object that resides nowhere and in nothing other than the shit or vomit that is expended, expelled or repelled by the machine: 'The whole thing I think is sick.'

The authentic rage of Slipknot is, then, neither purely mechanical nor non-mechanical, but reproduces, with the regularity of a technique and at the risk of cliché, the instance of the non-living, of the dead in the living. This becomes the locus of affect: 'Some feel I kill for fun / I kill for life! / They don't know I'm immortal / They don't know I'm just cattle / They don't know I'm eternal' ('Some Feel', 1998). The dead and the dead machine become the spectral fantasy of the dead as the principle of life and survival. Evoking the Hegel-machine, Derrida writes, 'this mechanical principle is apparently very simple: life has absolute value only if it is worth *more than* life' (Derrida, 2002: 86). The seriality and mechanical rage of the serial killer is an ideal figure with which to convey the communal rage of the maggots, the 'fat and ugly and uncool' Midwestern white trash who characterise Slipknot's fan base ('I am Hated', 2001). As a value, the rage of evil is both immanent and heterogeneous to the community to which it gives consistency. It is 'the pulse of the maggots', to use the title of Slipknot's tribute to their fans (see also the name of the official fan website, www.pulseofthemaggots.com).

Bataille writes that

> The very principle of value wants us to go 'as far as possible'. In this respect the association with the principle of Good establishes the 'farthest point' from the social body, beyond which constituted society cannot advance, while the association with the principle of Evil establishes the 'farthest point' which individuals or minorities can temporarily reach. (Bataille, 1973: 74)

Rage, as the expression of excess, establishes value precisely because it puts at risk the life that it affirms. Through the negating action of rage, value is pushed to excess above and beyond the living. It becomes a contagion (etymologically, the words 'rage' and 'rabies' are both derived from the Latin word '*rabies*' meaning rage). A disease is said to rage when it spreads rapidly and uncontrollably. Opening the space of death through its mode of replication, the rage of the machine accentuates the silence of the death drive that is 'at work in every community, every *auto-co-immunity*, constituting it as such in its iterability, its heritage, its spectral tradition' (Derrida, 2002: 86–7): 'Killers are quiet like the breath of the wind' (Slipknot, 'Killers are Quiet', 1998).

In their emphasis on serial killers and death, but also musically, Slipknot are close to the death metal genre and bands like Carcass, Morbid Angel and Immortal. Death metal is contemporary with the negative turn in hip hop and follows a more extreme trajectory than nu metal, as we will see in the next chapter.

## Notes

1   As Keith Ansell-Pearson argues, however, the novelty of this suggestion is a little exaggerated, since it is there in the continental philosophical tradition since Hegel (1997: 224).
2   But some of their most ardent supporters are no longer interested in maintaining the distinction, Nick Land for example (Land, 1993: 480).
3   Just as later when desiring machines are replaced by the broader notion of 'machinic assemblage', these assemblages are produced in the 'strata' (which replaces 'structure'), but operate in zones where milieus become decoded (Deleuze and Guattari, 1988: 40).

# 10

# Bass spirituality

You will give praise to Satan
Impaled vibration,
Crucifixion

(Deicide, 'Crucifixion', 1990)

## Inner experience of the maggot

While trawling the internet's darker corridors looking for inspiration, Slipknot's vocalist Corey Taylor came across a website located at www.crimescene.com (1998). The site recounted the case of a murdered college student. In March 1997, 20-year-old Ariadne Purity Knight was kidnapped by an ex-lover who eventually buried her alive in a home-made wooden coffin. In May the abductor sent three documents to the police, a map and two polaroids of Knight in the box, her face visible through a wooden grill. She was found dead on 9 June 1997. A man called Ben Archer found her body in the wooden box out in the woods where he had been walking his dog. Crimescene.com further reports that 'Archer described a child he saw crouched over the burial site. The child was identified as 9-year-old Dylan Tull. In the days before her death, the boy attempted to assist the victim. She gave him a note, pleading for help. The note was never delivered. It was later discovered in the university library.'

The story became the inspiration for the song 'Purity', written by Taylor.[1] The Slipknot fansite www.black-goat.com reports how much the story affected the vocalist. Taylor is quoted at length on the site, reflecting on the specific horror of the tale:

> I still think it's real – see the thing whether it's true or not, it's a real story – that we read about – that fucked our whole world up – can you imagine a girl being buried in a box and having all this lecherous bullshit drip down on her from this guy? And thinking that there is hope, because this kid is taking some bizarre note to this guy he doesn't even know – thinking that you are holding on to the shirt of hope – and you wake up and you're dead you're buried in mud – they find the note about a week later shoved in a library book for gods sakes – it just hurts

your head – it's a case of what is good and bad in people – the box alone is reason
enough to be like, 'I cant stand to be fucking human' – how can someone fucking
do this to somebody? What is inside of us that is so fucking wrong? He had written
quotes from Edgar Allen [*sic*] Poe and lots of fucked up things on the box.
(www.black-goat.com/song_slipknot.php)

The website claims to be the Yoknapatawpha County Law Enforcement Division Evidence File, and ghoulishly reproduces the abductor's photographs and
an image of a beautiful corpse, Purity Knight's face buried in the mud. These
images indicate that the site is a fake, as indeed it is. Ironically, as another Slipknot fansite, www.Maggot-land.com, notes, 'Purity' was apparently pulled from
*Slipknot* because of a dispute over copyright with crimescene.com itself.

Even though it is fiction, the story produces such an affect in Taylor that it
feels real. Drawing a distinction between the truth of the story and its reality,
Taylor apprehends the latter directly through his imagination. The song is written primarily from the point of view of the young woman's fear and anguish.
Characteristically, however, the song lurches at points over to the side of the
killer. Indeed, it seems to begin that way, 'psychopathic daze ... I create this
waste'. The song situates the singer/listener once again in the sovereign position of the ultimate predator who can empathise with prey or predator at will,
but this position is no longer one of comfort. Taylor recognises with horror the
human impulse that put her in the coffin: 'I can't stand to be fucking human.'
That is why the story is real, even though it is not true. There is no woman, it is
his own violence, fear and anguish that he feels. Taylor feels the absolute soli-
tude of the sadist and the imprisoned woman facing death, all light and all
hope fading in the mud. His song gathers both to the same point in the amoral
sovereignty of his imagination. Its stupidity and prurient cruelty, evident in
the original fiction itself, is nevertheless completely in accord with the 'unregulated cruelty of the universe, the cruelty of famine, of a hopeless sadism: God's
unfathomable taste for the extreme suffering of his creatures, suffocating and
dishonoring them' (Bataille, 2001: 197).

The contemplation of a horrible death is an unlikely topic for most mainstream pop songs, but is actually very common in some genres of metal, particularly death metal, with which Slipknot has many affinities. Moreover, such
material is not offered for quiet contemplation, as in a folk song or country
music, but for the occasion of *dancing* – a frantic and sometimes violent mode
of dancing, headbanging and moshing. Extreme heavy metal is essentially live
music that generates an intense experience outside the home, outside the clubs
and the malls, at extreme volume. In the mosh pit, beneath the 'hell-hop
polydrumming and nail-bomb showers of soprano-drone guitar and sampled
squeal' (Udo, 2002: 127), Slipknot's audience are a mass of swarming maggots
writhing in ecstasy. Slipknot themselves are noted for their high-energy, fren-
zied yet ritualised performances in which they are dressed up in prison dunga-
rees and serial-killer masks. Murder, violence, rage and anguish become the

condition of this musical ecstasy, a festive joy before death. For Bataille, writing just before the beginning of world war two, 'the practice of joy before death' is a method of atheological ecstasy, a kind of *mysticism* without God. "Joy before death" belongs only to the person for whom there is no *beyond*' (1985: 236). The method involves the anguished imagination of one's own imminent death:

> ceaselessly destroying and consuming myself in myself in a great festival of blood … Joy before death annihilates me … I remain in this annihilation and, from there, I picture nature as a play of forces expressed in multiplied and incessant agony … I imagine the gift of an infinite suffering, of blood and open bodies, in the image of an ejaculation cutting down the one it jolts and abandoning him to an exhaustion charged with nausea.
>
> I imagine the earth projected into space, like a woman screaming, her head in flames (238–9).

During the war and after, this idea developed into the notion of 'inner experience' that Bataille explored along with his fellow French author Maurice Blanchot. Paradoxically, this inner experience was sought as a form of communication. Accepting that (religious) communion was impossible, inner experience was to be a mode of negativity that negated the boundaries of the isolated being. Bataille and Blanchot determined that inner experience can only have as its principle and end the absence of salvation. It must give up clinging on to the shirt of hope, as Corey Taylor says, and affirm experience itself as the only authority, the only reality: an experience, furthermore, that contests and breaks apart the limits of the self, and thus the subject of experience. Inner experience is thus neither an experience in the sense that it is the property of a subject, nor inner since it sets the subject alight and projects it out into a space beyond itself in continuity with a violent universe.

Ronald Bogue in a very interesting chapter on death metal, 'Becoming metal, Becoming death …' (2004), emphasises the role of the music's volume in live performances and the transformative communal effect it has on audiences that participate in the experience. Adopting a mode of analysis from Gilles Deleuze and Félix Guattari, Bogue suggests that death metal provides 'illuminating instances of a musical becoming-metal' and a lyrical becoming-death 'that produces a sonic plane of consistency of affective intensities' (84). Lyrically, death metal shares with Slipknot an interest in 'psycho killer songs, first-person expressions of sadistic pleasures and tormented obsessions' but there is a more hyperbolic tendency in death metal that expands into third-person accounts of the deeds of mass murder, satanic rage and revenge. Unlike nu metal and Slipknot, death metal songs are 'seldom laments of self-pitying Angst, the tone of the lyrics generally ranging from icy detachment to manic exuberance' (103).

The most important factor, however, is the presence of the live concert sound, which is 'heard with the ears but above all felt with the body, especially the upper chest' (88). In death metal, as with grind core and other extreme forms of metal, the force of the low frequencies is particularly intense, with the bass and guitars usually tuned half a step or a whole step below standard tunings. The effect of this for Bogue is 'a music of intensities, a continuum of sensation (percept/affects) that converts the lived body to a dedifferentiated body without organs' (88). The music bypasses the brain, Bogue suggests, and conveys the 'brutality of fact'. A violent reality is experienced even though the brain, the subject of experience, knows nothing about it as it is shredded along a shared plane of sonic intensity.

But it is not just the communion of maggots and other death metal fans that is at stake in the live concert. The maggots do not constitute a purely organic mass. In their inner experience they 'develop a specific potential within the basic loudness a line of variation that plays across an electronic–industrial–commercial machinic phylum [that] entails a continuing experimentation on the body' (88). The becoming-metal of the maggot is also a becoming-machine in that it takes part in an assemblage of non-human becomings. The organic elements of the death metal machine assemblage are largely anonymous. In relation to the pulse of extreme volume, even the band and the instruments that provide it are continuous with the maggots. Slipknot's ostentatious anonymity – the lurid masks and uniforms, the adoption of numerals, from 0 to 8, as performing aliases – is both an expression of this facelessness and a rage of the machine that demands and necessitates it: 'We did it because we were degraded constantly … No one gave a fuck, no one cared, so we were never about our names or our faces, we're just about music' (Joey Jordison cited in Udo, 2002: 127).

This element of uniformity and anonymity is consistent with death metal generally, usually in a less ostentatious way. As Bogue notes, 'death metal groups have the requisite vocalist and lead guitarist, but sonically they tend toward anonymity' (94–5). Every vocalist has guttural growls and screams, every guitarist plays grinding riffs. The subject of enunciation, then, is not so much the vocalist nor even the guitarist, but the machine assemblage. And that is the case not just for a particular performance but also for the proliferating genre itself. The musical form has thrived despite the virtual absence of airplay, by word of mouth, concerts, CDs and also internet connectivity and downloads. Bogue comments that 'performers and listeners self-consciously, and often astutely, negotiate the development of the genre, ensuring its commercial viability while insisting that it remain extreme and marginal to the mainstream of pop music culture' (87).

There are hundreds and hundreds of death metal groups recording and performing in the Americas, Europe and Australia, so many that it sometimes seems as if there are as many death metal bands as there are fans. So while the most famous groups are, as Bogue says, Morbid Angel, Deicide, Cannibal Corpse, Dying Fetus, Cryptopsy, Immolation and Nile, the very success of these groups means that they are always on the crest of 'selling out', that is, distinguishing themselves from the rest of the community and leaving or being expelled from it. Moreover each group aims to outdo the others in its singular relation to death, shock and outrage. Bogue quotes Jon Sutherland of *RIP Magazine*, 'the never ending list of extreme metal bands related to death has been growing for years. Each new band who picks such an evil, degrading, socially unacceptable moniker is certainly not looking for acceptance from the moral majority' (84). Certainly, Bogue agrees, the names are there to offend people, particularly the US Christian coalition, but 'above all, the names are meant to evoke the music which is 'heavy, full, fast, brutal, intense, horrifying, aggressive, and extreme' (84). The never-ending list of shocking names, allied to increases in speed, aggression and volume, describes the line of variation that plays across the 'electronic–industrial–commercial machinic phylum' and entails a continuing experimentation on the social machine, playing with, provoking and distending its organs.

The names support the music in its emphasis on the metallic quality of the machine: its hardness, sharpness, lethality. Bogue writes, 'practitioners of death metal frequently refer to the sound as crunching, grinding, and shredding, the guitars resembling buzzsaws, chainsaws, and (less frequently) jet engines. The project of this music is to create an aggressive sonic machine of destruction, an electronic nonhuman sound shredder' (91). Death metal provides not just the sound track of a war machine, but its very modality in form, speed and intensity. The 'themes of chaos, death, violence, and destruction' (102) enhance the death metal machine to the point of it becoming the double of war in a heightened form. So much so that Christopher Coker claims that such music is used to compensate for the absence of intensity in contemporary warfare. For fighter pilots, wired into a cockpit linked to a network of computers, remote from the effect of their actions, war has become cerebral rather than visceral. 'In the Gulf War', therefore, 'US bomber pilots flew missions with heavy-metal music pumping through their headsets while graphic-simulated displays helped guide their bombs to their targets' (Coker, 2004: 117).

Death metal is the perfect simulacrum of the experience missed by the US fighter pilot as he or she wreaks his or her shock and awe upon unknown populations. The horrific visions of death metal are often, Bogue suggests, simply 'verbal collages, ready-mades constructed from the clippings and footage of daily carnage and abuse' (105). This reportage is thus integrated into an aural package ready to be unleashed on its hearer like a destablising weapon. The US military has also used heavy metal (though not specifically death metal) in military actions against Iraqi insurgents in Fallujah and to torment Iraqi prisoners (see DeGregory, 2004 and BBC News World, 2003). Beyond transgression, reportage and critique, Bogue argues that 'the most fundamental motive in death metal lyrics is to evoke an experience of the body, a libidinal dissolution of the self and of the organism as integrated system … an intensive, acentred, prepersonal, and preindividual affective continuum, an ecstatic, disorganized body of fluxes and flows' (105). 'I MYSELF AM WAR' wrote Bataille in 'Joy Before Death' (1985: 239). And the joy of death metal negates the isolation of the individual in order to render it continuous with the forces of annihilation projecting the world into space, like a woman screaming with her head in flames.

## Atheological ecstasy

One major problem that Bogue acknowledges he has in 'Becoming Metal, Becoming Death...' is in remaining consistent with Deleuze and Guattari's concept of becoming. This is because they assert that 'all becomings commence with and pass through becoming-woman' (277). Since death metal is performed almost exclusively by men for an audience that mostly comprises men, it is difficult to see where one might comfortably become-woman in such a context. But Deleuze and Guattari's concept of becoming-woman is itself highly problematic, not to say paradoxical since it is something that even women have to do if they are to engage in any kind of becoming. The 'woman' in becoming-woman does not refer to any actual woman or to woman as a term of gender. Becoming-woman does not simply involve being born and designated a girl and passing through adolescence – quite the contrary. Becoming-woman does not refer to a 'woman defined by her form, endowed with organs and functions and assigned as a subject' (275). The woman in becoming-woman does not exist as such. Becoming-woman, therefore, would be just as difficult if not more so at a Women's Institute garden party as at a death metal concert.

So what does becoming-woman involve? Given the overt masculinity of the genre, Bogue is reluctant to directly ascribe an incipient becoming-woman to death metal, particularly its lyrical content. Instead he emphasises music that he claims is 'a highly deterritorialized medium susceptible to various becomings through a direct experimentation with abstract sound' (2004: 107). But it seems to me that Bogue does suggest indirectly that there is an incipient becoming-woman in his description of the musicality of death metal, especially in the affects – the joy – that it produces. This joy is not 'phallic' in the sense of building to a violent climax, but involves waves or plateaux of intense affect:

> Musical elements that might be considered masculine are denatured, but through exaggeration rather than elimination. The orgasmic rise to a musical climax becomes in death metal a plateau of constant orgasm, and hence a plateau devoid of climax in the usual sense. (106)

The distinction Bogue makes between a musical climax and a plateau devoid of climax chimes with Deleuze's opposition between pleasure and joy that informs Deleuze and Guattari's concepts in *A Thousand Plateaus* (1988). Deleuze does not give any positive value to pleasure because pleasure interrupts 'the immanent process of desire' (2006: 130–1). Deleuze's distinction between pleasure and desire and its relation to joy is partly worked through a critique of psychoanalysis and Jacques Lacan's concept of desire. For Lacan, unconscious desire is directed by the law of the father in the form of a 'castrating' paternal prohibition. Pleasure is the economic compensation for this prohibition and 'limits the scope of human possibility – the pleasure principle is a principle of homeostasis' (1976: 31). Pleasure places a limit on desire, thus sustaining it as a desire to cross that boundary of pleasure into jouissance (a beyond-of-pleasure, pain).

In its relation to pleasure, Deleuze's conception of desire is quite similar to that of Lacan. The key difference is Deleuze's refusal to accept that desire is determined by some form of paternal authority. He also rejects the term 'jouissance', preferring the term 'joy'. For Deleuze, desire is a process that unrolls a plane of consistency (Deleuze and Parnet, 2002: 89), and 'the process of desire is called "joy", not lack or demand' (100). Joy, the immanent process of desire, replaces both paternal authority and the pleasure principle that is defined by Deleuze as the 'pleasure-interruption' in which desire culminates in a 'sordid' discharge (orgasm). In order for desire to unroll a plane of consistency, it must be transformed from the desire that is established as an effect of the 'castrating' paternal prohibition that produces the 'lack' that is constitutive of desire for Lacan. This transformation can take place through a form of ascesis. Deleuze argues that 'ascesis has always been the condition of desire not its disciplining or prohibition' (Deleuze and Parnet, 2002: 100–1). For Bogue, similarly, 'death metal can undergo a genuine becoming, primarily through an ascetic concentration on and intensification of certain possibilities inherent in rock music' (106).

Ascesis traditionally has a religious reference that is pertinent to death metal in a negative sense, but one of Deleuze's favourite examples is courtly love. The ascesis of courtly love – the abasement, the service, the tests, the whole 'military service' of love – replaces the lack. Furthermore, the process of desire inherent to courtly love is similar, for Deleuze, to masochism. The organisation of humiliation and suffering is not a means of playing out anguish or perversion, nor is its goal the attainment of forbidden pleasures. Rather, it is a 'procedure ... to constitute a body without organs and develop a continuous process of desire ['joy'] which pleasure, on the contrary, would come and interrupt' (Deleuze and Parnet, 2002:101).

For Lacan the climax or pleasure-discharge that results from desire's encounter with its lack is called phallic jouissance. This is also known as the masturbatory jouissance, or the jouissance of the idiot. Lacan actually seems to have as low an opinion of the jouissance of pleasure-discharge as does Deleuze. The jouissance of pleasure-discharge is ultimately aiming at something else, and is always unsatisfactory. But phallic jouissance in Lacan is defined against the jouissance of the Other, sometimes known as feminine jouissance. 'Other jouissance' is located by Lacan 'beyond the phallus', but can be experienced by either gender, although under different conditions for men than for women. Women have available to them both phallic jouissance and the jouissance of the Other, but for men it is one or the other. To experience the jouissance of the Other, men have to give up on phallic jouissance.

Access to this Other jouissance would be a Lacanian way of understanding becoming-woman, since it lies beyond the phallus and the phallic (or 'molar') projection of woman that turns her into a subject and a signifier of patriarchy. Lacan argues that the jouissance of the Other does not lead to transcendence but rather to immanence since it 'puts us on the path of ex-sistence' (Lacan, 1999: 77). That is to say, it puts us on the path of the real which, since it is unsymbolisable, does not exist but ex-sists. Lacan's specific example of the jouissance of the Other, moreover, is not dependent on gender. 'Feminine' jouissance, as opposed to phallic jouissance, has been historically an effect of the ascesis of religious ecstasy, the ecstasy of male and female saints and poets. Accordingly, Lacan further suggests that it is possible to interpret 'one face of the Other, the God face' as being based on feminine jouissance.

In its relative absence of crescendi and decrescendi, musical ups and downs, rises in sentiment, climactic moments evocative of deep feelings, and so on, death metal seeks to evoke a 'distilled affective intensity', aspiring 'to music of constant orgasm' (93). Lyrically, this joy of constant pulsing orgasm, supports one face of God through its 'becoming death', its sadistic violence against women and its blasphemous rage. In death metal, God and women are located in a position of negative equivalence, in a way that is structurally the same as the poetry of Neoplatonism (Dante, Petrarch). Some groups specialise in songs about killing women (Cannibal Corpse, for example, whose album *The Bleeding*, 1994 includes tracks such as 'Fucked with a Knife' and 'Stripped, Raped and Strangled') while others concentrate on killing God. Yet Deicide's indefatigable blaspheming of God in the name of Satan discloses a deep ambivalence towards Him and his double: 'God is the reason we live in dismay / It is his will that this world's suffering / ... / You are the one who killed his own son / We are the ones you're blaming it on ('Blame it On God', 1997). Satan's own reign, however, simply promises more dismay and suffering, 'When Satan rules his world / Disease, run free, killing / When Satan rules his world / Religion, infliction, obscene / When Satan rules his world / Witness, dismissed, executed ('When Satan Rules His World', 1995).

The correlation of God, women and the jouissance of the Other that supports it in an intensely ambivalent passion of love-and-hatred (or *hainamoration*, to use Lacan's neologism) recalls Bataille's short story *Madame Edwarda* (1989). Elisabeth Roudinesco, the historian of psychoanalysis in France, records that the seminar in which Lacan spoke about the jouissance of the Other, 'the jouissance of the (under erasure) woman' as an experience of unknowing, was turned into 'an act of homage to the Bataille of *Madame Edward*, to the absolute figure of the hatred and love of God' (Roudinesco, 1990: 524). *Madame*

*Edwarda* is a short story of the narrator's visit to a Parisian brothel and his revelatory encounter with a prostitute:

> She was seated, she held one long leg stuck up in the air, to open her crack yet wider she used her fingers to draw the folds of skin apart ... 'Why', I stammered in a subdued tone, 'why are you doing that?' 'You can see for yourself', she said, 'I'm GOD'. (150)

God reconfigured as the genitals of a crazy whore is a blasphemy that links atheological inner experience to eroticism. God is a cunt: an impossible object of desire that comprises both finite being and unknown infinity, offering a glimpse of sacred excess. Her divinity, moreover, is guaranteed by the joy she experiences in a sexual encounter witnessed by the narrator:

> fountain of boiling water, heartbursting furious tideflow – on and on, weirdly, unendingly; that stream of luxury, its strident inflexion ... Her body, her face swept in ecstasy were abandoned to the unspeakable coursing and ebbing ... from the bottom of my desolation I sensed her joy's torrent run free. My anguish resisted the pleasure I ought to have sought. Edwarda's pain-wrung pleasure filled me with an exhausting impression of bearing witness to a miracle. (158)

The narrator encounters not simply a woman experiencing an orgasm but a different plateau of experience that seems consistent, for him, with the exuberant continuity of things, the divine totality. Joy's torrent flows beyond bodily constraints and boundaries to engulf even the narrator who gives up on his own (phallic) pleasure to be filled by the miracle of hers. Eroticism, then, for both male and female characters in different ways, involves an opening on to something entirely other, becoming-woman, perhaps, the gateway to every other kind of becoming ... becoming-animal, becoming-machine, becoming-metal ...

For Bogue, while 'death metal is all male in its tonality', it remains 'curiously plotless and floating in its structure, its movement devoid of conquest or return. The death vocal, finally, deepens and hence hypermasculinizes the voice, but to the point that it ceases to sound human, its groans and growls resembling those of some unspecified animal or machine' (2004: 106–7). In the intense volume of the low-pulse and high-speed blastbeats, bizarre as it may seem, the mass of lumpen and abject masculinity, the scuffed leather and ripped denim, 'the bodies heavily tattooed, the expressions tough, mean and angry', experience their plateaux of joy as the mosh pit becomes a vulvo-uterine space of constant orgasm.

That this hypermasculinised yet vulvic space of becoming also pulses with a rage against God is essential, although it varies in its significance. Judging by the relative lack of attention given to it by Bogue, it is the aspect that attracts and interests him least. He regards it as an expression of 'atheistic materialism' that sometimes seeks a justification in the writings of Anton Szandor La Vey, founder of the Church of Satan, or simply a provocative 'resistance to conventional Christian morality' (103). For provocative Christian moralist Alice

Cooper, it is simply a gimmick (quoted in Dunn and McFadyen, 2006). This is certainly not the case in Norway, however, where violent anti-Christianity has involved black metal and Viking metal group members burning down churches in the name of a return to its ancient Norse traditions.

If it isn't bound up in some ethnic or cultural battle, blasphemy is of course illogical. Yet Nick Land, in his book *Thirst for Annihilation* (1992a) – a book whose title and themes seem very consistent with those of death metal – insists on the importance of blasphemy and in so doing makes a case also for the importance of Satanism to death metal. So what is the point of raging against something you know to be an illusion? To do so is either to rage pointlessly into the void or make a hysterical attempt to wake God up. For Land, the fact that 'God has wrought such loathsomeness without even having existed only exacerbates the hatred pitched against him. An atheism that does not hunger for God's blood is an inanity' (62). Land contends that 'anyone who does not exult at the thought of driving nails through the limbs of the Nazarene is something less than an atheist; merely a disappointed slave' (63). Deicide's 'Crucifixion' (1990) on the group's debut album similarly exults obsessively in the torture and death of 'the chosen, righteous one', setting the tone for all their subsequent recordings.

The crucifixion is for Christians the most sublime of all symbols, the Passion of Christ being an object of ecstatic contemplation for religious mystics throughout the ages. These are precisely the people, Lacan suggests, who 'get the idea that there must be a jouissance that goes beyond' the 'phallus' (76). This is a jouissance based in love and hatred, or rather a hatred that is indistinguishable from love and beyond both, an emotion worthy of God and God's own jouissance and the 'measureless expenditures of energy' (Bataille, 1992a: 18) that would represent. For Bataille, in elevating and nailing Christ upon a cross, 'humankind attains a summit of evil. But it's exactly from having attained it that humanity ceases being separate from God' (18). Lacan comments drily that through such a correspondence, Christianity 'ended up inventing a God such that he is the one who gets off (*jouit*)!' (1999: 76), who comes. The 'communication', in Bataille's sense, of human beings is guaranteed by this evil (1992a: 18), and the participation in God's jouissance that expands into a collective joy before death. Christian communication and community is therefore sustained in relation to evil and the apprehension of death, but it is the same with the community of death metal, since their 'zero belief sustains belief in zero', in the definitive emptiness of death, that only sustains life in its fullest intensity.

Commenting on the lyrics that are characteristic of death metal, Bogue highlights its 'obsession with death ... with the death at the heart of life, the desire/ death of zero intensity, which is figured as life in death or after death, the living death of zombies, vampires, ghouls, and devils, the undead, the already dead, the living dead: a becoming-death in the lyrics to accompany the becoming metal of the sound' (2004: 105). There is an obsession with death in two senses, then. The immanence of death that illuminates life's intensity, and the productivity that is generated through the operativity of zero, the life-in-death of the 'nihil from which creation proceeds, the undifferentiated cosmic zero' (Land, 1992a: 90) that is figured in the form of the zombie, vampire, and so on.

If poetry is a kind of money, since it is the measureless measure of all literary exchange, then so too is zero, suggests Land. It is 'a redundant operator; adding nothing in order to make things hum' (90–1). Karl Marx, famously, regarded capital as a vampiric system. 'Capital', Marx wrote, 'is dead labour which, vampire-like, lives only by sucking living labour, and lives the more labour it sucks' (Marx, 1976: 342). Capital establishes value neither in the living nor in the dead but simply in terms of exchange and money in the ghostly form of the commodity. Once exchanged, the destiny of the commodity is to haunt the landfills as waste, or as redundant information, accumulating a reservoir of uselessness and valuelessness. This introduces a third area where death operates in death metal. Becoming-death is also related to becoming-capital, an essential element in the 'electronic–industrial–commercial machinic phylum' that provides the substratum for its existence. Becoming-capital denotes a locus of success and redundancy, selling and selling out, reduction as at best vinyl or at worst pure digital information circulating on discs or floating through bandwidth, substanceless pure vibration.

Land points out that when Marx associates capital with death he is only drawing the final consequence from the correspondence between money and zero: 'Surplus value comes out of labour-power, but surplus production comes out of nothing. This is why capital production is the consummating phase of nihilism … Modernity is virtual thanocracy guided insidiously by zero; the epoch of the death of God' (1992a: 91).

The joy before death that is immanent to the process of desiring capital is, in supercapitalism, also a desire for war: 'War in its intensive state is desire itself, convulsive recurrence, unilateral zero' (149). Furthermore, this war does not stop and does not fail to engulf everyone as it rages across the globe.

> There has been a revolution in Hell
> Satan hangs from a gibbet and rots
> wreathed in the howls of anarchy
> out there beyond the stars
> the cold wind of zero rages without interdiction

(132)

## Notes

1    The song 'Purity' was on the original master for the debut *Slipknot* (1999) album, but ultimately left off, apparently because of a legal dispute. It reappeared on the *Disasterpieces* DVD (2002).

# 11

# All is war

Attack at dawn with sonic horns
Quranic forms and phonic guns
Sufi surfing on boards of steel
Laser sim tars coded zikar
Love and hate approach the state
The statue of liberty falls prostrate ...
Dream team salahuddin
The citizens they build a mosque on ground zero

(Fun'da'mental, 'All is War', 2006)

## 11 September 2001

The epoch in which America has been known as the Great Satan is more or less the same as the epoch of the naming of rogue states generally. Consolidated by the end of the cold war, that epoch has, according to Jacques Derrida, been brought to a close by the attack on the Pentagon and the World Trade Center on 11 September 2001 (2005: 95–107). The cold war that was defined by the nuclear stand-off between the US and USSR after world war two began to un-wind with the USSR's debilitating war in Afghanistan in which the US-funded Mujahideen insurgents exposed the weakness of the Soviet military outside their spectacular Kremlin displays. The war crippled an already weak Soviet economy, forcing President Gorbachev to withdraw his troops in 1989, the year the Berlin Wall came down. Ironically, a civil war between the victorious Mujahideen saw the emergence of the hard line Islamicist regime of the Taliban. The Ayatollah Khomeini, already in power after the Iranian revolution of 1979, named America the Great Satan, for his own reasons, on 5 November of that year. The USSR entered Afghanistan a month later, on Christmas day, at the request of the imperilled Marxist government that had became further threat-ened by the proximity of Iran and Islamic militancy. These were the events that determined the end of the cold war and what followed.

The Iranian reference to Great Satan the seducer is more of a warning to devout Muslims to beware the secular attractions of the West than a direct provocation. The Great Satan is a reference of jihad not because he represents the infidel against which Muslims must wage war. Jihad or holy war refers to the battle of renunciation that one must engage in against oneself, a renunciation threatened by the satanic, seductive pleasures on offer in the land of secular states. It is America that takes its way of life as a measure and guarantor of universal good in the field of international relations, thereby raising the stakes to a metaphysical level. Thus, it is the USA, in the voices of successive American presidents, that evokes the language of evil in a direct challenge to other states who constitute an 'axis of evil' or who support 'evil doers' and enemies of freedom. The axis of evil is comprised of a number of 'rogue states', and it is in relation to these states that America justifies itself as the 'great protector', in the worlds of Colin Powell. To understand why America's role as 'protector' necessitates that it become satanic, it is helpful to look at Derrida's argument on the fate of the rogue state in the post-cold-war period. This fate seems to herald one of a number of possible ends of the state, not just rogue states, but the state-form generally and with it, necessarily, America.

The phrase 'rogue state' has been used as a denunciation intermittently since the 1960s to describe the internal, non-democratic politics of various nations. But it is only since the end of the cold war that it has gained currency as an indicator of international behaviour breaking the spirit of international law. This extension, Derrida shows, increased during the presidency of Bill Clinton in the context of what was being called international terrorism. For Derrida the setting and stage for the use of the rhetoric of rogue states derives from the fact that the United States and its allies can no longer rely on a majority in the General Assembly of the United Nations because of the decolonisation of the past few decades. The exception perhaps is in the case of 'international terrorism', where it is backed up by notional rogue states that threaten the sovereignty of all states. But even though the General Assembly of the United Nations may have been becoming more democratic, and therefore frustrating to some states' own interests, it has no power to make binding or enforceable decisions. That power lies with the Security Council which, since the end of world war two, has been biased, through the possession of the power of veto, to the permanent members, the USA, UK and USSR (now Russia), with the later addition of France and China. In the context of the United Nations, it is only the Security Council that has the force of effective sovereignty.

Derrida's argument is not just that the United States and its allies have, in their actions inside and outside the Security Council, abused that power through a highly interested use of the veto. It is not just that they have demonstrated that 'the most *roguish* of rogue states are those that circulate and make use of a concept like "rogue state", with the language, rhetoric, juridical discourse, and strategico-military consequences we all know' (2005: 96). Derrida cites works by Noam Chomsky (2000), William Blum (2000) and others which provide evidence of this and other abuses by America and its allies, but his analysis seeks to go deeper. Derrida's concern is more with developing a political thought that works through the history of the concept of sovereignty itself that can deconstruct its structure and logic (102).

While it is true that, as Bataille claims, his own notion of sovereignty has little to do with that of states, a satanic link with this concept of sovereignty is disclosed as Derrida pursues its logic to the point of impossibility. At the heart of the logic of sovereignty is a satanic principle: *non serviam*, the Devil's motto, 'I will not serve' (Bataille, 1990: 34 see also Botting and Wilson, 2001b: 40). 'I will not serve' is the impulse from which the modern secular state emerges out of theocratic, monarchical and absolutist regimes and states. As Derrida shows, this principle of satanic sovereignty must necessarily remain in reserve, silently at the heart of the state, even when its role is to protect and serve the people and their democratic institutions:

> A pure sovereignty is indivisible or it is not at all … This indivisibility excludes it in principle from being shared, from time and from language … The paradox, which is always the same, is that sovereignty is incompatible with universality even though it is called for by every concept of international, and thus universal or universalizable, and thus democratic, law. There is no sovereignty without force, without the force of the strongest, whose reason – the reason of the strongest – is to win out over [*avoir raison de*] everything. (2005: 101)

The sovereign force of the strongest power is necessary to guarantee democracy, but as such it necessarily cannot be subject to it, and must always threaten it with betrayal or abuse. It is the satanic aporia at the heart of any sovereign state whatever its constitution or democratic institutions and process. Any form of universal democracy beyond the nation-state and citizenship, would require a 'supersovereignty' that also could not but betray it. Therefore, the 'monstrous' abuses of the Security Council of the United Nations 'or of certain superpowers that sit on it permanently, is an abuse at the very beginning, well before any particular, secondary abuse. Abuse of power is constitutive of sovereignty itself' (Derrida, 2005: 102). Since every state, even a notional universal state (and the state-form as universal), is always already a rogue, then there can be no specific rogue states. But that is not why the epoch of rogue states is coming to an end. It is not just the facile reversal which determines that if everyone is a rogue, then there are no more rogues. There may be multiple rogues with devilment in their make-up, but there is only one Great Satan.

Great Satan was already defined by his rage before the attack on the World Trade Center confirmed itself, for itself, as the sole protector of the West. In an address to the United Nations in 1993, President Clinton inaugurated the 'politics of retaliation' by declaring that America 'would make use whenever it deemed appropriate of article 51, that is, of 'the article of exception' and 'act multilaterally when possible, but unilaterally when necessary' (Derrida, 2005: 103). Subsequently, as various Secretaries of State (both Democrat and

Republican) have asserted, the US will maintain, militarily if necessary, 'uninhibited access to key markets, energy supplies, and strategic resources' (104). That is to say, whatever the Americans deem threatening to their interests would give them good reason, without the requirement to consult the international community of nations, to attack, destabilise or destroy another state, hence, up to 9/11, America's need for rogue states to justify its actions (that of acting as the most powerful rogue state). After 9/11, the United Nations, somewhat redundantly, officially authorised America to act as it had already been doing throughout the 1990s when it approved all measures deemed necessary 'to protect itself anywhere in the world against so-called international terrorism' (104).

The irony, of course, is that the United States was not attacked by a state, not even a rogue state. That certain states have suffered the consequences of Great Satan's rage does not change that. America is now committed to expending ever-increasing amounts of rhetorical, financial and military resources in the name of homeland security and the 'war on terror'. But, as Derrida insists, the threat to America 'can no longer be contained when it comes neither from an already constituted state nor even from a potential state that might be treated as a rogue state' (105). All such expenditure does is produce more combatants, across innumerable states, inside and outside America, whose means can only escalate.

For Derrida, the biggest trauma of 9/11 is the 'apprehension of a threat that is *worse* and still *to come*' (104). What is the worst that can happen, for Derrida?

> The worst to come is a nuclear attack that threatens to destroy the state apparatus of the United States, that is, of a democratic state whose hegemony is as obvious as it is precarious, in crisis, a state assumed to be the guarantor, the sole and ultimate guardian, of world order for all legitimate, sovereign states. (105)

Derrida looks towards a horizon as bleak as any American presidency could wish. The destruction of America heralds the end of civilisation both in the form of modern sovereign states and the new world order promised under US protectorate. Great Satan's rage must be sustained by the prospect of being thrown into the lake of nuclear fire that he is showing every sign of bringing about through trying to prevent it. When homeland security requires the negation and the remaking of the whole world in its own image through the combination of economic and military force, all that is left is the pure negativity that is defined by death. The trumpet of freedom that is borne on the cold winds of ground zero resounds in the silence of absolute destruction: 'the battleground we're given' (Ministry 'Great Satan', 2005).

In the instances of popular cultural negativity that have been discussed in the previous chapters, America can be seen as a negative-land set on a train of negative-becoming, a becoming nonAmerican in necessarily multiple ways. Indeed, at the antipodes, becoming nonAmerican denotes both the threshold of absolute destruction but also, if it can be avoided, the threshold of the 'democracy-to-come'. The latter would see, at the very least, the end of the reign of Great Satan, protector of Western values, and of the wholesale transformation of the 'strange and supposedly all-powerful institution called the Security Council' (Derrida, 2005: 98).

## Becoming nonAmerican at the end(s) of the state

> You are either with us or with the terrorists (George W. Bush)
>
> Nous sommes tous Americaines (*Le Monde*)

A postcard depicting the smoking ruins of the World Trade Center in lower Manhattan on 9/11 bears the legend 'All of us are American', translating the famous cover of *Le Monde* issued on 12 September 2001. The statement echoes President George W. Bush's announcement to the rest of the world that 'You are either with us or with the terrorists', and his declaration that 'we wage a war to save civilization itself ... We have our marching orders. My fellow Americans, let's roll!' (President Bush quoted in *Le Monde diplomatique*, 2006). America is thus identified as the bearer and protector of civilisation itself, and all the people of the world must recognise themselves as American in so far they must become part of, and identify with, this transnational, global 'us' or face war with America.

The supposition thus arises that 'we' Americans are on the path of a new global politics in which the pre-eminent question concerns becoming nonAmerican. As Derrida comments, in its declaration of the war on terror, America as a sovereign state no longer opposes itself essentially to 'an enemy that takes either an actual or virtual state form' (2005: 155). The war on terror, that is to say a war that takes no nation or state as its object and yet is prosecuted over the terrain of other nations, including America itself, announces a profound change in international relations. Indeed, it declares that there is no such thing as an international relation. In its sovereign right to defend itself in this global war, America may respect no national boundaries, no other national interests, no other jurisdictions. The statement 'you are either with us or with the terrorists', while it is addressed to states actually abolishes them through homogenising all the different independent states into a polarity of 'us and them'. It may seem simplistic, but Bush speaks a truth about the polarising logic of his country's pre-eminence; it is not just a peculiarity of his own regime in the White House. Bush's statement discloses a necessary logic inherent to America's position of overwhelming military and absolute nuclear supremacy that divides the world into an actual 'us' and a virtual 'them'.

Bush's statement makes it clear that no state, however tiny or insignificant, may safely express disinterest in, disagreement with, or even reservations concerning this war on terror without risking American condemnation and accusations about harbouring its enemies. This does not mean that a particular state will receive automatic sanction from the US, but the threat is implicit. Whether we recognise it or not, whether we like it or not, we have all become subject to American power and become servants of its interests, mobilised by a transcendent empiricism that finds foes wherever they may be, irrespective of national boundaries or the laws of states. Just as rogue states were defined by Robert S. Litwak, a member of President Clinton's team who served on the National Security staff, as 'basically whomever the United States says it is' (cited in Derrida, 2005: 96), so America's enemies are wherever they find them. At the same time, these empirically found objects transcend all national affiliation. They represent no one and are afforded no legal protection.

America can act in this way, of course, precisely because of its unmatched and unmatchable might. No sane state will ever declare war on it, certainly Afghanistan and Iraq did not oppose the US in any formal way before they were attacked. Nor does America need to act unilaterally, since there are always peoples beyond America's borders ready to heed the call to defend 'us' and 'our' way of life, or to provide logistical support. Any liberal or Democratic administration, no matter how theoretically committed to the ideal of international law, can default to this position at any time, and indeed carries this position with it to any negotiating table. All that the Bush regime has done is to make this default position explicit in its policy of pre-emptive strike.

Bush's statement exposes and nakedly defines a state of affairs extant since America's power became unmatched and unmatchable: that is, since the end of the cold war. This state of affairs had been largely implicit since that moment. Subsequent to that point, and the announcement of the new world order, it had seemed, especially given the Republican desire to continually 'roll back the state', that America was content to be the subject of globalisation. Government ceded to management, law to contract, power to technological forms of control and the economics of transnational corporatism. The attack on the World Trade Center, however, brought America back to its national desire with a vengeance. To use the discourse of Alexandre Kojève, a discourse, as we have seen, favoured by some around the White House, America appeared to be losing itself in its simple negation of the Other, only to be awoken to self-consciousness by the Other's desire. From being the contented subject of globalisation, America suddenly became subject to the globalised force of the Other. The response was to rouse a national consciousness back to itself. In his address to Congress shortly after the attack, George W. Bush announced, 'this country will define our times, not be defined by them' (The White House, 2001b).

The statement betrayed the anxiety that America had become subject to global forces even as it expressed a determination to resist that subjection. This resistance took the form of the reassertion of unconditional rights of national sovereignty, and the immediate prosecution of devastating wars in Afghanistan and Iraq which made no sense in terms of wars against threatening states, and which did not require any justification in international law.

This sudden hostility to the arrival of another globalised force provides the context in which Bush can threaten war on all of you who are not explicitly with us. All of you who do not share our interests: that is, subsume your own interests to our interests. It goes without saying that no other nation on earth could even think of making such a statement, issuing such a challenge.

Bush's statement makes symbolic America's desire not simply to become an empire of culturally and economically colonised or subjugated nations or the hegemonic power of a cabal of developed nations exploiting and controlling the growth of undeveloped ones, but practically to become the last state. It could be argued that at the end of the twentieth and the beginning of the twenty-first centuries America has been the only meaningful state effective in the world. There has been, and is, America and there is the world of markets, resources and populations friendly or hostile. These populations are of course organised into nations and states, for domestic purposes, but the latter have no consequences internationally. There is no effective international domain. For this situation to change requires an alliance of Russia, China and Iran as nuclear powers based around Russian and Iranian oil. It is the goal of America to prevent that coalition at all costs, and for it to remain pre-eminent as the last state. Yet, America as the last state necessarily sets itself on the path of becoming nonAmerican.

One way or another, the pre-eminent question of global politics in the twenty-first century concerns, in a variety of different ways, becoming nonAmerican; it is the formula for twenty-first-century politics. A formula not in the sense of a programme for the future, but in the sense of a pure form that does not determine any specific content. The formula connects with other ideas concerned with the subject of becoming and of the coming of a future politics or a future conception of the political. While the notion of 'coming' or of a future 'to come' (*l'avenir* – in Derrida's terms) is not at all the same as the notion of becoming, the former will be, or is already (or will have been), intimately related to the latter. That is to say that the coming (or indeed the arrival) of the Other is an event coterminous with becoming nonAmerican. A number of points plot the horizon for becoming nonAmerican that seem to me to be axiomatic.

## Axiomatic

1    As it seeks to define and determine its times and its space, America begins to encompass the whole world, therefore overrunning its own national boundaries and identity. As the great protector of civilisation, America's interests in the international sphere become overwhelmingly everyone's interests; there are no other interests. Or rather, other interests, other

possibilities take a purely virtual form that describes the locus of becoming nonAmerican. This means that there is a virtual or potential 'them' immanent, to the civilised 'us' that can emerge at any time, irrespective of nationality or cause.

2    Becoming nonAmerican is the formula for twenty-first-century politics (and a new concept of the political) precisely because it has a purely formal structure that contains no specific cultural content. Further, it predetermines no content. Therefore it is not a question – and this cannot be stressed enough – of being anti-American. It is not a question of loving or hating America for whatever reason, justified or not. It is not a question of simply rejecting this 'we' that mobilises us all as American and negating it on the basis of one's national, cultural or ethnic identity as Arab or Irish or Chinese or Somalian. The category of the American 'us' already encompasses and hyphenates these national differences in the pre-existing form of Arab-American, Irish-American, Chinese-American, Somali-American, and so on. 'We' can hyphenate endlessly over the backdrop of a virtual 'them' that is supposed to refuse the paradox of an American multiculturalism. Similarly, it is not a question of rejecting American culture, as if that were possible, and refusing to drink Coca-Cola or read Susan Sontag. Correlatively, it is not a question of rejecting the hyperbolic expansion of America on the *basis* of a specific American identity or culture, as if there were one. Always heterogeneous, linguistically, ethnically and culturally, the idea of a single shared American national culture is a mirage, an effect of a historical European desire, and a hegemonic class currently dominant in American culture and politics. A quotation from a classic of that hegemonic culture, Herman Melville's *Redburn*, gives fine expression to the irony inherent in America's eurocentric world-wide heritage:

> You can not spill a drop of American blood without spilling the blood of the whole world. Be he Englishman, Frenchman, German, Dane or Scot ... we are not a nation, so much as a world ... we are without father or mother ... We are the heirs of all time. (cited in Deleuze, 1995: 85–6)

The quotation places Bush's statement claiming the world into a history of similar statements, just as it perceives the world as primarily European. But it is important to take seriously the claim that America is the world, that 'we are the world' as Michael Jackson sang, and perceive the world in all its heterogeneity rather than homogeneity. There is no necessity that the coming of American national cultures should be determined by its colonising/migrant European history. There is every possibility that it could be dissolved in the creation of something quite different along pragmatic, that is to say, quintessentially American lines: 'We understand the novelty of American thought when we see pragmatism as an attempt to transform the world, to think a new world or new man in so far as they *create themselves*' (Deleuze, 1995: 86). Pragmatics would do nothing to stop and would perhaps precipitate America becoming nonAmerican culturally according to a principle of heterogeneity. Whether politically or culturally, then, becoming nonAmerican is a formula that formulates an essentially contentless principle in which 'we Americans' are transformed along with 'our' culture.

3   As Derrida suggests in *Rogues*, the extraordinary war on terror begins to disintegrate the concept of the state the moment it fails to take the state as its object and therefore totally opens up the concept of war. Since the enemy is immanent to all states, America's own terrain cannot fail to become a field of engagement like any other, has already become one. Because of the transcendent empiricism of the constitution of the enemy, its existence below the threshold of domestic administrations and jurisdictions, power enters a different domain and modality. It is no longer sovereign authority operating exceptionally in a zone of indistinction (Agamben, 2005), nor is it disciplinarity operating in the institutional shadows of the law (Foucault, 2003). Rather, the moment it dispenses with the state, power opens itself to the war immanent to both sovereign authority and disciplinarity. For Foucault, in the lectures collected as *Society Must Be Defended* (2003), politics is war by other means. If politics begins to disintegrate when the state no longer takes itself as its object, this disintegration threatens to unleash the war that state politics had stratified in institutions, economic inequalities, language, law, discipline, and so on. The particular relationship of power maintained by laws and state institutions is disclosed and unleashed and America itself risks unravelling in a general conflagration of heterogeneous forces. 'I would rather be fighting them here than in New York', commented Paul Bremer, head of the American civilian command in Iraq (cited in Pieterse, 2004: 122), in a statement that betrayed an anxiety not that Iraq might launch an invasion of the American Eastern Seaboard, but that the war might erupt within the boundaries of America at any time.

This is where the formula differs from the analysis of Giorgio Agamben. I do not see the Guantanamo detainees so much as instances of the 'bare life' over which sovereignty erects its biopolitical authority. Rather, the camp where the detainees are placed outside of state legal protection and entitlement, stripped of all forms of identity, is the site and symptom of the event of becoming nonAmerican in a world dominated by the last state, America.

## Form and event

The idea that America constitutes the last state should be distinguished from the notion of the universal homogeneous state that was publicised by Francis

Fukuyama at the time of the end of the cold war. For Fukuyama, the universal homogeneous state is supposed to mark the triumph of capitalism and liberal democracy and be exemplified by the American way of life. At the same time, it is significant that ideas drawn from Alexandre Kojève and Leo Strauss have been very influential to a number of the neoconservatives prominent in both the anti-Clinton campaigns and the Bush regimes. These political 'Straussians', as some of them are known, appear to have a highly ambivalent view about America as the embodiment of the universal homogeneous state, and correlatively of the American consumer as the embodiment of Nietzsche's last man. The idea is neatly summed up by Alexandre Kojève:

> The *American way of life* was the kind of life proper to the post-historical period and that the presence today of the United States in the World prefigures the future 'eternal present' of all of humanity. Thus Man's return to animality seemed no longer a possibility still to come, but an already present certainty. (cited in Derrida, 1994: 72)

For Kojève and the Straussians, the American way of life is a problem not just because it marks the end of history, but because it also marks the end of humanity, philosophically speaking, since it returns 'man' to the 'animality' proper to a life of consumption. This view is essentially shared by Giorgio Agamben, for whom animality is another figure for the bare life over which the biopolitical state erects its sovereignty (see Agamben, 2004a: 76). It seems possible, as we have seen, that this is a diagnosis both shared and welcomed by the Straussians. Furthermore, in identifying an Islamicist enemy that invokes the austere martial legacy of the early years of Islam, the neoconservatives could not have a more perfect and useful foe. The Islamicist desire to evoke the early embattled legacy of Islam as a means of fomenting a holy war against the West, finds its mirror image in the neoconservative desire to re-enchant politics and reinvigorate 'man' through war. In the image of quasi-mythical figures like Osama bin Laden, jihad is indeed transformed from a personal struggle to a war against the infidel.

In a chapter on Islam as 'the conquering society', Bataille cites a French study by Emile Dermenghem on the values of Islam which argues that early Islam saw that one means of ensuring the discipline for the personal jihad lay in the permanent practice of war. Bataille notes that it is one thing to inspire people with religious enthusiasm, but it is equally important to give them something to do. The imams of the Muslim community, Dermenghem argues, felt it their duty to incite jihad against the peoples that bordered and threatened their territory. The military commanders first had to establish that these adjacent people knew the teachings of Islam, and that they refused to follow them. If that was the case, then they had to be fought: 'The holy war was permanent, therefore, at the borders of Islam. There was no real peace possible between Moslems and infidels' (cited in Bataille, 1988: 84). While Dermenghem sees this perpetual war as a purely theoretical notion that could never be practically sustained, involving of necessity pragmatic accommodation of the infidels, Bataille sees in it the formula of a means of expansion and indefinite growth: 'Islam is a discipline applied to a methodical effort of conquest' (84). Reminiscent of puritanism in so many ways, particularly in its austerity and iconoclasm, early pious Islam renounces the spectacular rituals and sacrifices of Christianity, just as it renounced the wasteful expenditures of Arab tribal cultures, indeed 'any expenditure of force that was not external violence turned against the infidel enemy' (89). In its synthesis of religious and military forms, curtailing sacrifice and limiting religion to morality, Islam provides a robust mirror of militant American puritanism.

The problem is that early Islam is not actually the mirror that confronts the Great Satan. The spectaculars claimed and promised by Osama bin Laden and his followers have nothing to do with Islam. Precisely *as* spectaculars, they are manifestations of satanic seduction in negative form, the power of which they presumably seek to turn back on itself. Their introduction of sacrifice in the form of a death cult of mass murder and suicide is a grotesque perversion of Islamic religious discipline turned to martial ends. Given their Western context and connections, it is perhaps possible to see in this perversion the *père version* which Lacan suggests involves both veering away from and veering towards the father by way of the symptom, or *objet petit a*: 'perversion (*père version*) being the sole guarantee of this function of father, which is the function of the symptom, as I have written it' (1982: 167). The spectacular actions of Al Qaeda indicated that they are turning away from Islam and Allah, even as they turn towards Great Satan in an attempt to stir up his rage. These acts are *for* America, just as they are products *of* supercapitalism, using all its technological and financial resources, its systems of communications and networks, that are staged for the gaze of the West for no other reason than to become the perverse object of its rage and desire. They are the acts of 'hyphenated' Americans, first because the negativity of Qutb and Bin Laden owes more to an ambivalence towards America than it does to any affirmation of Islam. And second, as Paul Berman argues in *Terror and Liberalism* (2003), the roots of their cult of death owes nothing to Islam and everything to a European heritage of anarchism and nihilism from eighteenth-century libertarianism to twentieth-century Fascism (see Berman, 2003: 50; see also Grey, 2003: 27–43 for the suggestion that Al Qaeda is a modern rather than premodern phenomenon).

The declaration of the war on terror, then, brings America back to its (historical) desire, but through confronting nothing other than that desire in reverse form, in the mirror of globalisation. Like Travis Bickle in Scorsese's film *Taxi Driver*, America is held in a stand-off with its own image, the great protector preparing in the mirror his act of terror aimed at cleaning the evil-doing scum off the streets – 'Are you looking at *me*?' The absolute negativity of the challenge 'You are either with us or with the terrorists' envisages a stand-off that would ultimately plunge America back to the mythical origin of history, and therefore, to the inauguration of a different, essentially nonAmerican history in which it finds itself no longer the state of liberated slaves, but the master-state engaged in a vain search for a recognisable foe. As anyone familiar with the dialectic knows, the future does not belong with the master.

This potential renaissance, which necessarily sets, or resets, history on the path of becoming nonAmerican, recalls Derrida's very brief reading of Kojève in *Specters of Marx* (1994). There Derrida notes how Kojève changed his opinion concerning the fate of humanity in the 'eternal present' (or enduring freedom) of the American way of life. Derrida shows how, through revising his view, Kojève acknowledged that any renaissance of historicity for post-historical man necessarily implied some form of becoming nonAmerican. Famously, it was a trip to Japan which provided the occasion for his change of view.

What is significant is not the speculation concerning the specific non-American content (Japan) of Kojève's change of view on the beginnings of a historicity 'beyond man and beyond history' and certainly as such beyond America, but its emphasis on form. Kojève determines that 'post-historical Man' should 'continue to *detach* "forms" from their "contents", doing this not in order to trans-form the latter actively, but in order to *oppose himself* as a pure "form" to himself and to others, taken as whatever sorts of "contents"' (cited in Derrida, 1994: 74). Derrida's reading highlights in Kojève's formalism and this 'indifference to the content' not a negation of content, but an opening to any content whatever. This indifference marks the 'opening to the event and to the future as such' since it 'conditions the interest in and not the indifference to anything whatsoever, to all content in general' (73).

Similarly, becoming nonAmerican is simply a *formula* for the future in which any content is possible, indeed a multiplicity of contents become possible. Becoming nonAmerican is a 'purely formal' formula for the future, for any future. As such it is also 'the necessarily pure and purely necessary form of the future as such, in its being-necessarily-promised, prescribed, assigned, enjoined, in the necessarily formal necessity of its possibility' (73). It does not promise this or that, but simply promises 'some historicity' and 'a future-to-come' (73). In its pure formalism, then, becoming nonAmerican has the same structure as that which Derrida nicknames 'the messianic without messianism' (73). It has the same structure as the 'emancipatory promise as promise' (75), which promises a democracy to come. Only through becoming nonAmerican will we approach the democracy-to-come. The democracy-to-come bears no relation to the democracy 2go (served with freedom fries) that is exported and imposed by American violence and conquest.

Indeed, the group Negativland disclose how specifically American content can mark out a locus of becoming nonAmerican precisely through extenuating the negativity of that content, hollowing it out into pure form, particularly that associated with its advertising and marketing. Over the past twenty years

Negativland have exposed the negative-land that is immanent to American supercapitalism. After *Escape from Noise* (1987) Negativland pioneered the method of aural collage that utilised samples of copyrighted material to anti-corporate, anti-copyright ends. Although representative of the Californian underground, the brief notoriety achieved by this album helped to give further definition to the political issues associated with other more commercially suc-cessful forms reliant on sampling like rap and nu metal. Negativland were among the first American groups to build their work and reputation around samples that assemble a montage of citations and startling aural juxtapositions. They construct aural collages that function like a nightmarish suburban unconscious. It is an audio world 'where scenes of guerrilla warfare or starvation are arbi-trarily mixed with bra commercials and public service announcements for Gulf Oil' (Thom Holmes, *Recordings Magazine*, cited in Negativland, 2006). On tracks like 'Car bomb', 'Methods of Torture', 'Time Zones' and 'Christianity is Stupid', *Escape from Noise* negotiates the relation between information and noise, hu-man and machine, advertising and propaganda, and (cold) war and terror with subversive humour. 'The Playboy Channel', for example, documents how a sub-scriber to the porn cable station is tormented by the interference of an indus-trial noise that continually prevents his orgasm. The demonic insistence of the drill-like noise survives six visits from the Playboy technician (he is eventually fired) to the point where the consumer realises that this noise is much more important than him or his orgasm. 'That noise is more important than your whole life', confirms the narrator of the song, as its object suffers total onto-logical collapse.

While they have been operating since 1975, the group achieved notoriety in the late 1980s and early 1990s through two events associated with their work. In 1987 they released a bogus press statement announcing that their live shows were being cancelled because 'Christianity is Stupid' from *Escape from Noise* was responsible for a recent axe murder. The media furore is documented in *Helter Stupid* (1989) which details and satirises the process whereby the media 'sell the past in a future that hasn't happened, but which becomes old news' (Negativland, 2006). In 1991 they were involved in a long and ruinous copy-right battle with U2 over the use of copyrighted material on their record 'These Guys Are from England, and Who Gives a Shit?' Despite this setback, they have persisted in their principle of 'fair use' and of the recycling of culture deploying digital means and utilising the internet.

The internet is of course another form that is open to any content whatso-ever; indeed, it is rarely content or information that is at issue on the internet but access and navigation. Negativland utilised the world wide web for anti-corporate purposes, disseminating information about circumventing copyright law and showcasing their work. The anti-corporate logic of Negativland both feeds into and complicates the transvaluation of classical economic logic caused by network culture. Groups/sites like Negativland provide exemplary critical models that operate in the context of radical change in the economy of cultural production. It is no longer the cultural product – its meaning or affect – that is important and profitable, but possession of a list that would enable one to access it. The compilation of lists and the efficiency of search engines dominate the activity of cultural production and consumption. Control and deployment of the archive is essential in the battle to exhaust and exploit history.

Negativland's mode of aural collage is essentially nostalgic through producing a 'homesickness' in a double sense. Commenting on their anti-cola work *Dispepsi* (1997), one critic wrote, 'the album plays like a disturbed, impersonal scrapbook of my life and times ... true to its creator's name, *Dispepsi* is consummately negative, causing me to grit my cola-rotted teeth in anger as I view my existence as one big beverage commercial' (Stephen Thompson, *The Onion*, 1997, cited in Negativland, 2006). The memory of a past saturated with commercials produces a nausea that provides the affective means of establishing a different relationship with the past. It is an affective mode of historicism geared at archiving for a different future.

Another technique of *Dispepsi* demonstrates and attempts to subvert the way that marketing preserves through exploiting 'a certain relationship between the concept and the event' (Deleuze and Guattari, 1994: 10). 'The Greatest Taste Around' uses a jolly advertising jingle to show how brands like Pepsi attempt to brand various events, all of them, in this instance, disastrous. It begins with the sampled voice of an advertising executive saying 'The condolences of everyone at Pepsi Cola are with you', as the singer begins jauntily:

> I got fired by my boss – *Pepsi!*
> I nailed Jesus to the cross – *Pepsi! ...*
> Children dying of disease – *Pepsi!*
> Leading helpless teens astray – *Pepsi!*
>
> (Negativland, 1997)

The album relentlessly assembles and disassembles aural scrapbooks from the media archive, voices and jingles repeatedly drifting in and out, being reset to signify differently in a variety of contexts. Negativland negatively recompose history as an infinite series of possible futures, lost and found in the digital archive. In this history, at one possible end of the state, all events have become branded in the context of cola wars and corporate conflagrations, even the event of becoming nonAmerican. As a Coca-Cola executive from the 1980s affirmed, 'This product is more durable, more self-correcting than the Roman Empire. Coca-Cola is destined to outlive the USA' (cited in Prendergrast, 1994: 409).

## Cultural translation

The sound of becoming nonAmerican can be heard in Great Satan's rage, reverberating in his thunderbolts from space and in the pulse of his music. The former will result inevitably in his destruction, the latter offers the possibility of his transformation.

In so far as culture provides the possibility for welcoming the future to come it is because it provides a variety of forms in which the formula of becoming nonAmerican can be practically implemented. It is not a question of an authorial or subjective intention to implement any formula, however. The formula for becoming nonAmerican works all by itself in relation to an America that can be surpassed only at the point of its own dissolution. It is not therefore a formula for overcoming or even opposing America: on the contrary. While America marks the horizon beyond which neither 'we' Americans nor 'you' the terrorists (in relation to which 'we' are constituted) can see, becoming nonAmerican describes a movement, a locus of possibility and an openness to the new and the event. This event would be the coming of the 'other' who is neither 'we' nor 'you', but emerges from a process of translation from one to the other.

Becoming nonAmerican is a necessary consequence of the constant process of cultural translation that cultural forms allow. It goes without saying that in any form of translation, the source text is never completely surpassed. It should be stressed that this idea of cultural translation does not primarily refer to the translation of specific works, but of forms and practices. The appropriation of foreign forms and practices can have a profoundly transformative (and even formative) effect on the host culture. An excellent example would be the cultural translation that resulted in the origin of modern Western subjectivity in so far as it was developed in secular love poetry from the troubadours. Up to about the twelfth century, there is little or no recognisable modern poetry outside of religious liturgy and epic narratives bearing the history of the tribe or race. The birth, in the South of France, of 'the poetry of passion' led to the development of courtly love in the courts of Northern Europe and ultimately the achievements of Petrarch, Dante, Ronsard and Shakespeare, among many others. These works feature prominently as landmarks in the development of recognisably modern, individualistic subjectivity defined in relation to love, that is to say private passion, and self-love. As Bataille comments, this tradition extends back, via Andalusia, 'to those poetry competitions of the [Arab] tribes … which maintained a tradition of chivalrous valour in which violence was combined with prodigality, and love with poetry' (Bataille, 1988: 90–1). These Arab practices, examples of wasteful expenditure, migrated north even as they became subject to the austere strictures of the prophet Mohammed. Centuries later, the Northern European reformation would, in some respects, repeat the pious revolution of Mohammed. But Protestantism, particularly in the court of Elizabeth I, would eventually ally itself with the amorous Neoplatonism of the poets, sustaining love (rather than submission) as the means to an affective and personal relation with God.

In this book, it has been American popular music that has provided the formal and technical (in the oldest and fullest sense of *techne*, as art, skill and

technique that can include the technological) support for trans-cultural becoming. Because of its multiple strands and origins, American popular music
has always been on a virtual trajectory of becoming nonAmerican and has been
translated and transformed differently throughout the world. Indeed, it is ar-
guable that the disparate forms of blues, rhythm and blues, country, gospel
and rock and rock required British translation (the Beatles, the Merseybeats
and so on) before it could be retrospectively homogenised and identified as
American pop.

American heavy metal is an effect of precisely this trajectory, usually finding
its origin in 1960s Britain as the result of the cultural translation of African-
American blues by British beat groups. As Walser notes, Black Sabbath's invocation of the occult is pre-empted in Robert Johnson's pact with the devil or
Howlin' Wolf's 'meditation on the problem of evil' (1993: 8). Musicians credited with inaugurating the distinctive guitar sound of metal – Jeff Beck, Jimmy
Page, Eric Clapton – essentially produced highly amplified and distorted riffs
that had been appropriated or stolen from black American musicians accompanied by heavy drums and bass.

While it remained pre-eminently British throughout the 1970s, American
heavy metal was kick-started in the 1980s by the new wave of British heavy
metal (led by Motörhead, Iron Maiden, Def Leppard, Saxon) to become 'the
dominant genre of American music' (Walser, 1993: 11). In its multiple varieties (thrash metal, speed metal, glam metal, industrial metal, grindcore, rap core,
alternative metal, nu metal, death metal, black metal, Viking metal … ), it has
spread to countries throughout the world, including Japan and China.[1]

Of course the proliferation of American popular music across the world has
been alongside and in relation to American capitalism, its popular culture helping to advance capitalism throughout the world, often with destructive effect.
At best consumer culture may provide a platform and some income for local
groups, but usually the economies of scale afforded to the big companies of the
music industry and the homogeneity of global retail outlets marginalise local
differences in favour of American acts. At the very minimum, commodification
detaches and deforms the value of cultural production from the specific site of
its emergence, vampirically draining its expenditure and transforming it into
exchange value. But music is never completely constrained by the commodity
form. Indeed, capitalism requires that music and other cultural forms retain a
sovereign charge precisely in order to provide a locus of innovation and the
new that can be commodified. Music and other cultural forms exceed
commodification precisely through maintaining the minimal distance necessary for econopoietic production or creation. Music retains a minimal freedom in a sense that is both opposite and integral to the idea of the free market.
That is to say that in relation to this market it is sovereign, indifferent. It will
not serve the dictates of the market, but neither does it wish to subordinate it
in the name of any other sovereign power, be it of a nation or theocratic state.

In so doing it becomes an operation of loss – the loss of meaning and significance, that is at the same moment one of ecstatic affirmation. American music's
sovereignty provides a locus of becoming, of becoming nonAmerican, both
outside and inside America.

Metal is second only to hip hop in its multiple proliferation around the world.
Tony Mitchell's collection *Global Noise* looks at 'emergent global hip hop that
has evolved from Tunis to Honolulu' (2001: 1–2). His book also shows how
much of this music has a political edge, seeking to intervene both in the traditional culture for which it marks a break and in American consumer culture
from which it seeks to sustain a difference. The essays in Mitchell's volume
discuss

> Japanese b-boys struggling with the hyperconsumerism of Tokyo youth culture,
> Italian posses promoting hard-core Marxist politics … Basque rappers … Rappers
> in Bosnia [who] declare their allegiance with the violent lives of gangsta rappers
> in South Central Los Angeles, a rap group in Greenland [that] protests that
> country's domination by the Danish language. Rap in Korea and Bulgaria …
> [and] its Islamic and African manifestations in France and the United Kingdom,
> and its indigenization in Australia and Aoteroa-New Zealand. (1)

As Mitchell states, hip hop cannot, therefore, 'be viewed simply as an expression of African-American culture' (1). Rather, it is a form open to any content
whatsoever, radical or conservative (there is even an orthodox Jewish rapper
called Etan G).

One of the chapters in *Global Noise*, by Ted Swedenburg, concerns European Islamic hip hop, focusing particularly on Aki Nawaz of the UK-based
group Fun'da'mental, Natacha Atlas, formerly of Transglobal Underground, and
the Sicilian Akhenaton. Swedenburg discusses the conflicted complexities of
their ethnic, political, cultural and religious emplacement and their activist
responses to Islamophobia of both active and passive kinds, involving either
hatred or neglect. Evidence of the latter, for Swedenburg, is the fact that the
'transglobal Islamic underground' has been ignored in America despite 'its clear
affinities with the Islamic rhetoric of much African-American hip hop culture'
(14).

Fun'da'mental appear to have, in any case, quite an ambivalent attitude to
American popular culture and American rap. The opening track on their 2006
album *All is War*, 'I Reject', provides a litany of rejection of American and British cultural practices, beliefs and cultural objects. 'I reject your beauty and Barbie
doll figure / Reject the rappers that use the word ...' ('I Reject', 2006). The line
refuses even to quote the 'n' word that rhymes with 'figure'. Yet Fun'da'mental
appropriate the form of American hip hop, although they combine it with other
styles, beats and instruments drawn from Indian subcontinental traditions.
Clearly they have more in common with Chuck D than NWA, and in their
sampling of speeches of Martin Luther King and Malcolm X make connections
with the civil-rights movement. Indeed, an earlier album of remixes takes its

title from a quotation from Martin Luther King concerning 'Why America will go to Hell' (1999). As this title suggests, in spite of their appropriation of the hip hop form and of samples taken from American speeches and American records, Fun'da'mental take a largely negative view of America.

Perhaps Fun'da'mental's most controversial recording is *All is War* (2006), which seems to acknowledge and take on the declaration of George W. Bush on 12 September 2001. But Fun'da'mental correlate 9/11 with another event that heralds the overcoming of America – the torture of Iraqi detainees at Abu Ghraib prison. The cover of the album features the image 'Liberty' by Leon Kuhn, a UK artist specialising in political art that uses the technique of digital photomontage. Kuhn's image sees the Statue of Liberty replaced or rather morphed into one of the hooded victims of US torture whose photograph circulated the world's media in 2004. In the image, Liberty's torch powers the electric torture cable.

In a short piece on 'War Porn' (2006) Jean Baudrillard also connects the events of the attack on the World Trade Center and the publication of the torture photographs. Or rather he regards the former as an event and the latter as its abject negation, the non-event of an atrocious yet obscene banality that will nevertheless prove fatal to the USA. Like Leon Kuhn and Fun'da'mental, Baudrillard lights on the image of the hooded figure:

> this most ferocious image (the most ferocious for America), because it was the most ghostly and most 'reversible': the prisoner threatened with electrocution and, completely hooded, like a member of the Ku Klux Klan, crucified by its ilk. It is really America that has electrocuted itself. (Baudrillard, 2006: 88).

Kuhn's image concurs with this view, though the substitution works on many levels. The beacon of liberty that symbolises for America its status as freedom's great refuge and protector has turned into an instrument of torture and oppression. This substitution and the consequent monumentalisation and indeed sacralisation of the image of the hooded figure, however, implies a massive act of contrition. In its grandiose self-abjection and abasement, the sacred monumentalisation of this Christ-like figure is an authentically Christian gesture. And, indeed, it is appropriately American since torture by crucifixion has been replaced by electrocution, America's distinctive contribution to the technology of execution.

All of which makes it a curious image, perhaps, for Fun'da'mental to choose in their call to arms, particularly given Islam's conventional prohibition on iconography and idolatry. In the context of the album, the image appears to suggest the conclusion of a war between East and West in which the forces of Islam have triumphed and occupied New York. This is the scenario envisaged by the title track on the album. '786 All is War' (2006) anticipates a future dawn attack on New York by the 'dream team salahuddin': 'replicant Sufis' surfing on boards of steel, accompanied by 'cyborg mujahids', 'robotic maidens of paradise', 'mechanoid' martyrs, 'shabab clones' in 'crescent starships' pulling over the Statue of Liberty and annihilating the 'Pharoah's sons'. With 'Jihadi jetskis' patrolling the Hudson river, 'the citizens they build a mosque on ground zero'. The conquest of America is complete, and yet the highly technologised vision of a future Islamic cyberutopia with its surfing, jetskis and starships is quite reassuring, from the point of view of an American used to correlating wealth and comfort with technological progress. A mosque may have been built on ground zero (Why not? What a good idea!), but in every other respect life remains as normal. And if Fun'da'mental are providing the soundtrack, hip hop and rap remain in the new world, as American forms offering an opportunity for further negative-becoming in relation to any content whatever.

America is not surpassed in Fun'da'mental's Islamic cyberutopia but enhanced, its way of life remaining the horizon beyond which we do not see but in relation to which the challenge remains to become nonAmerican. '786 All is War' provides an exemplary image of the paradox and impossibility of becoming nonAmerican even as it moves along that trajectory. It deliberately provokes Great Satan's rage, thereby sustaining it in a performance that gestures towards an Islam that is also on a path of becoming, one that necessarily broaches the risk of the arrival of an altogether different future.

## Notes

1    For a current list of Japanese rock and metal bands, see ww4.et.tiki.ne.jp/~sophia/
     english/japanese.html; for China, see www.rockinchina.com/index_metal.html.

# Bibliography

Agamben, Giorgio (1998) *Homo Sacer: Sovereign Power and Bare Life*, Stanford, CA: Stanford University Press.

Agamben, Giorgio (2004a) *The Open: Man and Animal*, Stanford, CA: Stanford University Press.

Agamben, Giorgio (2004b) 'Interview with Giorgio Agamben – Life, a Work of Art without an Author: The State of Exception, the Administration of Disorder and Private Life', *German Law Journal*, No. 5 (1 May) (Special Edition), www.germanlawjournal.com/article.php?id=437.

Agamben, Giorgio (2005) *State of Exception*, Chicago: University of Chicago Press.

Angelico, Irene (1998) *The Coca-Cola Conquest: A Trilogy*, DLI Productions in association with Channel 4 Television, the Canadian Broadcasting Corporation and Télé Québec.

Ansell Pearson, Keith (1997) 'Life Becoming Body: On the "Meaning" of Post Human Evolution', *Cultural Values*, 1.2: 219–40.

Apple, Michael A. (1975) 'The Hidden Curriculum and the Nature of Conflict', in William Pinar (ed.), *Curriculum Theorizing: The Reconceptualists*, Berkeley, CA: McCutchan.

Azerrad, Michael (1994) *Come As You Are*, New York: Main Street Books.

Bataille, Georges (1973) *Literature and Evil*, London: Marion Boyars.

Bataille, Georges (1985) *Visions of Excess: Selected Writings, 1927–1939*, ed. Allan Stoekl, trans. Allan Stoekl with Carl R. Lovitt and Donald M. Leslie, Jr, Minneapolis: University of Minnesota Press.

Bataille, Georges (1986) *Eroticism: Death and Sensuality*, London: Marion Boyars.

Bataille, Georges (1988) *The Accursed Share, I: Consumption*, trans. Robert Hurley, New York: Zone Books.

Bataille, Georges (1989) *My Mother/Madame Edwarda/The Dead Man*, London: Marion Boyars.

Bataille, Georges (1990) 'Letter to René Char on the Incompatibilities of the Writer', trans. Christopher Carson, *Yale French Studies*, 78: 31–43.

Bataille, Georges (1991) *The Accursed Share, II: The History of Eroticism and III: Sovereignty*, trans. Robert Hurley, New York: Zone Books.

Bataille, Georges (1992a) *On Nietzsche*, trans. Bruce Boone, New York: Paragon House.

Bataille, Georges (1992b) *Theory of Religion*, trans. Robert Hurley, New York: Zone Books.

Bataille, Georges (2001) *The Unfinished System of Nonknowledge*, ed. Stuart Kendall, Minneapolis: University of Minnesota Press.

Baudrillard, Jean (1993) *The Transparency of Evil: Essays in Extreme Phenomena*, London: Verso.

Baudrillard, Jean (2005) *The Intelligence of Evil and the Lucidity Pact,* trans. Chris Turner, Oxford: Berg.

Baudrillard, Jean (2006) 'War Porn', *Journal for Visual Culture*, 5(1): 86–8.

Bauman, Zigmunt (2001) 'Excess: An Obituary', *parallax*, 18: 85–91.

BBC News World (2003) 20 May, http://news.bbc.co.uk/1/hi/world/middle_east/3042907.stm. Accessed on 20 August 2006.

Beardsworth, Richard (1995) 'From a Genealogy of Matter to a Politics of Memory: Stiegler's Thinking of Technics', *Tekhnema*, 2 (Spring): 85–116.

Berlinger, Joe and Bruce Sinofsky (2004) *Metallica: Some Kind of Monster*, Paramount Home Entertainment DVD.

Berman, Paul (2003) *Terror and Liberalism*, New York: W. W. Norton.

Blake, William (1984) *Complete Writings*, ed. Geoffrey Keynes, Oxford: Oxford University Press.

Bloom, Allan (1987) *The Closing of the American Mind*, New York: Simon and Schuster.

Blum, William (2000) *Rogue State: A Guide to the World's Only Superpower*, Monroe, ME: Common Courage Press.

Bogue, Ronald (2004) *Deleuze's Wake*, New York: State University of New York Press.

Borger, Julian (2003) 'US Planning Global-reach Missiles: Allies not Required', *Guardian Weekly*, 3–9 July.

Botting, Fred and Scott Wilson (1997) *The Bataille Reader*, Oxford: Blackwell.

Botting, Fred and Scott Wilson (1998) *Bataille: A Critical Reader*, Oxford: Blackwell.

Botting, Fred and Scott Wilson (2001a) *The Tarantinian Ethics*, London: Sage.

Botting, Fred and Scott Wilson (2001b) *Bataille*, London: Palgrave.

Botting, Fred and Scott Wilson (2004) 'Toy Law, Toy Joy, *Toy Story*' in Leslie J. Moran et al., *Law's Moving Image*, London: Glasshouse Press.

Boyle, Francis A. (2002) *The Criminality of Nuclear Deterrence*, Atlanta, GA: Clarity Press.

Brinkley, Douglas (1994) 'Educating the Generation Called X' from 'Stop Making Sense of Generation X, *Washington Post Education Review*, 3 April.

Calvert, John (2000) '"The World is an Undutiful Boy!": Sayyid Qutb's American Experience', *Islam and Christian-Muslim Relations*, Vol. II.1: 87–103, 98.

*Capitalism Magazine* (2001), www.capitalismmagazine.com/2001/december/jj_walker.htm.

Caplow, Theodore and Jonathan Simon (1999) 'Understanding Prison Policy and Population Trends' in Michael Tonry and Joan Petersilia (eds) (1999) *Prisons, Crime and Justice: A Review of Research*, Chicago: University of Chicago Press.

Caygill, Howard (1996) 'Drafts for a Metaphysics of the Gene', *Tekhnema* 3/'A Touch of Memory, Spring, http://tekhnema.free.fr/3Caygill.htm.

Cebrowski, Vice Admiral Arthur K. and John Gartska (1998) 'Network-Centric Warfare', *Proceedings*, www.usni.org/Proceedings/Articles98/PROcebrowski.htm. Accessed on 20 October 2004.

Chang, Jeff (2005) *Can't Stop, Won't Stop: A History of the Hip-Hop Generation,* London: Ebury Press.

Chomsky, Noam (2000) *Rogue States: The Rule of Force in World Affairs*, Cambridge, MA: South End Press.

Coker, Christopher (2004) *The Future of War: The Re-Enchantment of War in the Twenty-First Century*, Oxford: Blackwell.

Coole, Diana (2000) *Negativity and Politics: Dionysus and Dialectics from Kant to Poststructuralism*, London: Routledge, 2000.

Coupland, Douglas (1991) *Generation X: Tales for an Accelerated Culture*, New York: St Martins Press.

Crimescene.com (1998) www.crimescene.com/purity/index.html.

Curtis, Adam (2002) *The Century of the Self*, BBC Four Documentaries.

Curtis, Adam (2004) *The Power of Nightmares*, BBC Productions, www.archive.org/details/ThePowerOfNightmares.

Davis, Mike (1990) *City of Quartz: Excavating the Future in Los Angeles*, New York: Verso.

DeGregory, Lane (2004) 'Iraq 'n' Roll', *St Petersburg Times Floridian*, 21 November.

Deleuze, Gilles (1983) *Nietzsche and Philosophy*, trans. Hugh Tomlinson, London: Athlone Press.

Deleuze, Gilles (1993) 'Ethics and the Event' in Constantin V. Boundas (ed.), *The Deleuze Reader*, New York: Columbia University Press.

Deleuze, Gilles (1995) *Negotiations*, Columbia University Press.

Deleuze, Gilles (1998) *Essays Critical and Clinical*, trans. Daniel W. Smith and Michael A. Greco, London: Verso Press.

Deleuze, Gilles (2003) *Desert Islands and Other Texts (1953–1974)*, New York: Semiotext(e).

Deleuze, Gilles (2006) *Two Regimes of Madness: Texts and Interviews 1975–1995*. New York: Semiotext(e).

Deleuze, Gilles and Félix Guattari (1984) *Anti-Oedipus: Capitalism and Schizophrenia*, London: Athlone Press.

Deleuze, Gilles and Félix Guattari (1988) *A Thousand Plateaus: Capitalism and Schizophrenia II*, London: Athlone Press.

Deleuze, Gilles and Félix Guattari (1994) *What is Philosophy?*, London: Verso.

Deleuze, Gilles and Claire Parnet (2002) *Dialogues II*, London: Continuum.

Derrida, Jacques (1994) *Specters of Marx*, trans. Peggy Kamuf, London: Routledge.

Derrida Jacques (2002) *Acts of Religion*, ed. Gil Anidjar, London: Routledge.

Derrida, Jaques (2005) *Rogues*, trans. Pascale-Anne Brault and Michael Naas, Stanford, CA: Stanford University Press.

Dimery, Robert et al. (2005) *1001 Albums You Must Hear Before You Die*, London: Cassel Illustrated.

Drury, Shadia (1988) *The Political Ideas of Leo Strauss*, New York: St Martins.

Drury, Shadia (1994) *Alexandre Kojève: The Roots of Postmodern Politics*, London: Macmillan.

Drury, Shadia (1999) *Leo Strauss and the American Right*, London: Macmillan.

Drury, Shadia (2003) 'Saving America: Leo Strauss and the Neoconservatives', Evatt Foundation, 10 September, http://evatt.labor.net.au/publications/papers/112.html.

Dunn, Sam and Scot McFadyen (2006) *Metal: A Headbanger's Journey*, Momentum Pictures.

Ehrmann, Jacques (1981) 'The Death of Literature' in Raymond Federman (ed.), *Surfiction: Fiction Now and Tomorrow*, Chicago: Swallow Press.

Evans, Dylan (1996) *An Introductory Dictionary of Lacanian Psychoanalysis*, London: Routledge.

Fink, Bruce (1995) *The Lacanian Subject*, Princeton, NJ: Princeton University Press.

Fink, Bruce (2004) *Lacan to the Letter: Reading* Ecrits *Closely*, Minneapolis: University of Minnesota Press.

Foucault, Michel (1984) *Language, Counter-Memory, Practice*, trans. Donald Bouchard and Sherry Simon, Ithaca, NY: Cornell University Press.

Foucault, Michel (1986) *The Order of Things*, London: Tavistock Press.

Foucault, Michel (1988) *Politics, Philosophy, Culture: Interviews and Other Writings 1977–1984*, ed. Lawrence D. Kritzman, London: Routledge.

Foucault, Michel (2003) *Society Must Be Defended*, trans. David Macey, London: Penguin.

Freud, Sigmund (1995) *The Freud Reader*, ed. Peter Gay, London: Vintage, 1995.

Fukuyama, Francis (1989) 'The End of History?', *The National Interest*, 16 (Summer): 3–18.

Fukuyama, Francis (1992) *The End of History and the Last Man*, Harmondsworth: Penguin.

Fukuyama, Francis (1999) 'Second Thoughts: Last Man in a Bottle', *The National Interest*, 56 (Summer): 16–24.

Fukuyama, Francis (2002) *Our Posthuman Future: Consequences of the Biotechnology Revolution*, New York: Farrer, Strauss and Giroux.

Gallagher, Noel (2005) *The Observer* Music Monthly, June, No. 22.

Genova, Nick de (1995) 'Gangsta Rap and Nihilism in Black America: Some Questions of Life and Death', *Social Text*, 43 (Fall): 89–132.

George, Nelson (1994) *Buppies, B-Boys, Baps and Bohos: Notes on Post-Soul Black Culture*, New York: Harper Collins.

George, Nelson (1998) *Hip Hop America*, New York: Viking Press.

Gilder, George (1981) *Wealth and Poverty*, New York: Bantam Books.

Goldman, Robert and Stephen Papson (1998) *Nike Culture*, London: Sage.

Goux, Jean-Joseph (1998a) 'General Economics and Postmodern Capitalism' in Fred Botting and Scott Wilson (eds), *Bataille: A Critical Reader*. Oxford: Blackwell.

Goux, Jean-Joseph (1998b) 'Subversion and Consensus: Proletarians, Women, Artists', in Jean-Joseph Goux and Philip R. Wood (eds), *Terror and Consensus: Vicissitudes of French Thought*, Stanford, CA: Stanford University Press.

Greimas, A. J. (1987) *On Meaning*, trans. Paul Perron and Frank Collins, London: Pinter.

Grey, John (2003) *Al Qaeda and What it Means to be Modern*, London: Faber and Faber.

Guattari, Félix (1992) *Chaosmosis*, trans. Paul Bains and Julian Pefanis, Sydney: Power Publications.

Guattari, Félix (1995) *Chaosophy*, New York: Semiotext(e).

Hardt, Michael and Antonio Negri (2004) *Multitudes: War and Democracy in the Age of Empire*, New York: Penguin Press.

Harris, Eric (1999a) Online Journal. www.acolumbinesite.com/eric/writing/plans2.gif.

Harris, Eric (1999b) Online Journal, http://members.aol.com/rebdomine/pissed.htm.

Hillis Miller, J. (1995) 'The University of Dissensus', *Oxford Literary Review*, 17: 121–43.

Hoffman, Bruce (2002) *Lessons of 9/11*, Santa Monica, CA: RAND Corporation.

Hollier, Denis (ed.) (1988) *The College of Sociology, 1937–39*, Minneapolis: University of Minnesota Press.

Jahn, Karl (2000) 'Leo Strauss and the Straussians', http://home.earthlink.net/~karljahn/Strauss.htm.

Joxe, Alain (2002) *Empire of Disorder*, New York: Semiotext(e).

Kelly, Kevin (1998) *New Rules for the New Economy: Ten Ways the Network Economy is Changing Everything*, London: Fourth Estate.

Kennedy, Randall (2002) *Nigger: The Strange Career of a Troublesome Word*, New York: Pantheon.

Kincaid, James (1998) *Erotic Innocence*, Durham, NC: Duke University Press.

Kitwana, Bakari (1994) *The Rap on Gangsta Rap: Gangsta Rap and Visions of Black Violence*, Chicago: Third World Press.

Klein, Naomi (2000) *No Logo*, London: Flamingo.

Kojève, Alexandre (1969) (1989) *Introduction to the Reading of Hegel: Lectures on the Phenomenology of Spirity*, Ithaca, NY: Cornell University Press.

Lacan, Jacques (1976) *Four Fundamental Concepts of Psychoanalysis*, tr. Alan Sheridan, Harmondsworth: Penguin.

Lacan, Jacques (1982) 'Seminar of 21 January 1975' in Juliet Mitchell and Jacqueline Rose (eds) *Feminine Sexuality*, Basingstoke and London: Macmillan.

Lacan, Jacques (1986) *Ecrits: A Selection*, trans. Alan Sheridan, London: Routledge.

Lacan, Jacques (1992) *The Ethics of Psychoanalysis, 1959–1960. The Seminar of Jacques Lacan*, Book VII, ed. Jacques-Alain Muller, trans. with notes by Dennis Porter, London: Routledge.

Lacan, Jacques (1999) *On Feminine Sexuality, the Limits of Love and Knowledge, 1972–1973. Encore: The Seminar of Jacques Lacan*, Book XX, ed. Jacques-Alain Muller, trans. with notes by Bruce Fink, New York: Norton, 1999.

LaFeber, Walter (1999) *Michael Jordan and the New Global Capitalism*, New York: Norton, 1999.

Land, Nick (1992a) *Thirst for Annihilation*, London: Routledge.

Land, Nick (1992b) 'Circuitries', *Pli: Warwick Journal of Philosophy*, 4.1–2: 217–35.

Land, Nick (1993) 'Machinic Desire', *Textual Practice*, 7.3: 471–82

Luttwak, Edward (1999) *Turbo-Capitalism: Winners and Losers in the Global Economy*, London: Orion Business Books.

Lyotard, Jean-François (1984) *Postmodern Condition*, trans. Geoffrey Bennington, Manchester: Manchester University Press.

Lyotard, Jean-François (1993) *Political Writings*, trans. Bill Readings with Kevin Paul Geiman, London: UCL Press.

Lyotard, Jean-François (1994) *The Inhuman*, trans. Geoffrey Bennington and Rachel Bowlby, Stanford, CA: Stanford University Press.

McIver, Joel (2002) *Nu-Metal*, London: Omnibus Press.

McLaren, Peter (1995) *Critical Pedagogy and Predatory Culture*, New York: Routledge.

Malik, Suhail (2006) 'Fucking Straight Death Metal', *Journal of Visual Culture*, 5(1): 107–12.

Marx, Karl (1976) *Capital: A Critique of Political Economy,* Harmondsworth: Penguin.

Mendelssohn, John (2004) *Gigantic: The Story of Frank Black and the Pixies*. London: Omnibus Press.

Miller, Jacques Alain (1988) 'Extimité', *Prose Studies,* 11: 125–6.

Milton, John (1983) *Milton Poetical Works*, ed. Douglas Bush, Oxford: Oxford University Press.

Mitchell, Tony (2001) *Global Noise: Rap and Hip-Hop Outside the USA*, Middletown, CT: Wesleyan University Press.

*Le Monde diplomatique* (2006) President Bush Discusses War on Terrorism in an Address to the Nation World Congress Center, Atlanta, Georgia, November 8, 2001, www.monde-diplomatique.fr/cahier/irak/discoursgwbush–3.

Moore, Michael (2002) *Bowling for Columbine*. Momentum Pictures Home Entertainment.

Mulholland, Garry (2002) *This is Uncool: The 500 Greatest Singles Since Punk and Disco*, London: Cassell Illustrated.

Murdian, Albert (2005) *Choosing Death: The Improbable History of Death Metal*, London: Feral House.

Murphy Jr, John F. (2001) *Day of Reckoning: The Massacre at Columbine High School* Xlibris Corporation.

Negativland (2006) Welcome to Negativworldwideebland, http://negativland.com.

Nietzsche, Friedrich (1968) *The Will to Power*, ed. Walter Kaufmann, New York: Vintage.

Nietzsche, Friedrich (1969) *Thus Spoke Zarathustra*, trans. R. J. Hollingdale, New York: Vintage.

Nietzsche, Friedrich (1984) *Beyond Good and Evil*, trans. R. J. Hollingdale, Harmondsworth: Penguin.

Norton, Anne (2004) *Leo Strauss and the Politics of American Empire*, New Haven, CA: Yale University Press.

Ord, Douglas (2005) 'From Absolute Other to Eric and Dylan', http://home.eol.ca/~dord/
    FCHED1.html.
Pieterse, Jan Nederveen (2004) 'Neoliberal Empire', *Theory, Culture and Society*, 21(3): 119–
    40.
Potter, Russell (1995) *Spectacular Vernaculars*, New York: State University of New York Press.
Postell, Danny (2003) 'Noble Lies and Perpetual War: Leo Strauss, the Neo-Cons and Iraq',
    *Information Clearing House*, www.informationclearinghouse.info/article5010.htm.
Powell, Colin (2002) 'Be Heard: An MTV Discussion with Colin Powell', US Department of
    State Website, 14 February 2002.
www.state.gov/secretary/former/powell/remarks/2002/8038.htm. Accessed on 13 August
    2006.
Prendergrast, Mark (1994) *For God, Country and Coca-Cola*, London: Orion.
Prestowitz, Clyde (2003) *Rogue Nation: American Unilateralism and the Failure of Good In-
    tentions*, New York: Basic Books.
Quinn, Eithne (2005) *Nuthin' But a G Thang: The Culture and Commerce of Gangsta*, New
    York: University of Columbia Press.
Risen, Clay (2006) 'The Danger of Generals as CEOs. War Mart', *The New Republic online*.
    www.tnr.com/doc.mhtml?i=20060403&s=risen040306. Accessed on 3 April 2006.
Rose, Gillian (1996) *Mourning Becomes Law: Philosophy and Representation*, New York: Cam-
    bridge University Press.
Roach, Jay (2001) *Meet the Parents*, Universal Studios.
Rose, Tricia (1994) *Black Noise: Rap Music and Black Culture in Contemporary America*,
    London: Wesleyan University Press.
Roudinesco, Elisabeth (1990) *Jacques Lacan & Co A History of Psychoanalysis in France*,
    trans. Jeffrey Mehlman, London: Free Association Books.
Salecl, Renata (1998) 'Cut in the Body: From Clitoridectomy to Body Art', *New Formations*,
    35: 28–42.
Sandford, Christopher (1995) *Kurt Cobain,* London: Orion.
Saunders, Clayton D. (2002) *Al Qaeda: An Example of Network-Centric Operations*,
    www.stormingmedia.co.uk/85/8511/A851104.html?PHPSESSID=383b80d6cdd578a7f
    53f4a239b41bacb.
Schloss, Joseph (2004) *Making Beats: The Art of Sample-Based Hip-Hop*, Middletown CT,
    2004, 65).
Serpick, Evan (2006) 'Soundtrack to the War', *Rolling Stone*, 24 August: 20–2.
Stelarc, 'From Psycho to Cyber Strategies: Prosthetics, Robotics and Remote Existence', *Cul-
    tural Values*, 1.2 (1997), pp. 241–9, 246.
Stiegler, Bernard (1998) *Technics and Time*, 1, trans. Richard Beardsworth and George Collins,
    Stanford, CA: Stanford University Press.
Strauss, Leo (1963) *On Tyranny*, Ithaca, NY: Cornell University Press.
Tarantino, Quentin (1995a) *True Romance,* London: Faber.
Tarantino, Quentin (1995b) *Natural Born Killers,* London: Faber.
Tonry, Michael (1995) *Malign Neglect: Race, Crime and Punishment in America*, New York:
    Oxford University Press.
Tonry, Michael and Joan Petersilia (eds) (1999) *Prisons, Crime and Justice: A Review of Re-
    search,* Chicago: University of Chicago Press.
Toop, David (1984) *The Rap Attack: African Jive To New York Hip Hop*, London: Pluto.
Udo, Tommy (2002) *Brave Nu World*, London: Sanctuary.
Ullman, Ellen (1997) *Close to the Machine: Technophilia and its Discontents*, San Francisco:
    City Lights.

Upshal, David (2005) *Hip-Hop Nights: Porn with Attitude,* Lion Television, for Channel 4.

Walser, Robert (1993) *Running with the Devil: Power, Gender, and Madness in Heavy Metal Music,* Hanover, NE: Wesleyan University Press.

Webber, Julie (2005) *Failure to Hold: The Politics of School Violence,* Lanham, MD: Rowman and Littlefield.

Wernick, Andrew (1999) 'Bataille's Columbine', ctheory.com/a76.html www.ctheory.net/articles.aspx?id=119. Accessed on 3 November 1999.

White House, The (2001a) 'The National Security Strategy of the United States of America', www.whitehouse.gov/nsc/nss.html. Accessed on 5 November 2005.

White House, The (2001b) President George W Bush, Address to a Joint Session of Congress and the American People, www.whitehouse.gov/news/releases/2001/09/20010920-8.html.

Žižek, Slavoj (2000) 'Desert of the Real' *Lacanian Ink,* 16: 64–81.

## Further websites

www.black-goat.com/song_slipknot.php
www.capitalismmagazine.com
www.crimescene.com
ww4.et.tiki.ne.jp/~sophia/english/japanese.html
www.guardian.co.uk/climatechange/story/0,,1754276,00.html
www.Maggot-land.com
www.myspace.com/wthanb
www.newamericancentury.org
www.pulseofthemaggots.com
www.rockinchina.com/index_metal.html
www.snopes.com/horrors/madmen/doom.asp

# Discography

Biohazard (1994) *State of the World Address,* Warner Brothers.
Biohazard (1999) *New World Disorder,* Mercury/King.
Cannibal Corpse (1994) *The Bleeding*, Metal Blade.
Carcass (1988) *Reek of Putrefaction*, Earache.
Chuck D (1996) *Autobiography of Mistah Chuck*, Mercury.
Coal Chamber (1999) *Chamber Music*, Roadrunner.
Deftones, The (2000) *White Pony*, Warner Brothers.
Deicide (1990) *Deicide*, Roadrunner.
Deicide (1995) *Once Upon the Cross*, Roadrunner.
Deicide (1997) *Serpents of the Light*, Roadrunner.
Dr. Dre (1992) *The Chronic*, Death Row.
Eazy E (1994) *It's On (Dr. Dre) 187um Killa*, Priority.
Fear Factory (1995) *Demanufacture*, Roadrunner.
Fun'da'mental (1997) *Erotic Terrorism*, Beggar's Banquet.
Fun'da'mental (1997) *Why America Will Go To Hell*, Beggar's Banquet.
Fun'da'mental (2006) *All Is War,* Five Uncivilised Tribes.
Ice Cube (1990) *Amerikkka's Most Wanted*, Priority.
Ice Cube (1991) *Death Sentence*, Priority.
Ice Cube (1992) *The Predator*, Priority.
KMFDM (1996) *Xtort,* Wax Trax!
KMFDM (1997) *Symbols*, Wax Trax!
Korn (1994), *Коял*, Immortal.
Korn (1996) *Life is Peachy*, Immortal/Epic.
Korn (1998) *Follow the Leader*, Immortal/Epic.
Korn (1999) *Issues*, Immortal/Epic
Lil' Kim (1996) *Hardcore*, Undeas/Big Beat.
Lil' Kim (2000) *Notorious K.I.M*, Queen Bee/Undeas/Atlantic.
Lil' Kim (2005) *The Naked Truth*, Atlantic.
Limp Bizkit (2000) *Chocolate Starfish and the Hotdog Flavored Water*, Interscope.
Machine Head (1994) *Burn My Eyes*, Roadrunner.
Ministry (1992) *Psalm 69*, Sire/Warner Brothers.
Ministry (2005), *Rantology*, Mayan.
Negativland (1987) *Escape from Noise*, Seeland.
Negativland (1991) *Heifer Stupid*, Sst Records.
Negativland (1997) *Dispepsi*, Seeland.

Nirvana (1989), *Bleach*, Sub Pop.

Nirvana (1991) *Nevermind*, Geffen.

NWA (1988) *Straight Outta Compton,* Priority/Ruthless.

NWA (1991) *Niggaz 4 Life*, Priority/Ruthless.

Pixies (1988a) *Surfer Rosa*, 4AD.

Pixies (1988b) *Come On Pilgrim*, 4AD.

Pixies (1989) *Doolittle*, 4AD.

Public Enemy (1988) *It Takes a Nation of Millions to Hold Us Back*, Def Jam.

Rage Against the Machine (1992) *Rage Against the Machine*, Epic.

Rage Against the Machine (1999) *Battle of Los Angeles*, Epic.

Slipknot (1998) *Mate. Feed. Kill. Repeat*, Bravado.

Slipknot (1999), *Slipknot,* Roadrunner.

Slipknot (2001) *Iowa*, Roadrunner.

Slipknot (2002) *Disasterpieces* DVD, Roadrunner.

Slipknot (2004) *Vol.3: The Subliminal Verses*, Roadrunner.

Snoop Doggy Dogg (1993) *Doggystyle*, Death Row.

Snoop Doggy Dogg (1996) *The Doggfather*, Death Row.

Snoop Doggy Dogg (1999) *Doggystyle* DVD, Hustler.

Static-X (2001) *Machine*, Warner Brothers.

System of a Down (2001) *Toxicity*, Columbia.

System of a Down (2002) *Steal This Album*, Columbia.

# Index